M8

# JOURNEY TO POLAND

EUROPEAN SOURCES

*LITERATURE*

American Journals
ALBERT CAMUS

Diary of an Unknown
JEAN COCTEAU

Fragments of a Journal
EUGENE IONESCO

Journey to Poland
ALFRED DÖBLIN

Letters to Gala
PAUL ELUARD

Letters to Merline
RAINER MARIA RILKE

Souvenir Portraits
JEAN COCTEAU

*HISTORY*

Berlin Underground: 1938–1945
RUTH ANDREAS-FRIEDRICH

Battleground Berlin: 1945–1948
RUTH ANDREAS-FRIEDRICH

Series Editors
Russell Epprecht and Sylvere Lotringer

# JOURNEY TO POLAND

## ALFRED DÖBLIN

TRANSLATED BY JOACHIM NEUGROSCHEL
EDITED BY HEINZ GRABER

PARAGON HOUSE PUBLISHERS

NEW YORK

First American edition, 1991

Published in the United States by

Paragon House
90 Fifth Avenue
New York, NY 10011

Originally published in German under the title *Reise in Polen*.
Copyright © Walter-Verlag AG Olten, 1968
English translation copyright © 1990 by Joachim Neugroschel.

Library of Congress Cataloging-in-Publication Data
Döblin, Alfred, 1878–1957.
  [Reise in Polen. English]
  Journey to Poland/by Alfred Döblin; translated by
Joachim Neugroschel.
    p.  cm.—(European sources)
  Translation of: Reise in Polen.
  ISBN 1-55778-267-9: $21.95
  1. Döblin, Alfred, 1878–1957—Journeys—Poland.  2. Authors,
German—20th century—Biography.  3. Jews—Poland.  4. Poland
—Ethnic relations.  5. Poland—Description and travel—
1901–1944.  I. Neugroschel, Joachim.  II. Title.  III. Series.
PT2607.035Z46813   1991
838′.91203—dc20
[B]                                                              90-40595
                                                                    CIP

This American edition is based on Walter Verlag's edition of *Reise in Poland* which is part of *The Collected Works of Alfred Döblin* edited by Walter Muschg in collaboration with the author's sons and Anthony W. Riley.

Manufactured in the United States of America

The paper used in this publication meets the minimum requirements of American National Standard for Information Sciences— Permanence of Paper for Printed Library Materials, ANSI Z39.48-1984.

"FOR EVERY BORDER WIELDS A TYRANT'S POWER."

These words are aimed at all states
And at the State per se.

# CONTENTS

EDITOR'S INTRODUCTION                                    ix


Warsaw                                                    1
The Jewish District of Warsaw                            50
Wilno/Vilnius                                            83
Lublin                                                  118
Lwów/Lemberg                                            136
The Petroleum District                                 174
Cracow                                                  181
Zakopane                                                211
Lodz                                                    228
Departure                                               256
Map                                                     265
Bibliography                                            267


NOTES FOR THE INTRODUCTION                              269


NOTES FOR THE TEXT                                      272

# EDITOR'S INTRODUCTION

*Journey to Poland* was first published in German in November 1925 by S. Fischer Verlag in Berlin.[1] Döblin had traveled through Poland during 1924. He supplies no precise dates, and his text offers few leads; at most, the religious holidays and historical events that he mentions allow us to establish a chronology case by case. While the author's posthumous papers contain a few notes specifying places and times, the sequence of these references is defective, seldom revealing how long the author spent at his various stations or how long his entire trip lasted. The date he set out on is uncertain; it can only be guessed. Going chiefly by an indication in the text, we may assume that Döblin began his trip during the final days of the month of September.[2] We are better informed about when his trip ended: He kept a hotel bill dated November 24/25 in Danzig (Gdansk) —his last stop before returning to Berlin. Thus, his entire trip probably lasted about two months.

Döblin cared little for traveling and less for the opinion that travel is broadening. He was far more interested in studying his immediate environment; he himself was always intensely preoccupied with the world around him. His world was Berlin, where he was settled and sedentary since 1888. He couldn't do without Berlin; he felt he could work nowhere else. ("I'd be lying if I concealed the fact that I often feel like running away, but I don't have the money; however, I'd return just as often. Sampson demanding his hair.")[3] Döblin seldom left Berlin and usually only for a very brief while. Perhaps an outing to Prague, a cruise down the Rhine, a holiday in France may have interrupted the daily flow of his modest medical practice at a health plan office in the eastern part of Berlin.[4]

Of course, this physician led a double life; his far greater wanderlust is demonstrated in his voluminous novels—the products of an overheated imagination that ranged chiefly through remote, exotic climes, while the author felt trapped in the Public Library. China and the Thirty Years' War were fields of activity for his urge for transformations. In 1924, he published *Mountains, Oceans, and Giants*, a flight from the present into the future and back to a prehistoric era. After this "exhausting strain," the author traveled to Poland; but this was no vacation. He went on this trip despite a number of difficulties. He did not know the language of the country, and almost no one in Poland admitted to knowing German. He was dependent on information that he could not verify, and he was not always fortunate enough to meet people who knew what he wanted. And just what did he want?

Döblin wanted to find out what was happening in Poland; he wanted to understand the political and social conditions of this country, the relations of the ethnic minorities to one another and to the state. He wanted to know which forces were ruling officially and which unofficially. The fact that his trip to Poland had a political component is blatant in his book; this is already indicated by the epigraph, the first and most compelling Schiller quotation to occur in these pages: "For every border wields a tyrant's power." And this Poland was the test case. Repeatedly divided and tyrannized by the surrounding major powers, Poland had only just been resurrected in 1918 after their collapse, regaining its political autonomy. Döblin had a great deal of sympathy with these developments. He admired the resolute desire of a long-suppressed nation to rebuild, and he shared Poland's joy about its tasks and their solutions. Nevertheless, he had no illusions, for he also saw the dangers facing the young state: economic crisis and internal ethnic disintegration, unsettled borders, threats from the outside. "Poland has to be afraid!" The darkest skepticism proved correct.

A book by Döblin about Poland is a political book, but its political interest is not exhausted in the current situation, nor is it limited to Poland. This state merely serves as a background and point of departure for comments on the "State per se," which is addressed in the initial epigraph. The general political reflections, prompted by specific phenomena, are not voiced systematically; they are noted in a casual sequence—indeed, scattered throughout the book. Their thrust, however, is consistent. They are aimed at the totalitarian state as an obsolete institution that prevents the free development of the new impulses of nations.

The solemnity of the epigraph is imbued with personal experiences. Döblin already got to know the state as an instrument of suppression in his schooldays as a scholarship student. The high school in Berlin pounded not only the misnamed "humanistic" education into the Jewish boy, but also Prussian patriotism. School, as a place of nationalist orgies, always remained a nightmare for Döblin. Even at fifty, he suffered from these memories and tormentedly cited the shades of his teachers to his court of law. The sheer thought of the "barracks of youth" made him feel disgusted and ashamed that he had once been so terrorized. Moreover, as a member of a notorious minority, Döblin tended to agree with the definition of the state as an equilibrium of suppressors and suppressed, whereby he never left any doubt as to which side he stood on. In 1918, he had committed himself to a new social system. He regarded a thoroughgoing change as the inevitable consequence of World War I. Hence his profound disappointment at the outcome of the revolution in Germany. Exposing the Weimar Republic as "imperial," he attacked it first with the weapon of political satire. As of 1919, *Die Neue Rundschau* ran his commentaries under the pseudonym Linke Poot, which, in 1921, were collected in a book entitled *Der deutsche Maskenball* (The German Masquerade). In 1918, Alfred Döblin joined the Independent Social Democratic Party of Germany (USPD); in 1921, after the Party Convention in Halle, he switched over to the Socialist Party of Germany (SPD). He traveled to Poland as a Socialist; he wanted to know: "Who has the power and who the word? . . . Who starves in this country, and who is sated?"

In this book, Döblin does not talk about the chief purpose of his trip. His motive became noteworthy only after an interval of many years:

> In the first half of the nineteen-twenties, pogromlike events took place in Berlin, in the eastern part of the city, on and around Gollnowstrasse. They occurred against the lansquenet backdrop of those years; Nazism let out its first shriek. At that time, representatives of Berlin Zionism invited a number of men of Jewish origin to meetings to talk about these events, their background, and also the aims of Zionism. In connection with these discussions, a man came to my apartment and tried to talk me into going to Palestine, which I had no intention of doing. His influence had a different effect on me. I did not agree to visit Palestine, but I felt I had to get my bearings about the Jews. I realized I didn't know any Jews. I had friends who called themselves Jews, but I could not call them Jews. They were not Jewish by faith or by language; they were possibly remnants of an extinct nation that had long since integrated into a new milieu. So I asked myself and I asked others: "Where do Jews exist?" I was told: Poland. And so I went to Poland.[5]

In reading Döblin's book, one senses that the chief concern of his trip was Jews: the biggest and best portion of his book is devoted to the Jews of Poland—who were Jews in both faith and language, clinging to a spiritual world that had not changed essentially since late antiquity. Döblin was shocked and agitated by the sight of these people in medieval garb, with their own language, religion, and culture. He was startled by how poor, despised, and hated they were. He went to the old Jewish cemeteries, visited the graves of the holy men, and literally "lapped up" the legends he was told. He could not get enough of it all; he was "filled with an eeriness." He had Jews translate passages of Cabbalistic writings for him, and he admiringly saw that the reality of this nation, for whom school and house of worship are one and the same, consisted in its spirituality. He followed the pious to their synagogues on holy days, but he did not understand the rituals. He was fascinated; but at times he felt as if he had wandered into an exotic tribe. Everything was alien to him —and therefore all the more fascinating.

Judaism had not been a decisive factor either in Döblin's upbringing or in his education. He had received, if possible, even less of that "nothing" which Kafka discusses in his *Letter to His Father*. Döblin spoke about it later:

> At home, back in Stettin [Szczecin], I heard that my parents were of Jewish origin, and that we were a Jewish family. But I noticed little more of Judaism within the family. On the outside, I encountered anti-Semitism as a matter of course, and these experiences were no different for me than for schoolmates who had heard the same things in their homes. We did not attend Protestant religious instruction, and the Jewish instruction was unsteady and more voluntary. We had no school on Christian holidays, and we could get off two or three Jewish holidays. These were the things we saw and observed. My parents celebrated two major holy days: New Year's and the Day of Atonement. Dressing up, they attended synagogue, usually in the evening and in the morning, and they did not work. When they went to temple, they took along books containing prayers and excerpts from the Old Testament as well as psalms, all of which were printed bilingually, in German and Hebrew. In my (quite sporadic) religious lessons, I learned a little Hebrew, but never got beyond the rudiments. What interest could I have in learning Hebrew, too, along with Latin, Greek, and French, since the study of these empty linguistic shells always repelled me? Between the Iliad and the Odyssey, the Edda, *The Lay of the Nibelungs*, and *The Lay of Gudrun*, I knew little about the early history of the nation of Israel, which was subsequently scattered and disbanded. As for the doctrines, the actual religion—I read them and heard them. It was and remained a shallow reading. I felt nothing in particular, no rapport was established.[6]

Hence, it is not surprising that later on, when Döblin was on his own, he officially left the Jewish faith.[7] In so doing, he severed a link that had never spiritually bound him. However, anti-Semitism may have shown him the relative value of this step, reminding him that he was a Jew. Still, Döblin's sole reaction to anti-Semitism was mockery. At the time, he still believed that he could parry the assaults of stupidity with witty and impudent aphorisms. During the early nineteen-twenties, he still dealt with the Jewish issue entirely in the style of Linke Poot: "How is the Jew to realize that he is a Jew? Other people say so. But saying does not make you anything. He wants to become something else, but he merely becomes a Zionist."

The existence of East European Jews, mentioned in this connection for the first time, is, at present, nothing but an unsubstantiated rumor: "The issue of East European Jewry is a chapter unto itself. In case it is true that great masses of Jews, millions, live there as a cohesive group. . . . We would have to determine whether millions of East European Jews really do live in Poland and Galicia. . . . A geographic expedition would have to be fitted out to confirm this question."[8]

Three years later, Döblin set out to look with his own eyes and discover the Jews of East Europe for himself.

There were, no doubt, other reasons for his trip. Although he had been living in Berlin for over three decades, he had spent his childhood in Stettin. His mother had grown up in Samter, in the province of Posen (Poznan), where her father ran a small housewares shop. He still spoke Yiddish, while his children already spoke mainly German, as well as Polish, and a little Yiddish. During the eighteen-sixties, the brothers of Döblin's mother had moved to Breslau and Berlin, where they became well-to-do lumber merchants; their firms were still thriving when Döblin traveled to Poland.

His father, Max Döblin, was born in the city of Posen. In Stettin, he owned a cutting shop. He was an artistic man of many talents, but with no real backbone—a problematical person. At forty, he fled to America with a girl from his shop and then eventually settled in Hamburg. The father's guilt haunted the son until he was fifty. Only then did the writer work up the courage openly to confront his father, whose buried gifts had blossomed in him, the son. In 1928, Döblin, looking back autobiographically, gives a faltering, wavering account of his father's flight and its impact on the writer's life. The image of his father,

loudly cursed and silently admired, oscillates in his son's judgment: He condemns and justifies him. It was only after tackling
it three times that he came up with something worthwhile; Döblin says about his father: "He was—ethnologically—the victim
of resettlement. All his values were reevaluated and devaluated.
. . . Only in my generation has the memory, including the joyous memory of our background and the old respect, been heavily and gradually revived. I—survived the great resettlement."[9]

So that is the point of departure: A man who survived resettlement goes back. Can one go back? That is the very question
that Döblin asks himself in Poland: "Could I, could anyone else
return to this level?" His manuscript reveals how deeply haunted
he was by this question even though it was settled for him; the
relevant passage is thoroughly revised. Two versions can be de-
ciphered. First, Döblin wrote: "I feel I could not go back to that
level." Then he wrote: "I feel I am on this level; or approaching
it, I had only moved away from it, like someone forgetting something."

However, this addition was crossed out; the process of resettlement was irreversible. His fascination with this exotic world
was tremendous, but the sense of being alien predominated.
The foreigner was suspect, his attempts at striking up conversations with the leaders of Judaism thwarted. Instead of being
welcomed, he was eyed with hostility as an intruder, and he felt
left out. His efforts at getting closer simply pointed out the
insuperable gap. On the eve of a Jewish holy day, he walks alone
through the dark streets of the Cracow ghetto: "Window after
window is bright; they sit around the father at the festive candlelit table. He sits royally, he sings."

The father in the family circle, in harmony with tradition,
comfortable in the faith of the fathers—all the things that Döblin had been deprived of are mirrored in this scene. His memory
of his childhood preserved a similar image, but characteristically
altered:

My mother could read Hebrew, and on the high holidays, it was
poignant to see this woman—who worked hard and who went to
so much trouble for us and who could barely read a newspaper

xv

—quietly sitting off to the side somewhere in the room. She would hold one of her Hebrew books in her hand and read for a while in an undertone. At times it was only a murmur. When I think of Jewishness, I see that picture of my mother. She dashed around, wearing herself out for us children, whose father, her husband, had settled down in Hamburg with that girl, occasionally remembering his large family with letters.[10]

After being deserted by her husband, the mother, with her five children, had moved to Berlin, where a rich brother put them up and supported them. Alfred Döblin was ten years old at that time. Over forty years later, after leaving Germany, he recaptured that early period, when Berlin itself had been a place of exile; he conjured it up in his autobiographical novel, whose title *Pardon wird nicht gegeben* (No Mercy is Shown) could serve as the implacable motto of his youth.

An early and lasting impact on Döblin was made not by the circumstance that his family was Jewish, but that it was uprooted and déclassé. The shocks he suffered in his childhood sharpened his social consciousness forever. The father's desertion, the loss of a homeland, the relocation to Berlin, the destitution: "That was how I grew up. That was what I got at home. It remained in me that we, that I, belonged to the poor. This had marked my entire mentality. I belonged to this people, to this nation: the poor."[11]

Döblin's commitment to the poor was immune to sentimentalization, for he lived in close contact with the social reality. In Poland, he was confronted with an undreamt-of degree of poverty and the filth accompanying it. He walked through the slums with the eyes of a physician and a social-minded man: "People in such houses. And someone dares to speak of the beauty of the archway."

In the face of indigence, the enjoyment of art is barbarous. Döblin's vehement disavowal of classicism is to be understood against that background. Nowhere can one see as clearly as here the way his aesthetic protest is tied up with his social protest. His very skepticism about traveling stems from an antibourgeois passion; it is a distaste for the tourist, who flees his everyday life in order to enjoy the everyday lives of other people. On the whole, it is a dislike of a hedonistic attitude toward the world and of anything that inspires such an attitude. Döblin describes himself as a new brand of tourist; on principle, he avoids anything that a guidebook touts as noteworthy. Sometimes, in an exuberant mood, he makes references to this purely for the sake of parody. In Wilno, he plays the role of tourist guide in order to show the castle to a native, and he discovers a new meaning in the tourist attractions by also finding them worth smelling. He listlessly plods through museums, circles around statues at an appropriate distance, and flaunts his indifference to the past that is hewn in stone. His plebeian disrespect comes from Linke Poot's conviction: "You shouldn't talk about heroes too much, the masses have something on the ball too. If the masses didn't have such a thick skin, they wouldn't be able to endure the many heroes. The skin too is worth celebrating."[12]

It is Linke Poot who, when standing in front of a painting, is irresistibly drawn to its dusty back, and who is so deeply touched by the mute canvas that the painted, shaped front surface strikes him as superficial. Thus, Döblin always prefers the despised back to the façade, because the former seems more true and more real. He sticks to the homely, indeed, ugly side of life: "I sense disquiet, filth, poverty, suffering, formlessness." His focus is on living, urgent things that are not yet frozen into form. He always seeks the human being and he find him on the street, in the throng, in the teeming marketplaces, in the beggar and the worshiper. The trip to Poland is a trip to poor people.

The unsystematic structure of the book corresponds to the external form of the trip; the sequence of chapters is dictated by the travel route. Döblin does not visit "land and people"; his stations are almost exclusively cities—not only because that was where the Jews were concentrated: In the countryside, the passionate urbanite is helpless, needing the pulse of city life. The traveler's situation is also mirrored in the syntax. Thus, in their disjointed rhythm, the jottings about the street follow Döblin's observations of the passersby. In Warsaw, he encounters officers; he describes them and remarks: "The Poles haven't had a military for long, they relish it. Trolleys rattle by. . . ." Now the trolleys distract the stranger, the military theme vanishing with the perception that evoked it. The promiscuously noted impressions could easily become the point of departure for a digression. At every step, the present offers a chance for the narrator to shift from the reporting present tense to the narrative past. His Polish trip is studded with episodes and anecdotes that reveal Döblin the storyteller. The story itself functions mainly as an impetus to tell stories. For a traveling storyteller, the historical digression is a legitimate device of narrative. More than in official history, he is interested in, say, the actions of the Polish Socialist Party during its underground period or the legends of holy men, which the author attentively absorbs and recounts. He often refuses to edit what he hears. In the oral translations which he depended on, he discovered a unique linguistic charm, which he preserved when writing them down. The incorrect sentence structure guarantees the authenticity of the statement. Episodes like that of the merry war of the Jews of Radom with their rebbe contribute a great deal to the atmosphere imbuing the text. Döblin never selects, he commits himself to the moment and to chance, even noting the number that is attached to him when he enters a restaurant. Selection would presume overview, hence a firm stance. The traveler, however, is in motion, en route. He knows that his horizon is restricted, and he makes sure that the reader won't forget it. Nothing is done to change the impression belatedly by adding something that was missing. "A name is written on it, ending with 'pole,' I can't read it." Such passages, devoid of any informational value, gain meaning from a different side; they remain as is out of fidelity to the momentary truth. For here, immediacy is more important than information. Its primacy keeps perception from being retrospectively filtered and distilled into an essence. Mistrust of abstraction is a characteristic of the narrator, who does not sacrifice concreteness to concept. As so often in Döblin, the joy of storytelling finds elementary utterance in counting and recounting; it leads to the lists of Jewish names or the catalogues of the merchandise hawked at the markets. But, at lucid moments, things appear as forcefully as signs, and concreteness becomes a symbol. Even the most random detail is given its specific place: "And nothing is unclear, uncertain, everything is completely present, open—transparent and exposed to its innermost core."

If reality turns into signs, then, vice versa, a sign can be filled with reality and represent reality. At St. Mary's Church in Cracow, Döblin stumbles upon a crucifix that Veit Stoss "hauled . . . out of his agonized soul." Döblin is stunned; it hits him like an illumination: "Pain, woe are in the world: a tremendous, illuminating emotion." Shaken, he comes to the "executed rebel." However, Döblin's declaration of faith is nondenominational, it is undogmatic; the executed man is also, in Jewish terms, the tsadik, the righteous man, the pillar on which the world rests. The Cross proclaims no evil tidings; instead, it becomes the sign of an unredeemed, struggling world that suffers in every limb. Even inanimate objects take part in the universal suffering. The water faucet with a pail hanging in front of it looks like a suffering thing. The bowels emerge from destroyed houses. In Poland, Döblin, who was justly viewed as representing the literary movement known as *Neue Sachlichkeit* (New Objectivism), discovered feeling as a reality. The religious turn is a shift to the reality of suffering. It is in this context that one must see Döblin's vehement rejection of the aesthetic; this rejection is religious: "Under Veit Stoss's crucifix, Döblin realized that his dislike of all classicism was Christian."[13]

This change should not be interpreted as a complete transformation, and we should not assume that Döblin was a different person when he returned from Poland. His development was not unilinear. Several tendencies existed simultaneously in him, operating next to and against one another. The visible ones were merely those that dominated the latent ones. And *Journey to Poland* offers insight into this cluster of strands; we see that Döblin was aware of and accepted his inner contradictions. The forgotten thing that he stumbled on in Poland was the religious stratum, the realm of feeling and suffering, which was covered over with his inculcated Prussian virtues of "rigor, matter-of-factness, sobriety, hard work." However, his experiences do not remain purely subjective; he came to realize their more-than-personal validity. In Poland, he found traces of a spirituality that had vanished from Western Europe. He saw enlightenment, science, and imperialism as replacing it.

Döblin reacts to everything he encounters with the sensitivity and vehemence of a magnetic needle. He is drawn or repelled, and he formulates likes and dislikes with the same lack of restraint. He, who equated existence with action, cannot observe and describe, he can only commit himself. He feels called upon to decide, and he has to take a stand. Upon seeing the poverty and destitution, he turns against classicism and aestheticism, commits himself to Christ and the red banner, whereby, as it later turned out, Christianity and revolution are by no means mutually exclusive; Döblin's profession of faith has a social tinge, his social protest a religious tinge. In the uncanny and mysterious world that he encounters in Poland, he questions the present and progress. Among the East European Jews, who are devoted to the Bible, he turns against the West European Jews, to whom he himself belongs. The purpose of all these decisions for and against, these critiques and engagements, is self-knowledge, the need to pinpoint his own position. "I, neither an Enlightener nor a member of these national masses, a West European passerby." The author's self enters the scene and remains constantly present. It is the subject of the report, it makes itself the subject, and at times it also reveals itself in a soliloquy. In *Journey to Poland*, Döblin talks about himself such as he has never done before. He had always been an enemy of the personal. The elimination of the "I" was the maxim he adhered to in all his previous works; they are concerned not about individuals, but about collective forces. The novelist was most excessive in *Berge Meere und Giganten* (Mountains, Oceans, and Giants). (This opus was completed by the time the author went to Poland, and at one point it is alluded to without its title.) In this novel, Döblin takes the technological era beyond itself to a point at which technology, in its struggle with nature, cancels itself out, throwing mankind back to a primitive level. The crude shape of this work is the expression of unresolved conflicts. They involve nature, the position of the individual, and the role of the mind in nature. As demonstrated by several of his essays, Döblin had been delving into such issues since the early nineteen-twenties. His trip to Poland was probably a welcome opportunity to break away mentally from that novel, and it helped to clarify the situation he found himself in. The conclusion indicates that the author himself saw his trip as a process of clarification. Thus, in this book, we also witness an important phase of his development.

The autobiographical character of *Journey to Poland* is symptomatic; its first-person narrative is merely a signal that the individual is speaking up, and that his demands are being heard. The individual is now given more clout in Döblin's work. The valorization of the individual has a political gist: "People have become persons, the nations have been called upon to practice self-determination, the ancient monstrosity of the state cannot survive."

Here, Poland once again has an exemplary significance: as a national individual, as an indivisible entity that, in the long run, will not be suppressed by greater organizations. Even in the face of an imminent totalitarianism, Döblin wanted to fortify the sense of individual responsibility. All his projects as a writer during the next few years served as warnings against the imminent danger.

Döblin's transformation in his view of nature—a process that took years—was visibly completed in a piece of natural philosophy whose title recorded the position he had reached: *Das Ich über der Nature* (The Self Above Nature, 1927). Unmistakable are the traces left here by his trip to Poland. The self moves entirely into an unattainable position that was first adumbrated in *Journey to Poland*; the individual becomes what Döblin saw in the tsadik in Poland: the pillar on which the world rests. At the same time, these ideas were treated artistically in *Manas* (1927), a poetic work about the power of suffering and of the self; this opus shows how radical Döblin's transformation was. Taking over the writer, it releases unsuspected energy, producing a new form akin to the ancient verse epic. This would not have been possible without the discovery of the self. In the next work, the novel *Berlin Alexanderplatz*, the self assumes narrative functions. Döblin's previous output met the author's need for self-denial; his attitude was that literature must "not appear to be spoken," it should appear "to be present."[14] This actually Naturalist demand is dropped, the author no longer has to deny himself, he can and should speak up, interrupting the narrative account and process and put in his personal word. Judgment is not left to the reader. The "I" enters the narrative, establishing itself as an authority that judges.

Pogromlike events in Berlin had sparked Döblin's interest in Judaism, inspiring him to go to Poland. Here too, he encountered anti-Semitism. In a shop window in Lodz, he saw German racist literature and a poster proclaiming: "Poles, don't buy from Jews!" In Gdansk's *Völkische Rundschau*, he reads: "Ethnic Germans! Do your Christmas shopping only in Christian stores!" (This newspaper, from which the author quotes, was preserved in his posthumous papers.)

During his nocturnal train ride to Gdansk, Döblin meets a Polish nationalist who is filled with unspeakable hatred of the Jews: "He doesn't even know whether it makes any sense to wipe them out completely, smash them and suck them up." In the rolling of the train, Döblin hears the true wording of those appeals to boycott the competition: "Strike them dead, strike them dead, strike them dead!" The end of his trip is darkened by the shadow of a future that realized the wildest dreams of hatred, fully surpassing them in reality.

In Poland, Döblin did not fail to perceive the economic and political dangers of the Jewish situation. After his trip, he was ready to commit himself publicly to Judaism. In 1928, upon being received into the Prussian Academy, he had to fill out a form; when asked about his religion, he wrote, "None," but then added: "I will not forget I come from Jewish parents." The focus on and commitment to his origins were the results of his trip to Poland. Döblin studied the history of the Jewish people, immersing himself in the Jewish past in order to find solutions for the present. He commented on Jewish issues and took stances with a resoluteness that matched the growing threat of National Socialism.[15]

During his first few years of exile, he deployed a great amount of activity. In this context, his position was determined by his experiences in Poland, which he repeatedly brought up in his writings. "Flucht und Sammlung des Judenvolks" (Flight and Gathering of the Jewish People) and "Jüdische Zerstreuung" (Jewish Dispersion) are passionate appeals to the Jews, the ultimate watchwords in a time when the "Final Solution" to the Jewish question was being prepared. Obtaining land somewhere for the homeless remnants of the Jewish people struck him as the only way to save them from annihilation and to end two thousand years of calamity and disastrous wandering. In Paris, he joined the Territorialists, whose goal was a Jewish state outside Palestine. As a member of the League for Jewish Colonization, he worked on its magazine *Freiland* (Free Land) and issued declarations at its meetings.[16] But no matter how passionate his official advocacy of the Territorialist plans, his chief goal was not land, but an overall spiritual renewal of the Jewish people. He thus once again revealed the deep impact of his trip in 1924. After seeing the Jews as a nation in Poland, he envisioned this original form of Judaism, and the idea of peoplehood was fundamental to all his thinking about the Jewish situation: "For the Jews really exist, even as a people. One should seek them not on the streets of Western Europe, but in Poland, Rumania, and Lithuania."[17]

Later on, it was precisely the national factor in Judaism that made it seem limited in Döblin's eyes, alienating him more and more from the Jewish cause. In a letter of 1942, which looked back at his activities in Paris, he resignedly described them as "taking the wrong route—that of Jewish nationalism." He was already on the broad road of a religion for all mankind. He had already discovered Kierkegaard and German mysticism in Paris, and, while still in exile, he converted to Catholicism.

A *Journey to Poland* shows that this step was not due simply to the events of the period; its roots lie further back than is commonly assumed. Döblin's conversion was prefigured in the religious shock he suffered in Poland. During the years after his trip, the effects of his Christian experience subsided; it went into his writings before being revived. Once again, Döblin was traveling. This time through France, fleeing the German invaders after the general collapse, which he experienced as a personal defeat. In *Schicksalsreise* (Fateful Journey, 1948), his other travel book, Döblin depicts his escape from Paris to the south of France, where he was interned. At the Cathedral of Mende, as earlier at St. Mary's Church in Cracow, he stumbled upon the crucifix. The two situations were similar; the second book contains passages that could have been taken from *Journey to Poland:* "I see Jesus with the crown of thorns on the cross as the incarnation of human suffering, of our weakness and helplessness. But this is not what I am seeking."[18]

Mentally, he was no longer in the same place as in 1924. What he was looking for now was a solace in this suffering, something he could cling to, rather than succumbing to resignation. Now, Jesus was not so much the example of human suffering in the world as the manifestation of its ultimate divine reason. Döblin effortlessly included Christ in his speculation; converting to Christianity would be only a small step, which he implemented in all due form after finding refuge in the United States.

At the publication of *Journey to Poland,* few people realized that the book has a religious core, signaling a transformation. Contemporaries ignored this, because Döblin's conduct belied the text. And how could anyone have figured out the true crux of a book combining various, seemingly contradictory, tendencies? So everyone read it by his own lights. In Poland, of course, the political remarks were given special attention. But on the whole, it was felt that a German reader would learn little about Poland from Döblin's book.[19] Jews in Western Europe had different reactions to it. The alert ones sensed what the author was after. His penetrating depiction of the Jews as a people was hailed, as were his indications of the spirituality revealed in Jewish religiosity; nor was the value of the book in this respect overlooked: "Never have the Jewish people of the present day been comprehended and drawn with such a powerful strength of impression. Döblin's work belongs among the very great travel accounts. For us, who share his passionate love for this subject, his tale of discovery is breathtakingly suspenseful."[20]

For others, it was an irritant. Indicting Döblin's lack of solid knowledge, they focused on his misinterpretations of Jewish religious customs and found them unforgivable. Nor would they forgive him for siding with the Yiddishists against the Hebraists among the conflicting trends within Judaism. Some were offended by his casualness, denying him all competence and simply accusing him of ignorance.[21]

In contrast, Joseph Roth, a native of Galicia who had visited Poland several times and loved that country, wrote: "Döblin saw the Jews with the unerring view that is a virtue of love. . . . He ought to have titled his book *A Journey to the Jews*. He got to know them better than do their West European 'brethren' of French, German, British 'nationality,' who, commiserating with their distant cousins, become charitable toward them and hand out clean collars and Enlightenment to the 'dull masses.' "[22]

Today, we cannot read Döblin's book without thinking about what came later. Twenty years after his visit, no more Jews were living in Warsaw. The ghettos in the cities, where the Jewish population had been locked up in order to be isolated, starved, and finally deported to annihilation, had been wiped out. The Jews of Eastern Europe were systematically exterminated, becoming a historical phenomenon. The world depicted here by Döblin no longer exists. Before our astonished eyes, his impressions freeze into snapshots of victims prior to the coming of their murderers. However, we also read Döblin's book as an autobiographical document that shows the author in a decisive phase of his life and creativity—in a crisis whose scope does not become clear until afterward.

The textual genesis of *Journey to Poland* can to some degree be reconstructed from Döblin's posthumous papers, despite the meagerness of extant material. The *Nachlass* of this book was kept in a legal folder. It comprises notes, handwritten portions of the manuscript, and newspaper clippings. Of particular importance are four packets totaling 128 sheets of paper (17.5 × 22 cm) and 44 slips. Each leaf has holes by the left-hand margin, is folded down the middle, and shows two columns of writing on each side. These are the first, quick jottings; they were done *in situ* with pencil or ink—the ink was normally used only for subsequent revisions. The writing is larded with shorthand and not very legible. This version, which Döblin brought back from his trip, served as the basis of the final draft. Extant are 151 unpaginated manuscript sheets of paper with writing in ink.[23] They contain portions of the chapter "Warsaw," almost the entire chapter "Lwów," and the chapter "Cracow." (Aside from two passages, which the author subsequently inserted, this is the only complete manuscript chapter to come down to us.) Finally, one portion is about the excursion to Gura Kalwarja, in the book an episode from the chapter "The Jewish District of Warsaw." In the manuscript, the episode is set off and has its own title: "With the Spiritual Prince of the Jews of Gura Kalwarja/By Alfred Döblin." The author developed this episode separately in order to publish it on its own, perhaps in a newspaper. Such a publication was posthumously preserved: *Das Leipziger Tageblatt* ran "Die Tür" (The Door) in its Sunday issue, December 14, 1924. This was the first known serial publication before the appearance of the book. Other pieces may have come out in other periodicals, but there could not have been many; the prepublication rights were owned by S. Fischer Verlag, which printed the book. In 1925, *Die Neue Rundschau*, which belonged to Fischer Verlag, ran four large excerpts from the book.[24]

Comparing these excerpts with the final book version, we find that they were revised by the author: He cut out sentences, shifted or removed sections, disregarding the ensuing gap, which could be felt as a lacuna by the reader. One example is the passage describing Döblin's arrival in Warsaw; this passage is missing. First, the author is in the train—then he is suddenly in the city. The missing part can be read in the magazine. There, Döblin's arrival in the station and his finding a place to stay are described in two sections.[25] Döblin eliminated them. He did the same with a few other passages.[26] Normally, however, their removal left no perceptible gap, since the book as a whole consists of disconnected pieces. The text obviously emerged from notes; long stretches maintain the character of jottings. In many instances, however, the ellipses were subsequently filled with verbs. Then again, the reverse can also be observed: Something that looks like a first, fleeting note in the printed text might

have resulted from a process of shortening. In some passages—
either in the manuscript or later on—Döblin cut out verbs. He
also removed adverbs of time, place, and manner, conjunc-
tions, numerals, and articles—words that modify the statement
but can be dispensed with. Furthermore, all the precise indications of time, which were in the magazine versions, were left
out of the book: "I've been in Cracow too long (two weeks)."
Such omissions, like most of the changes, are products of stylistic reworkings.

Nevertheless, we find an inchoate tendency that goes beyond
this framework: The stylistic change can affect the content and
alter the substance. At such times, the stylistic focus on form is
stronger than the interest in content and information. A com-
parison of the magazine version with the book version reveals
variants that contradict one another factually.

Take the start of the chapter "Lwów": "From provincial Lublin (it welcomed me with a tremendous starry sky, it sees me off
with a twinkling) to the south, to East Galicia."

The magazine version was different: "From provincial Lublin
(it welcomed me with a tremendous starry sky, it sees me off on
a gray afternoon." [27]

The book version of this sentence is apparently the product
of an aesthetic focus on symmetry rather than an attempt to
correct a factual error. In rewriting the magazine excerpts and
the manuscript, Döblin not only omitted, he also added. Statis-
tical data, quotations, historical digressions seldom occur in the
magazines.

The new German edition is based on the first edition. The
documents on which the latter was based are no longer extant.
The reliability of the text was tested by comparisons with the
manuscript—to the extent that it has come down to us—and
versions that appeared in periodicals. The latter helped in de-
tecting typographical errors in the original book edition. The
manuscript helped in tracking down a few errors and misunder-
standings on the part of the copyist. Obvious errors on the part
of the author were likewise corrected. On the other hand, his
spellings of geographical and personal Slavic names, some of

which are correct and some phonetic, were left intact. Similarly, no effort was made for a proper transcription of the Polish fragments and Yiddish verses.

The printing of the first edition was rife with commas. Döblin was not exactly in the habit of articulating his sentences precisely. Rather, even before *Mountains, Oceans, and Giants*, we cannot overlook his tendency to reduce punctuation. In the first edition of *Journey to Poland*, the punctuation marks or at least the commas, were not consistent with the author's original wishes—an assumption borne out by the magazine versions and the extant manuscript portions. Thus, Döblin rarely inserted a comma between adjectives, while main clauses linked by "and" were usually not separated by commas. In the new German edition, the chapter entitled "Cracow" follows the use of commas in the manuscript.

For the preparation of this book, I am grateful for the help given me by Frau Elli Muschg, who read the galley proofs. For information concerning individual questions, I am grateful to the Schiller-Nationalmuseum in Marbach, where Döblin's posthumous papers are preserved. Finally, for valuable information about Jewish and Yiddish matters, I am grateful to the Institute for Jewish Research in New York as well as Frau Dr. Salicia Landman, whose books *Jiddisch; das Abenteuer einer Sprache* (Yiddish; the Adventure of a Language) and *Der Jüdische Witz* (The Jewish Joke) (both: Olten and Freiburg i. Br., 1962) were used in explaining various words and items.

# WARSAW

*They now are dwelling in their very own homes.*

In the long railroad car, I sway over the tracks. The train zoomed off from Berlin like an arrow. The rails are endless. Now, I whiz along, jog along, with a wood-and-iron structure, inside a gurgling tube, into the night. The cars bounce. A chaos of noises has begun: a rhythmic thrusting from the wheels, a vibrating, a rolling, a clattering of windows, a buzzing, a hollow grinding, a sliding, a brief, sharp slamming.

I—am not here. I—am not in the train. We pelt across bridges. I—have not flown along. Not yet. I am still standing in the terminal, Schlesischer Bahnhof. They stand around me, but then I get into the train, I sit on the green cushion, amid leather valises, satchels, plaids, coats, umbrellas. I am caught. The train carries me off, holds me captive, rocks me along the rails into the night.

I looked out the window, across this metal bar. Now—two young men stand there, pull down the curtain, insert cigarettes into their mouths, smoke, chat in a foreign language. They have light-gray cotton gloves on, and caps over their dark, agile eyes; they smile. One man points to a newspaper he holds under his arm. An older man joins them; corpulent. The foreign parleying —trilled *r*'s, sibilants—keeps on. Now they make way. A little

1

girl—legs naked white up to the middle of her thighs, elegant patent-leather shoes, a short, loose velvet dress, unbound black hair—passes through, keeping her balance by holding on left and right. She gazes ahead, very earnest, very mournful.

I—am not here. The newspaper lies on my lap. "The Triumphal March of the Zeppelin," I read, with an intensely mounting anxiety, almost sorrow.[1] The train, the reverberating edifice, is taking me east. This is still Germany, I am still almost at home, here comes Frankfurt on the Oder: I can't believe it, I don't recognize the countryside. They are all traveling. These are the people with whom I'm traveling. The young man who was chatting at the metal bar saunters into my compartment, sits down next to me. He speaks. A voice addressing me. My voice comes to me. I arrange the suitcases for the night. Anxiously, I think of Poland, I let him talk about it. I think of my plans. But they are not my plans now, I do not recognize them.

Night. The train surges about us. The border is coming, three hours east of Berlin. The three elegant gentlemen occasionally speak a different language than before. I notice eyes moving, hunting peculiarly, shoulders shrugging in a certain way: the voices coo and carol Yiddish. They stick their heads together with their British caps. Then the train stops. A ceremonious act commences. The door at the end of the car has opened, all the passengers have left the corridor. Two men in green uniforms have climbed into the car, followed by a man wearing plainclothes and holding a notebook. They collect the passports, take notes. One man steps into our compartment, tells us to open our suitcases. Everyone is very silent. The officials wander from compartment to compartment. The train lumbers on. Black midnight has come. The train halts; is this a station? Tense hush. Again three men stride along the carpet. But now they are headed by a soldier in a black uniform, a policeman with an enormous polished cavalry saber. He distributes metal tokens for the passports. These are Poles, men, well-fed, with a healthy color, good-natured faces. Scores of passengers pour out of the train, as if a war were raging. We have to walk across dark platforms, down and up staircases, into gigantic wooden shacks —to the customs office. This is a foreign country. The train has

crossed the border. I am walking on foreign soil. That's how fast
it all went. I was only just thinking about it, two weeks, three
weeks ago, at home, weighing pros and cons. It was my plan.
Now it stands before me, moves, is no longer in my mind, rolls
down around me. I comb about in it. Now it is more powerful
than I. How dreadful this translation of an idea into visibility.

The signs on the staircase walls contain words, syllables,
whose meaning I can't surmise. They are probably just saying:
Such and such a train departs from the platform. But in the
foreign language, these words excite me, arouse my expectations. How could they help it? Now I begin to go dumb, go deaf.

Onward. I lie, drowsing—for hours or minutes—between the
canvas partitions of the sleeping car. Gray light through a gap
in a curtain. I sit up. Flat fields whoosh by, small forests. By
some water, below, at a wooden bridge, a peasant woman strides
barefoot, in a white kerchief. What's this? Herds of cattle. New
farmland. Many white geese. This is Poland. A troop of women
in particolored skirts, walking along a path. An old, gray railroad
station; people scurrying across the tracks to the train. My heart
is wrenched. I shake myself.

The faces of the Polish women: broad foreheads, not high;
full faces. The root of the nose starting low, sometimes with an
almost saddle-shaped recess. The nose sloping flat toward the
cheeks; very strong nostrils; the dark openings turned up. The
lips wide and fleshy. The eyes, under strong, almost horizontal
brows, straight, aligned, rather far apart. Their figures large. In
city streets, under hats, they are extraordinarily piquant. Bevies
of young girls, misses, young women populate the streets, arm
in arm, next to young gentlemen; they descend from hackneys,
gaze at their reflections in bright shop windows. Sporting light-
or flesh-colored stockings and elegant shoes, they glide very
gracefully from the coffeehouses and restaurants, walk down
the steps of churches. All the women are powdered, made up,
painted. They saunter aimlessly along the sidewalks; they obviously know how to aim Cupid's arrows. In a closed space, they
are less appealing.

Men and women, of a pure type, with light or brown hair.
The men massive, powerful—why, there are some enormous

3

specimens among them. Next to the Hotel Bristol lies a ministerial palace with a vast green front lawn.[2] It used to be a castle
belonging to magnates, the Radziwills; then it became the residence of the Russian governor. A bronze statue of Prince Paskevich stood in front of it: Paskevich Erivansky, a harsh, cruel
creature.

The Poles had a revolution in 1830/31. They planned to assas-
sinate Grand Prince Constantin, the Russian commander-in-
chief of the Polish army, disarm the foreign soldiers, and wrest
the country back from the Russians. The whole plan failed. At
Grochow, near Warsaw, the unfortunate Poles were defeated
by the Russian Dibich; and they were defeated once again near
Ostrolenka. Dibich was followed by that Paskevich. He dealt the
coup de grâce. Warsaw, Poland were lost.

The Poles have forgotten nothing. They got rid of his monument. But now, in front of the seat of the Polish government,
two live policemen in black uniforms stand with large sabers and
turned-down chin straps. Living colossi. I scrutinize them each
time I leave the hotel.

Cracow Suburb is the name of an avenue in Warsaw. Marshal
Street is the other one. Marshal Street is densely thronged; its
northern part, the movie district, is mobbed. Elegant stores.
The railroad station disgorges its masses. The sides of the street
have either odd or even house numbers. Each house identifies
itself very courteously: a bilateral streetlamp juts out over the
entrance archway, indicating the number of the house and the
name of the street; evenings, the lamp is lit.

In the morning, I walk along Cracow Suburb. Many officers.
The general staff is nearby; the country is well fortified; it has a
memory. The officers salute with two fingers, indolently; sub-
ordinates salute with their palms forward. Their caps: loose, flat
kepis in the French style, shoved backward, baggy-looking, and
with four corners. On the front of their collars they wear silver
caterpillars in varying shapes; on their epaulettes, stars. All these
field uniforms are yellowish green. Pictures of the soldiers hang
in the photographer's showcases along these avenues: in the
pictures, they sport medals and ribbons galore.

The Poles haven't had a military for long, they relish it. Trol-

leys rattle by; red cars with trailers, their flanks marked with
Warsaw's coat of arms: a woman with the body of a fish, the tail
of a fish, a mermaid, a siren. She brandishes a saber, holds a
shield. The passengers hang from the trolley, stand on its steps;
indeed—a scary sight—they balance diagonally, with one leg on
the back bumper. Inside, they push forward; the exit is near the
driver. The passengers standing and swaying in the car clutch
the wooden straps. In a manner unfamiliar in any German city,
the people chase after the trolley, frantically jumping in and
out.

Military music, slow, solemn, sostenuto: a funeral. And they
march with glittering brasses; a soldier, bareheaded, carries a
large cross; priests in white vestments; the flower-covered
hearse. The people on the sidewalks doff their hats.

I cross the street; the roadway is covered with wooden blocks
and has deep holes. The placard pillar at the corner has adver-
tisements for the theaters; but wide death notices in black out-
lines are also pasted up: at the very top, the black cross; palm
fronds underneath. Fruit peddlers sit next to the pillar; their
apples and pears are in large glass cases with hinged lids. What
does that peasant woman in the red kerchief do? She sits behind
her basket, with her head drooping, ready to doze off in broad
daylight. The man next to her offers official cigarettes, *papierosi*, lying in a red crate on a tripod.

I stand on the corner, peering toward the right, into the wide
cross street. What a bizarre sight! What a stunning, no, confusing tableau. A tremendous, fantastic building stands there—a
Russian cathedral. Hackneys roll past me, an auto scoots by,
newsboys yell *"Curier Warszawski!"* modern store windows glit-
ter. And here, dreadful and paralyzing, yawn—dear God—the
steppes of the Volga. Anyone would be dumbfounded by this
sight, for terrifying Asia is frozen here in stone. Its name is the
Alexander Nevsky Cathedral. It took eighteen years to build.
Supposedly, it had five gilded domes; a high campanile stood
next to it. The campanile is gone; I don't see the five domes.
The stone creature rising from the vast square has only strange,
towerlike rotundas. Its large central tower, truncated, flat, is
surrounded by smaller ones. With porticos and gateways, the

creature protrudes far across the square. A castle with merlons. Colorful Byzantine images of saints are painted above the doors. But no one goes in. The entire circumference of the building is encircled by a wooden fence; movie posters attached to it; crossbeams lying about. The windows of the giant structure are empty, black, many are boarded up, some walled up. The square is called Saxon Square. This building looks terrifying, sinister, dark, unnerving; and it's now being torn down, killed. There's something painful, poignant, moving about the sight of this church, which was consecrated to a God, a God whom they deeply believed in—and as it stands there now, it is being demolished, as if it were evil.

Yet there is something else. I notice it. This thing here, this building, was not conceived of, not meant as, a church. It was supposed to be a fist, an iron fist, which descended on the finest square in the city, and its clatter was to be heard forever. This church was not to be ignored. It was to be a second monument to General Paskevich. What is this fence? The bars, the cage for locking up a monster. I feel grief, commiseration, but I cannot disagree with the solution.

The liberated nation feels a great pride and joie de vivre. Not far from the fence, a Poniatowski[3] stands in bronze, on a low stone pedestal. Under the Russian aegis, the Polish hero had to be fashioned as a Roman in an abstract toga; he was not to appear in the old uniform. Then a rebellion came, a defeat for the Poles; the victorious general was given the monument. He took it to his estate in Minsk; first, the bronze pride of the nation was disassembled, the bridges were too weak for its weight. For decades the pieces gathered dust in sheds on the general's estate; the Treaty of Versailles forced the Russians to hand the pieces over. Now, to the delight of the Poles, the hero once again shines in the light.

Streets and squares of the city have been renamed en masse; the memory of old unhappiness and degradation has been wiped out. Popular squares are named after the poets Mickiewicz[4] and Slowacki.[5] A major avenue is named Traugutta: Romouald Traugutt, leader of the uprising of 1863, was executed in the Warsaw Citadel. Since the centennial of Napoleon's death, the large square outside the main post office has been named Napoleon Square.[6]

Cracow Suburb is further south. A bizarre mixture of people: elegant upper-middle-class and aristocratic creatures, male and female students with white caps and red cords. A strong preponderance of crudely dressed petty bourgeois, peasants, peasant women in red kerchiefs with floral patterns. A monk, bareheaded, in a brown cowl and cape, girded with ropes, his bare feet in sandals, trudges along the sidewalk; he has a long, brownish-black beard. A row of women squat on the steps leading up to the entrance of the church: crones, beggars, and a young woman; she holds out her left hand. An opulent blonde prostitute in a white shawl is pushed across the street by a policeman; she continues to stroll, unfazed, in garish green shoes. The hackneys roll swiftly; the coachmen whip the horses. In between, two farm wagons trot by slowly, their sideboards bulging way out; the little peasant and his wife sit on straw in the middle; he holds the reins, toddling along.

I stand at a trolley stop, perusing the very obliging streetcar signs, which indicate every passing line and its route. All at once, a lone man with a bearded face comes toward me through the crowd: he wears a black, ragged gaberdine, a black visored cap on his head, and top boots on his legs. And right behind him, talking loudly, in words that I recognize as German, another one, likewise in a black gaberdine, a big man, with a broad red face, red fuzz on his cheeks, over his lips. He talks intensely to a small, poorly dressed girl, his daughter no doubt; an elderly woman in a black kerchief, his wife, walks alongside her, with a troubled look. I feel a jolt in my heart. They vanish in the throng. People pay them no heed. They are Jews. I am stunned, no, frightened.

I visit a government office. Provisional rooms, the town is too small for the masses of officials that it draws. Outside, wooden coat racks. In the waiting room, elegant men stroll to and fro, in pairs, arm in arm. One leans on a radiator, which leaves white stripes on his back.

A Russian scene: an old man sits at the telephone in a cubicle,

7

a low-level clerk; a stranger comes, asks; they bow deeply to one another. I walk through red curtains and up stairs, along corridors, past partially concealed kitchen facilities. A very calm, educated man speaks to me; he studied sociology in Berlin. He helps me very amiably.

They now are dwelling in their very own homes. It's a tremendous thing. Garibaldi appealed to the nations of Europe:

Do not abandon Poland!

It is the duty of all nations to help this unhappy nation, which demonstrates to the world the power of despair. Although disarmed, robbed of its best youths, who are either outlawed or imprisoned, held down by a huge army, this nation is rising up like a giant. The men are leaving the towns and plunging into the forests, determined to win or die. The women throw themselves upon the thugs, the kidnappers of their children, and scratch their eyes out.

Do not abandon Poland! Do not wait until you, like them, have been driven to despair—do not let your neighbor's home burn if you want others to help you put out the fire that is devouring your home.

Rumanians of the Danube, Magyars, Germans, Scandinavians—you are the military vanguard of the nations in a fight to the finish, which is now being waged on the glorious soil of a Sobieski and Kosciuszko.

This struggle is that of despotism against justice—a tragic episode of the robbery committed by the three Vultures of the North to doom the freedom and life of one of the most important nations of Europe. It is the fight of chaos, of brute force against the order of the man who wants to dwell in his hut and live by his hands—a chaos that will endure as long as people think only about their own bellies and leave their unhappy neighbor under the cudgel of the crowned butcher.

Do not abandon Poland! At least imitate your tyrants. They never abandon one another.

And you, guardian of the Alps, offspring of the men of Rütli: throw your republican rifle upon the scale of Europe, and you will know what it weighs. Today, it is the free nations that must restore order in the world, an order disrupted by the lusts of despotism.

Do not abandon Poland! If we all do our duty and help, we will perform a sacred obligation, and the world can then be constituted according to the benefit of the divinely blessed human race.

The Poles themselves:

And now we speak to you too, you Muscovite nation. Our traditional motto is freedom and brotherhood of nations; that is why we forgive you even for the murder of our fatherland, even for the blood of Praga and Oszmiana, the violence on the streets of Warsaw, the atrocities in the dungeons of the citadel. We forgive you, for you too are miserable, you are murdered, oppressed, tortured; the corpses of your children dangle on the tsar's gallows; your prophets freeze to death in the snows of Siberia. But if, at this decisive moment, you do not feel in your breast remorse for the past and a holier yearning for the future, if, in our struggle, you support the tyrant who murders us and crushes you underfoot, then woe! Woe unto you! For in the face of God and the entire world, we will curse you to the shame of everlasting servility and to the tortures of everlasting slavery, and we will challenge you to the terrible struggle of extermination, the final battle of European civilization against the savage barbarism of Asia.

They are now dwelling in their very own homes.
For every border wields a tyrant's power.
One must forget nothing, including oneself.
I have the official Polish Almanac for 1924; I will not allow myself to be intimidated by the statistics. According to the census of 1921, this Poland has four hundred thousand square kilometers of surface area, inhabited by twenty-seven million people. Eleven million of these people were supplied by the old Congress Poland, eight by Austria, four by Prussia. Four million are missing: they occupy the "Eastern territory," the district of Grodno, Wilno, Minsk, Volhynia. This makes 70.3 people per square kilometer. In Germany, there are about twice that number per square kilometer: 126.8. In England, 152.8. In Belgium, 245.3. So there's room in Poland. Nevertheless, I marvel at how

sparsely populated other countries are—say, the Scandinavian ones; and Spain has a mere 42.2 people per square kilometer; European Russia only 22.1; and Finland must be empty: there, all of 8.8 people live on a square kilometer. The earth has room for everyone.

During the last century, the Polish cities grew merrily: in 1860, Warsaw had one hundred fifty thousand people; twenty years later, double that number; and in 1900, some seven hundred thousand. More women than men: in the Warsaw area, 121 women to one hundred men. Because of the war, no doubt. This country has four hundred Catholic churches with seven thousand priests.

And I skim another column: statistics from the last war. To which this state owes its genesis. The combined number of casualties for all countries was: seven million dead, fourteen million wounded. Fifty-five million men were mobilized. Not counted are the sick, who starved at home because of the war. And the children whom the millions of men did not father. I have no doubt that these figures will shortly be forgotten. If only the dead do not forget them. I mean: the dead among the living today. The presumed seven million of the fifty-five million who will march off in the next war. Or the seventy million of the five hundred fifty million. There is a theory about human nature that people can be ordered about like cattle. There are also other theories. One can also will and think. The legal codes of all nations share this opinion; they make each person responsible for his deeds. But they exempt people from this responsibility for certain mass actions, especially when life is at stake. No one can renounce other people's rights. You should die only for things for which you want to live.

But I do not interfere in the private concerns of those who are doomed.

The simple layout of the streets: from north to south, the large parallel avenues: Cracow Suburb and Marshal Street and their extensions. In the southern area, villas and parks. In the western area, Wola, the working-class neighborhood. In the northern area, on the Vistula, the old city with the castle. West of it, the Jewish district.

This is an old city with mansions, patrician homes, slowly and intensively dilapidated; Russian mismanagement accelerated the ruin. The decay of an old, noble world can be traced from the castle and across the old market into all the outbound and distant streets and roads. There are terribly crumbling façades, shattered windows, dark vestibules. But if you enter them, you see a door that makes you wonder, a balcony with a beautiful cast-iron railing. Proletarian lamps hang above it.

Rows of modern buildings stand isolated, in groups, six to eight floors. Some sections—around Napoleon Square, at the main post office, toward the "New World"—are modern within these surroundings. Then again, ichthyosaurs of today and tomorrow hulking next to frail, poignant stone grannies lost in thought. I stroll northward along Cracow Suburb toward the Vistula. The river, this treasure, has been left outside the city; that may be good, I think to myself, its banks then lie silent and untouched by these terrible constructions. On the street, in a photographer's glass case, I gaze at the picture of a man without a necktie. He peers slyly. This is Witos, the former government minister. He wanted to be a farmer even as a big landowner, that was how he received the queen of Rumania: without a tie. Down at the corner, across from the bookshop, many people are entering a large café. They stand around inside, wearing hats; it used to be the black market, what can it be now? Midday, a warm sun, I have no coat on. A convict in gray-green linen is led along, a soldier with a rifle behind him. They are soon followed by two convicts with bound wrists. In the roadway, behind the trolley, two men run into one another. They heartily shake hands. They kiss one another on the cheeks.

Music from the north, from the castle. Boys run ahead, the sidewalk is full of moving people. A company of Polish infantrymen marches by, military gray, knapsacks, cooking pots on their backs, steel helmets sporting the white eagle. Robust boys with the dull look of all marching soldiers.

In the hustle and bustle of the little people, the peasants, the upper-class Polish woman keeps emerging, with fine footwear, lots of makeup, elegant movements; irregular, very soft to luscious piquant features.

A tremendous iron grating fences in a lawn. Amid trees and flower beds, stairs lead up to the pedestal of a monument. At either side of the pedestal, black forged torch holders. At a greater height stands a man named in the inscription: Adam Mickiewicz, bareheaded, in a long jacket, his cloak tossed over him, his right hand eloquently on his chest, his left hand suspended. In 1885, under Russian rule, the monument was unveiled very quietly. The man who wrote *Pan Tadeusz*. One of those who kept the soul of the already shattered nation awake. In winter the trees go underground. Now he stands here, the man who died in Constantinople. Every Polish town names squares and streets after him.

A church: passersby cross themselves, doff their hats. I go inside, past the clergyman who watches over a table with slips of paper, I put down change, he seems to thank me. What splendor, columns, Baroque altars, golden pomp. A shabby woman kneels in the center aisle. I am taken aback by the picture of a Mary: she floats on a silver sickle, a moon. In this way, her soul and God are connected with nature; the deity blurs into nature. Even outside, I can still see the magical image: the goddess on the sickle, a lunar goddess.

The boulevard ends at a square with a high stone column and an old yellowish edifice. This is the old castle.

An old, bald curator, quite refined, who speaks French, guides me through. How well he knows the rooms, how lovingly he talks about the objects. He has me step back, he shows me the shimmering sunlight that falls upon the room. Terraces with hanging gardens are located on the Praga side. The Russians neglected the elegant building, the delicate rooms; they poured paint, yellow and red, inside and outside, on the walls. There is a white Saturn Room: the metal Saturn, stooping low, bears a huge clock on his back. A lot of things were hauled off by the Russians and not returned.

I walk down boards into the basement: a gigantic library is

revealed; a long, bright vault. In the courtyard, they covered the old façade, walled up arches.

A metal bison, a colossal creature, stands outdoors.

To the right, a tremendous ironwork swings out, the arches of a bridge. The shore must be there. Trolleys swerve around. The yellowish construction, the castle, sinks down to the river. And that is the Vistula, the broad, shallow river. No current: the water sparkles evenly. Yellow masses of sand loom right up to the surface. Small boats wait at the riverbank. The sun casts the shadow of the bridge grating across the water. The opposite shore is sandy, grassy. Workers loaf about; tracks, steaming locomotives. The bridge is long, groups of poor people wander across. At the other end, a policeman is enthroned on his bay horse.

I have crossed into a shabby neighborhood, which delights me like all bleak disorderly lively places: I skid too quickly past churches, palaces. This is Praga. Peasant women in loose, flowery linen skirts haul baskets. Jews in caftans, their searching looks, their heavy sticky shuffling. They wear clodhoppers, wide trousers splashed with filth. Many are frail, most are stooped. They plod slowly toward the bridge.

A broad avenue leads off to the right. Woeful paving, small houses with unclean fronts. A crack opens between two houses: the entranceway to stalls. These are small red wooden stands, for fruit, clothes, boots. The peddlers are almost all Jews. Sometimes an entire family is stationed behind the small table. They hail the buyers. Often all they have is a crate, a basket. A few signs bear Jewish female names: Gitla, Freydla, Nicha, Chana, Estera. So many sorrowful faces, white-parchment complexions, the women with disheveled hair, elderly women with thick lips, big eyes, dreadfully ugly jowls.

But to the south of Cracow Suburb, New World and Ujazdowska Avenue stretch out, beautiful, modern, with a handful of stores, furniture, antiques. At the end, a park and a *château de plaisance*, Poniatowski's. You gaze across an autumnal pond at the chateau, a kind of Sanssouci. It stands in the middle of the water, naked rococo statues all around. The king's open-air theater is being renovated, it has a circle of broken columns: people used to delight in artificial ruins. The top of the amphitheater is wreathed by a ring of ancient statues: I do not complain that they are swaddled in wood. There's a second theater, which is closed. Its garden is now a café; wicker chairs, tables on the loose yellow sand, few people. Gentle autumn. A young soldier has placed his cap next to him on the table. On his knees, he holds both hands of his young, brown-braided girlfriend, who smiles at me with shiny eyes.

Southward, at the corner of New World and broad Jerusalem Avenue, behind a lovely glassed-in veranda, there is a restaurant; I noticed it in the evening. Many small light bulbs are inserted into the ceiling. They twinkle amiably like stars, illuminating the street. To the left, the boulevard is no longer called Jerusalem Avenue but Avenue of the Third of May. Construction is going on here, a temporary wooden fence blocks the street, leaving only a passageway for pedestrians. They want to renew the area, expand the railroad from the main station by running it underground here for a stretch and extending it through the city to the other side of Praga. The new Parliament Building is to be erected here; at present, the Sejm convenes in an old tsarist secondary school and boarding school for girls. I enter the narrow opening in the board fence and walk past a long fence.

Avenue of the Third of May is the name of this unfinished street. Around the time of the great French Revolution, the Polish Diet met for a long time, four years. Disaster, death were knocking at Poland's door. All abuses were acutely felt, discussed:

> The cattle are poor and degenerate, the soil is depleted, weedy and rocky, the meadows are swamps. The forests have been chaotically hacked out and pillaged. The land has been depopulated and demoralized by incessant wars and feuds of the past centuries, by fire and pestilence, by inadequate administration. The peasant class is utterly depraved. A bourgeoisie barely exists. The Notec District is almost deserted, Bygoszcz in 1772 does not have even eight hundred inhabitants.

14

The Constitution of May 3, 1791, abolished the electoral mon-
archy, the chief source of corruption in the state, and eliminated the outrageous privileges of the nobility: one single
nobleman could veto any measure. This was a fine constitution;
streets can certainly be named after it. One year later, several
Polish princes felt inclined to protect the old "Polish freedom,"
meaning their feudal power. Russia applauded. No street has
been named after the confederation that they formed in Tar-
gowica with the Russians. The tsar marched into the land of
Poland, against the Third of May.

I stroll along the fence, through the twilight. Baby carriages
head home. There are old people reading newspapers, couples
on benches, touching knees. The fence stops. Now a majestic
tableau, the most awe-inspiring in Warsaw: Josef Poniatowski
Bridge. The land below recedes. The hills and undulations were
bridged, then the piers and arches were built across the Vistula.
The bridge begins in front of me. It is enormously wide. You
have to walk a long time before you reach the water, the Vistula.
This bridge is worthy of the water. Massive gates usher you into
the structure, then the splendid avenue stretches out, the bridge
floor with tracks, sidewalks right and left. The trolley jingling
below, coal depots to the right, the black arching silhouette of a
forest beyond them. In the thickening dusk, houses loom black,
behind me and to my left; lights flash in some windows. Smoking factory chimneys. Stairwells lead down, women with fruit
sit inside. A big white star appears in the sky.

Then a fence cuts right across the bridge; I can't keep going.
The Vistula starts down there, and the bridge ends. In the penumbra, huge naked bridge piers rise from the viscous water.
Scaffolding surrounds several of the piers. The real bridge has
been blown up. The space between the piers is empty; the great
river, unvanquished, draws waves between them. I stand for a
long time, then turn around.

A clock strikes six. Darkness falls, terribly swift, palpable. To
my right, the sky is still radiant white. I saw the moon earlier,
wan, matte; now, there is a harsh, increasingly harsher disk, a
dazzling circular yellow-white; wisps of clouds upon it. Electric

15

candelabras are placed over the bridge. They already shone whitish during my walk home, I could see beyond them. Now they won't relinquish my gaze. The more darkness and blackness set in, the more violently the spherical, beleaguered lights rebel. No depth is left in the space to my side and to my right. Red lights twinkle right and left from the city, toward which I am heading. Where are the spires, the factory smokestacks?

The old *szlachcic*, the feudal nobleman of the *liberum veto*, was exterminated in a century of exilé. Mieroslawski, a Polish leader, addressing his countrymen at a commemoration of the Revolution of 1830, spoke first about the tsar:

> Study chemistry, but just enough to make saltpeter and gunpowder for the uprising. Study mechanics, but just enough to understand the laws of leverage, so that you can lift your buried mother from the grave. Study music, not to tame the Saul-like fury of the tsar, but to strike up the band for the Grim Reapers. If you have money and leisure, do not go to the Comic Opera of the Loretto Church, go to the temple of Molière.

But then he pounced upon the hated masters of Poland:

> Religion, family, property are the idols of civilization; in order to maintain the prestige of the tsar, the Polish counts, Jesuits, Jews are intimately bound up with him. . . . Our masters are speculators, who, by pretending to emancipate the Polish nation, vigilantly expropriate, disarm, and immobilize the people, thereby making them incapable of a national uprising.

He was vilifying the pseudo-freedom of the West.
Even the nationalist right wing calls itself democratic today.

I go down to the Vistula a second time. From New World to Tamka Street, only parts of which have houses. The road all the way down below was named after Kosciuszko, the greatest Polish revolutionary and man of freedom; his wild face is on the banknotes.
And to my right, in the water, I then see the destroyed bridge

16

in the broadest daylight—as I wished: four piers, massive, stony, two with scaffolds, without arches. The signature of a great fact, the war. The destroyed bridge stands very much alive. In the end, a gigantic power, the tsar, left the land. An immense picture, history without a book, terrifying, threatening, and premonitory.

In the blackish-gray water, wedge-shaped stripes emerge against the wind; they change. Harsh sunshine lies on the red spires of Praga. The trolley crosses the bridge over there. It's lovely and peaceful strolling along the water here. Ordinary people stroll with children in their arms; meadows are being planted with trees, benches. Karowa Street, beautifully paved, starts to the left; it climbs up to the city over wooden stairs. The Institute of Hygiene at a corner; white-capped girls go inside, briefcases under their arms.

In the afternoon, a wretched funeral procession trudges past the hotel. The coffin carried on a simple wooden bier by two men. Outside the hotel, the first pallbearer falls down, the coffin starts capsizing. Pedestrians rush over, grab it, push it aright. The trolley halts. The mourners, leading the way with a priest, notice only gradually that something is wrong, they look back. The first pallbearer straightens up, wipes his clothes, searches for his soiled cap. He turns around, grabs it. Reluctantly marching on, he complains about the other bearer to a worker on the sidewalk.

The city has no musical cafés. Indeed, few cafés at all; one across from the Hotel Bristol, a café for men and business, a small old one in the basement of the City Theater, at Theater Square, plus a couple more; mostly only pastry shops. Wonderfull small cakes, but they only look wonderful; they often have an unpleasant taste. The coffee is served in glasses, with milk and sugar added if you order a "white coffee." It doesn't taste good; they're no experts. The restaurants—that's their space. Here, the music, the cuisine are finer than in Germany. I frequently have a red-beet soup, borscht, with or without an egg. Everything is prepared with brio, the service is vivacious and elegant. Waiters and busboys in droves. The diners start with an enormous cold appetizer; they have a rendezvous with several

Polish liquors, high-proof schnapps, which burns your lips. Tips for waiters have been abolished; but you add something to the total, probably so that the check won't fly away. The eating begins at three P.M.; then the music is turned on, and whoever ate before that was a prole. I have my first meal at The Oasis. The music leaves my mouth agape. My appetite is already weak; but they play with so much sophistication—three musicians, one page-turner—I am utterly done for. I perish between loin of venison and *Tosca*.

Few signs of rickets on the street, few crooked legs among men and women and girls. My question is quite wrong: Who's got crooked legs in this country, men or women, children or adults? Legs go crooked only in Western Europe.

No one eats on the street, in the trolley. Well-mannered people do not even smoke outdoors. How marvelous. Anyone who knows sandwich paper knows what I suffer. Here, you can sit in any trolley car without worrying that a gentleman or a lady might open a briefcase and take it out, it—the chewing, lip-smacking human, the biting, swallowing beast. You flee from seat to seat and finally to the trolley platform—in Germany. In Warsaw, you rest in God's hands.

Supper after the theater, the concert, in the major restaurants, late at night, until one, two, three A.M. Few public places with dancing, no dance halls. Fabulous candy.

Movie theater: *Ossi Oswalda*. Lucky I don't understand the title cards; they all whisper them here as soon as the words appear; murmurs, hisses pass through the room. This music is pleasurable: nothing but a piano, two violins, and a viola; it's all familiar, including German things, but oh, that playing. Yesterday afternoon I was wakened by such music. Violins came from below, through an open window, shattering, overwhelming. How they play here! Oh, what the violins can sing! How the singing of the violins drifted up from the courtyard through the gray drizzle! And here. The film gave me—I don't know what. I watched it only now and then. The violins stole into my blood, celestially. Whenever I looked up, Oswalda had seduced yet another man; she had corrupted her boyfriend, driven him to shoot himself; in front of this one—she became pure. Just love intrigues, the "plots" are unimportant, you can see the situations over and over. It's the good life.

And what handsome young men and girls sit near me, caressed by the movie, watching as if hypnotized, longing to imitate what is happening onscreen. . . .

Westward, toward Wola, the working-class area. At the end of Chlodna Street, a long thoroughfare running from east to west, I get out of the trolley. The old city limits; two gate booths stand there. The street is very crowded, it's two in the afternoon. Here, a mounted policeman is planted in front of the booths. A huge, disorderly mass—people, workers, peasants, mill about. When I take a right, the mass grows thicker. I am in a gigantic workers' market. Its name is Rogatka Cerceli.

First it goes through a narrow passage, then it widens in back. At the entrance, by the wall over there, men are already standing about with trousers, fur coats. A young worker holds an old pair of pants, checking them, pulling them over his own. Now he examines a jacket, tries it on over his own. He is satisfied. Working-class women in kerchiefs arrive, mingling with the women who stand around in clusters; they have live geese on their arms, cages of chickens at their feet. Peddlers carry whole batches of shawls on their shoulders; others hold long leather boot-tops, high top boots. The men wear vizored caps of brown and gray cloth. To the right, in the houses, open shops. I see no shop windows at all; the glass is gone everywhere. They sell flour and grits, sacks of it standing there. In the middle of the road, two women, haggling with one another, spread red quilts between them. Some hawkers have wagons, small and larger handcarts. One has a small audience: he yells, beats. He has combs on his wagon board; he beats them with a club, so hard that they bounce away. He shouts, "They don't break"—that's how good his wares are. The thronging, the noise.

I pass through an entire street of peddlers in black top boots, a boulevard of fruit baskets. The market goes far, past the start of Ogrodowa Street, lined with houses on the right. Now come dozens of solid booths, bright loaves of bread on display, gigan-

tic round ones. Pots and pans. In between, small bookshops.
Women in colorful kerchiefs move outside and sit in the booths.
Way in the back, fruit stalls. Figs are threaded on long strings.
Finally, the colorful heartwarming vegetable stands: apples,
beets, carrots, bunches of hanging onions. I see that I have
wandered into a rectangular square between the rows of houses
at the entrance. An elegant young lady, an imposing figure, in
fur, powdered, stands in the middle of a passageway. Her big
white greyhound is after a peasant woman's goose. The lady has
the dog on a leash, he yanks vigorously. The peasant woman
laughs, the lady laughs, the goose bends its long white neck
down from the peasant woman's arm, flashing its yellow beak at
the dog; the dog barks, jumps high, is beside himself. An erotic
scene, it seems to me, between the peasant woman and the lady.
I pass baskets of white cabbages.

Halfway through the market, I elbow my way back. Toy
stands. Musical instruments; gramophones playing; pottery, variegated glasses. Peasants buying locks, cord. Small jackets for
children, cloths hung on jutting poles; you have to bend down.
White underpants with ribbons; shirts, handkerchiefs. Stands
containing dresses, suits. Here, black-bearded Jews as vendors,
elderly Jewish women. Heaps of lambskins, furs are hawked.
Food is sold from pots. Blond flat-faced peasants, lovely robust
faces, also women, pop up. Chocolate and pancakes are touted.
Young Polish girls stroll about, laughing. Female workers, female peasants wear fine shoes, but their legs are—bare. At first
I don't believe it, then I see it frequently; some even go barefoot
—a peasant custom. A heated argument between two elderly
women over a child's red jacket. Children throw wooden darts.
In the throng, policemen, turning their heads every which way.
Several civilians that I meet look like plainclothesmen; here,
shady purchases are quickly unloaded.

I move on, past the comb hawker, stroll back eastward along
Chlodna Street. A funny spectacle on the corner, at the trolley
stop: a five-year-old boy has put his little brother into a very tiny
fruit crate. The brother is unable to move, he screams, tries to
lift his legs. But the boy has thrust a rope through a hole in the
crate, tied a sturdy knot, and is now pulling his little brother

20

along the pavement. The little boy hollers, the other blissfully trots along as a horse. People laugh, make way.

Chlodna Street: tall new houses, then warehouses behind fences, decrepit one-story houses, some with remnants of decorative insignia.[7] The street packed with pedestrians, wagons, trolleys. A man in a caftan drags a crate of windowpanes: a glazier. Two big schoolgirls in black velvet caps, long brown braids, amble slowly in front of two schoolboys wearing striped caps. The girls giggle, the boys are earnest and diffident. The girls suddenly vanish inside a house. The boys peer through a hole in the cracked front door. Loud laughter inside, grins outside. The knob is pulled. Then the boys slowly open the door, slip inside. Several younger and older girls come along; a girls' high school is across the way. Past a church.

Chlodna Street ends at a square; its name seems to be Mirowski. Many wagons arrive. A huge yellow building stands athwart the square, a modern market hall. The entire left side of the forecourt is covered with piles of dirty straw, empty baskets. A small row of fruit stands runs all the way to the entrance. Then I pass through this hall: fish, fish, fish, basins of water, dead, live fish. A new market begins at the rear of the hall: gewgaws, clothes. And a second hall: butter, cheese, as well as fruit. Here, almost only Jews are dickering; in caftans, skullcaps. Candy is sold.

Outside, a boot bazaar. I am standing in a new square. Its name is Zelasna Brama, Iron Gate.

Previously, huge mobs were already buying, selling chaotically, merging and separating. Here, at this time of day, it's really overwhelming. The center of the square is occupied by a circle. A name is written on it, ending with "pole." I can't read it. Market wagons careen about wildly, the drivers warning, children screeching. Men with great masses of colorful balloons wander along the curbs. This circle in the middle is crisscrossed only by cloth stands; what a riot of scarves, shawls, kerchiefs; stands with splendidly dangling ribbons; cartons of buttons stacked atop one another. Groups of women wander through the hall, have textiles spread out for them on the tables, wonderful, but also loud, harsh textiles. The screams, the tussling of women. In the middle, a stall containing bronze and plaster figures.

Beyond the circle, a new corral of wagons with piles of straw, heaps of baskets. Now, straight ahead, I see a dense row of people. They are gazing upward. A building has collapsed, no, a whole group of buildings has collapsed, settling down into a heap of rubble, one story high, dreadfully chaotic, white and red, mortar, shattered stones, whole clusters of stones. The tremendous heap lies dry, shapeless in the afternoon light, like the shriveling innards of a dead animal. A fence surrounds the line of ruins, right by a street corner. The back walls of the buildings are still erect; from there, firemen and masons knock off jutting parts, banging with crowbars. Giant girders slant from the sides into the light. The red and blue paper on the back walls. Portions of the roofs sink down, about to drop off. Men with pickaxes stand on the wall remnants and pound on dangling things. All sorts of stuff keeps dribbling and pattering on the mountain of rubble, dust flies across the street, people rub their lips and eyes, step back.

The landlord overenlarged the cellar, trying to get more space; the building developed cracks, it buckled, sank.

This square, this teeming marketplace, Zelasna Brama, extends quite a distance, beyond a palatial edifice with green columns, beyond the collapsed building, all the way to the quiet Saxon Garden. Droshkies, green lawn, and benches in front of the park. An "American bazaar" has been established in a high wooden booth. Three men holler down in Polish and Yiddish, each unconcerned about the others: always a uniform price for three items, soap, notebook, suspenders.

Now come the iron bars around the park, the Saxon Garden. The streets end. The autumnal park. The beautiful yellow leaves on the branches, on the ground: they lie there like hearts. Gangs of kids are playing everywhere. Scores of governesses sit on the benches under the foliage, chatting women, young men, older men, smoking cigarettes. Whole benchloads of Jews, smoking, reading newspapers, conversing loudly; women and caftan wearers laughing and earnestly debating. I sit next to children. Two little girls, dressed coquettishly, argue as they walk in front of me; perhaps four years old. Suddenly the girl in the white sweater runs into the one holding the white doll umbrella, bumps into her back. The one with the doll umbrella looks horrified, falls—no, drops belatedly on her left hand. The right hand very apprehensively brandishes the doll umbrella. Then, straightening up momentarily, she waits a moment and grasps the situation. Lifts her dirty hand and yells, yells, terribly, systematically. The mother of the white child instantly grabs her, hits her on her hands, back, skirts, as the yelling starts, hits harder when the other child yells louder and stands in front of her mother, for apology, revenge, diversion. But the white child tears away, and, with her head and whole body, she makes a smug, rebellious movement toward her mother, stands there mulish and somber. Her mother's face turns crimson, agitated; she scolds the child, the child doesn't stir at first, but then, while the other child continues yelling at different sound levels, this child yells and yells as if switched on, she weeps, kicks. The two children raise their voices, competing as to who has suffered the greater injustice, the girl with the umbrella is with her mother, the other alone in the middle of the passageway, her tiny fist on her face, her eyes and nose dripping. The mothers gesture agitatedly.

I stroll through the rustling leaves. Baroque statues of women loll about on the lawn. The rows of columns of the General Staff Building. And once again, behind it, disconcerting, alarming, the Russian cathedral looms, without gold cupolas, beyond the fence covered with movie posters. Right next to the fence, a boy sleeps on a plank in the mild afternoon air, his legs drawn up, his cap upon his face. Elegant coaches, rubber wheels, roll soundlessly over the asphalt.

A street in the old city: the houses so close together that one can touch the facing wall. A staircase leads up. On one step, a pretty blonde woman sits with an open blouse, nursing her baby. Her calm eyes follow the passersby.

I have an address. The man does not live in this building. The two old people, the concierges, know his forwarding address, as I hear—but they can't write it down for me. They can't write.

Droshkies are popular; their rates are low. The cushions are worn out; a bizarre jerking and jolting. Stopping, starting, swerving, they graze the sidewalks. You advance briskly; a tin sign hangs on the coachman's back.

This is Airplane Week. An inflammatory poster is pasted on all fences: danger of war from Bolshevist Russia. Cars sporting yellow flags zoom along Cracow Suburb, a propaganda motorcade. The two front cars carry model airplanes, the propellers revolve. Behind them, gentlemen and ladies in flower-decorated cars; they wave posters, strew leaflets. A cinematographer at their head. In the evening, propaganda cars halt outside the cafés, wind players and young people pile in. They sing, toot, shout, dash into the cafés.

I pass through a museum that has just been set up, a provisional national museum. A chaos of Egyptian sarcophagi, paintings, coins, arts and crafts. Chopin's death mask above a grand piano. Pictures by younger artists, Kowalski, Gerson, Malczewski, Maslowski. I first hear the name Wyspianski, a celebrated Polish artist, painter and playwright, who lived in Cracow.[8] Collections of weapons, rooms serving history. A glass cabinet holding mementoes of Kosciuszko: his baptismal certificate, officer's commission, pictures. A room from the Napoleonic era. But then I gape at a glass cabinet holding German "souvenirs": a steel helmet, an Iron Cross, spiked helmets.

"Where'd you get these things?"

"They're from the disarmament in 1918."

I feel a jolt. This is hatred. They maintain their hatred for Germany. They cultivate it. I ask no further.

They show a lot of stuff about Napoleon. In 1921, there was a big centennial celebration in his honor. A committee proclaimed:

He was the first to shatter the gates of our prisons after our dismantlement in order to open our way to freedom. He gave the Grand Duchy of Warsaw a constitution, modern, strong, and elastic. He declared the liberty and equality of all citizens. We celebrate the memory of an immortal dead man. The soldier should remember the oath: for glory, for Poland, for the world.

But in 1812, Napoleon also said to Narbonne:

I love the Poles on the battlefield, they are a heroic race. But I don't like their debating assemblies, their *liberum veto*, their mounted parliaments with drawn swords. Europe has had more than enough of the silly *cortes* in Cadiz. I will wrest Moscow away from Alexander, I will throw him into Asia. But I will not tolerate a [political] club in Warsaw or Cracow or anywhere else.

During Napoleon's Russian campaign, the celebrated Kosciuszko held back: Napoleon had not openly declared himself for Poland. Whereupon Fouché forged Kosciuszko's signature on an appeal. Eighty thousand Poles followed Napoleon to Russia, eight thousand returned: Poland was quite in earnest. In Italy, General Dombrowski's legions fought for Napoleon, with dreadful casualties; but when the Peace of Lunéville came, Poland was not mentioned. In fact, the great emperor wanted to get rid of his Polish soldiers: they were ordered to quell a Negro uprising in Santo Domingo. They refused; cannons were set up. They set sail from Livorno and Genoa. In Santo Domingo, nearly all of them died.

They have had to make an endless effort. Hence, their wildness and blindness.

The aphorism of 1861 is magnificent: "Under a mild regime, the Poles rise up because they can; under a strict regime, because they have to."

Across the Castle Square. I creep more northward and westward. In a narrow street, a tall, high-ranking officer, his cap in his hand, his hoary head lowered, wanders before me through the open entrance of a cathedral. He kneels at a side chapel. On the stone floor of a side aisle, someone is stretched out, a man, a peasant or worker, in dirty top boots. He lies full length, on his belly and face. His arms are stretched out at right angles, he has spread himself out as a cross. His cap in front of his squeezed head. The stone slab is blackishly wet around his nose and mouth. Outside, the church is Gothic; inside, everything is atangle: altars, statues, busts; Baroque, Renaissance, rococo. The house was built in dribs and drabs, starting in the fifteenth century. And I enjoy seeing that everyone built according to his own whims. A church is for the people who enter it; the man lying there hasn't the foggiest notion of Gothic. I wonder when he'll stand up. This is a peasant of this nation. He too fought for his country, that is, for his Catholic Church and the Polish tongue. Ten minutes later, when I walk back down the aisle, he's still lying there.

It's good that beggars exist and that they show themselves. They arouse feelings. Seeing them is as necessary as seeing the martyries in churches. You can't buy your way out. Tomorrow, the day after tomorrow, they're back again, as certain as human misery, the whole of dark life. There are many churches: there's one across from Mlodowa Street, on Cracow Suburb: the Bernardine Church; one behind the Mickiewicz Monument on the same street: the Church of the Visitation Nuns; on Copernicus Square, the Church of the Holy Cross. Beggars always stand or lie there, starting in the morning; people go in, out, little people, many women, female students in white caps; they genuflect next to a bench, on the steps leading to a side altar where candles are burning. The figures of Mary, of the saints, whose decorated images are suspended here, move in the flickering of candles and before so much urgent love. Poignant the young men and girls whom I meet here early in the morning; with briefcases and handbags, they plunge through the rows of beggars. At the very back of the aisle, they kneel, lower their heads, look at the altar, move their lips, stand up, cross themselves, are outside.

These churches, brimming with costly objects, served by very healthy, sated priests, have a strange decoration, a genuinely Polish one: memorial plaques, gravestones of famous Poles. National glory reverberates together with prayers. Epitaphs on the Church of the Holy Cross: for Chopin, the musician, who died in Paris; for a novelist, Joseph Ignac Kraszewski; a writer, Plug; a sculptor, Proszynski; tombstones for an old cardinal, Michael

Radziapowski, and a clergyman, Tarlok. The Church of the Visitation Nuns on the other side of the street has marble busts of Casimir Brodzinski, a Romantic; the names Thadeus Czacki and Sniadecki. Nationhood, the pride of the nation, was driven from the streets and squares—into the inviolable churches. And not only the walls but also the churchmen took in the fleeing nationalism. Churches and monasteries became armories; religious orders and congregations joined the popular uprisings. During the eighteen-sixties, Field Marshal Count Berg ordered a raid on the Warsaw monasteries and congregations: at the Bernardine Monastery they found daggers, bullet molds, stirrups, assembly components, a printing press. Prior Zaremski was the revolutionary armorer. The Polish clergy was fined twelve percent of its annual income. The illegal Polish national government created "hanging constables" for its enemies; the idea came from a priest in the Holy Church, Mikozewski.

Clergymen—Marists, Trinitarians, Lazarists, Carmelites, Paulists—became gang leaders. The Bernardine superior Zaborek helped organize revolts. Franciscans took part in assassinations; in 1863, the Russians hanged Kowarski, a Capucine, for slaughtering a tsarist officer. When the tsar closed the Church of St. John and St. Bernard for political abuses, the clergy shut all churches, and the administrator of the archdiocese of Warsaw called for a nationwide state of mourning. Rzowuski, the suffragan bishop of Warsaw, would not revoke the ecclesiastic interdict or use the Imperial Russian chargé d'affaires to communicate with the Viennese nuncio, and he refused to let the government appoint abbots; so the Russians sent him to Astrakhan. A Catholic weekly, published by a provost, wrote: "The Polish nation is an indivisible whole by God's will"; and then came the strange words: "It is Poland's vocation to maintain, hand down, and develop the life of Catholicism." During the terrible times, every Pole was filled with the thought of Polish messianism; hindered, beaten back, the nationalism grew, ran riot:

Among us, on the cross of a martyred Poland, the old customs, the traditions of our forebears, the traditional religious practices are maintained sacredly and staunchly. Who can say whether

27

Poles, purified by the fire of long sufferings, shall not be virtually an example of how men can find their way out of the sad schism that is now dividing Christianity.

A prayer went through the nation:

> *God, you have surrounded Poland for so many centuries*
> *With the radiance of your power and glory,*
> *Your providence has shielded her*
> *Against disasters that were meant to bend her;*
> *We beg you in front of our altars:*
> *Lord! Restore our Fatherland, our Freedom.*
>
> *You were moved by our Fatherland's fall,*
> *You have supported the fighters for the Holy Cause,*
> *You wanted the entire world to witness their courage,*
> *You increased their glory even in misfortune.*
>
> *Restore the old glory to our Poland,*
> *Make the fields fertile, the devastated soil,*
> *Give them happiness and eternally blossoming peace,*
> *Stop punishing, O wrathful God.*

And the other:

> *With fiery intoxication and steam of fraternal blood,*
> *This voice penetrates to me, oh Lord!*
> *The most dreadful lament, the final sigh*
> *Of such prayers bleaches the hair.*
>
> *We have no song without lament,*
> *The crown of thorns has grown upon our brow,*
> *As eternal as a monument to your wrath,*
> *The supplicating hand looms toward you.*
>
> *How often have you already chastised us!*
> *And we, with fresh wounds not yet healed,*
> *Call again: He is propitiated,*

# Journey to Poland

*For He is our father, He is our Lord!*
*And we rise up again, purer in trust,*
*For your will lets our hereditary enemy subjugate us*
*And laughingly toss the question, like a pebble, at our breast:*
*"And where is the father? Where is God?"*

The most solid house of this Polish city was built by the Russians: the central prison. It stands on a quiet northern side street, six floors high: gray sandstone below, then three stories of red brick, the top floor white. A massive building, a whole fortress. Here, in 1904, ten revolutionaries were kept, condemned to death. It was not Catholicism that drove and strengthened them; theirs was a different sanctity. The Polish Social-Democratic Party, PPS (Polska Partia Socjalistyczna), decided to get them out. One day the police chief of this fortress received a telephone call from the office of the governor-general: A captain of the mounted constabulary was coming, a Baron von Bindberg. He would report to the police chief, who was to hand over the prisoners in exchange for a letter of indemnity. The captain came with a constabulary escort, submitted his written orders, conversed with the prison warden for two hours. At last, he formally confirmed the transfer and took over the ten prisoners in a vehicle belonging to the institution. The baron was Grozechowski; he is still alive today, a colonel in the Polish army. They then rushed off. The liberated prisoners had no idea what was happening. They thought they were going to be shot. The next day the jubilant proclamations of the outlawed PPS hung on the building walls.

Another Polish revolutionary was Sulkewicz. He came from a Tartar family, he was a student, he joined the PPS during the eighteen-nineties. The illegal Polish organization that was fighting the Russians had a printing press in London. Sulkewicz organized the smuggling. He got a job as customs official in Eydtkuhnen; from there, he guided the contraband across the border, with the help of women and skinny men who hid the newspapers and pamphlets under their clothes. When he was found out several years later, he took a false passport, fled, and lived illegally in Poland. Tracked down, he went to Cracow,

which was now in Austria. And here, in 1914, he was overtaken
by the war. Volunteering for Pilsudski's Polish legions, which
fought on the Austrian side, he died in combat at forty.

There was an Alexander Siedielinkow, the Russian commander of the so-called tenth pavilion, the section for political
prisoners. Siedielinkow was the intermediary between the inmates and the Party. In the cells, the prisoners could tell by his
face whether he had a secret letter for them. He would hide it
somewhere in the cell, say, under cigarettes, leave and then, to
make sure, soon return, claiming he had forgotten his pack of
cigarettes. He informed the inmates about the contents of pro-
tocols, warned them about provocations. His wife was Polish.
In those days, during the eighteen-nineties, the privileged in the
tenth pavilion were served roast meat for lunch, workers only
soup meat and vegetables. But Siedielinkow put workers in the
cells of the privileged. Without his help, Pilsudski's escape
would have been impossible. The commander was retired in
1913, he died in 1916 at the age of sixty-nine. His sons are Poles.

Pilsudski was an important convict in his pavilion. He was to
be gotten out by the Party, since they feared he would have to
endure a long sentence. His comrades on the outside consulted
a psychiatrist. He advised them to have the prisoner play the
savage, he gave them instructions about refusing food, about
poison. When he was hungry, he should ask for cookies and
chocolate. When Pilsudski was exhausted, Russian physicians
came to the prison, they realized he was faking. The authorities
spoke of sending him to Siberia, where he had already spent five
years. He was transferred to the hospital in St. Petersburg. The
outlawed group looked for a doctor and found Professor Mazur-
kiewicz. (He is now professor of psychiatry at the University of
Warsaw.) He requested and obtained a position at the St. Petersburg Hospital, worked near the prisoner. One day he gave the
patient's guards a few hours off. During that time, the prisoner
was freed by his comrades.

Montwit, an intellectual, was hunted in 1904 on suspicion of
belonging to the terrorist group of the PPS. The Russians went
to arrest him in his home. When they approached, he defended
himself, shooting two of the arresting officers, firing a hundred

more bullets before they overpowered him. The prisoner refused to give any information, he identified himself as Mirecki.
He was sentenced to death as Mirecki and hanged. After the
execution, the Party officially announced who he was.

Peter Chnupko was a textile worker. He was apprehended
around the same time as Montwit. He supposedly had taken
part in robbing one hundred thousand rubles of Russian government funds from a train near Rogow; the red flags of the revolutionary party were found at the scene. Chnupko called
himself Jan Kawapinsky. He was condemned to death. Still a
minor, he was sentenced to a lifetime of *katorga* [Russian for
"hard labor"]. He remained in prison for eleven years. In Oral,
he was liberated by the Revolution in 1917, fought in the Russian Revolution, returned to Poland. He is now the head of the
free labor unions.

That was the struggle for freedom. Whose heart does not
swell at the thought? I want to know what is going on in this
country right now, which forces, powers are organizing the
state, which forces govern officially and which unofficially. Who
wields power and who wields words. I soon throw in the towel,
because I don't speak the language, or rather, languages of the
country: Polish, Ukrainian, Byelorussian, Yiddish, Lithuanian.
I ask: Who goes hungry in this country and who is sated? What
are the political crimes here? Who and how many people are in
prison for political crimes? Which crimes are the most frequent?

Late in the afternoon I am taken to the printing plant and
editorial office of a left-wing newspaper. A ten-year-old beggar
girl stands outside my hotel, barefoot, in a wretched little jacket,
with a few matchboxes. How she runs, arguing over her place
with a little boy! She pursues everyone who is dressed better.
She scurries across the street like a weasel. Now she's gone. An
hour later, I encounter her on a different corner, in her little
red dress, she pesters me.

A dark narrow side street; an old, badly kept house, once
occupied by the Germans for printing a newspaper. I enter a
small-scale printing plant, manually operated. The editorial offices, vast, furnished, as though for a temporary stay, with tables, chairs. The entire right side of the room empty. Two

31

posters hanging on a narrow wall, colorful, Belgian appeals. One for the First of May, with a Mayishly cheerful, swaying crowd. The second, with the word *Pax* at the top, printed in July 1923, addresses the Belgian workers in regard to the Ruhr question: on the left, big, the pope in his tiara; on the right, Vandervelde;[9] in the middle, a man who resembles Zola; each with a quotation from a speech advocating peace. The Ruhr flows underneath.

The office of the editor-in-chief. A narrow room, again sparsely furnished. In the window corner, a leather-sheathed flag. A short, elderly man props his head on the desk. He looks sickly, his pince-nez is askew, his beard is dark, stringy. His speech is slow and soft, melancholy, reticent. He warns me not to listen to any partisan talk in the country or to the national minorities, who, he says, put down everything. The state is young and must first consolidate. I can barely get anything personal out of him. He was an émigré for a long time, fleeing the Russians. He returned home illegally. He stayed in a different house every night. The German military police were not as resourceful as the Russian. Later on, I hear that this man went hungry. In the greatest misery, he wrote a book, dedicated to his wife, whose sewing paid for the barest essentials. He was used up by the struggle. He is plagued by arteriosclerosis and asthma. Lost in thought, he lies in his armchair, makes cigarettes. We sit awhile. He stands up, the quiet, mournful man (his hard life hovers in front of me, I can see it) shakes my hand.

On the wall of the large editorial office outside, there is the picture of a young man, a member of the earlier terrorist group of the Party; he was executed by the Russians. Pilsudski and also the current head of state [Stanislaw Wojciechowski] worked on this newspaper. Both deviated; the head of state to devote himself to corporativism and the cooperative movement.

Rosa Luxemburg,[10] who perished in Germany, and Jogiches, who likewise perished in the revolutionary period, both of them Poles, considered Poland's link with Russia economically crucial. These people here connected Marxism with the Polish autonomy movement, gave the latter a Marxist underpinning:

class struggle, they said, can develop freely only in the nation
state.

As we walk through the human tides of the evening streets,
they tell me: there was an Austro-Polish solution for the Polish
question that aimed at attacking Russia. The solution offered by
Roman Dmowski, who translated Rosa Luxemburg into Marxism, involved the faith in Russia's invincible might and the distaste for the imagination of the Galician Poles. Incidentally, in
Austria, Tisza opposed the three-way breakup of the Hapsburg
Empire with a Poland next to Hungary and Austria; he wanted
a Poland inside Austria; the only issue was the degree of independence. However, the future was determined by imaginative,
active Galicia. For in the sober Russian land, in Congress Poland [as demarcated by the Congress of Vienna in 1815], the
bad Warsaw passivism grew. Even after the German occupation
of Warsaw, the passivism continued, the fear of Russia. Then the
Polish legions marched from Galicia; with them, Pilsudski, the
first activist, the man who had wrested power for Poland in 1918.

Pilsudski himself: he is a revolutionary à la Mazzini, a revolutionary to the core. He is anticlerical, he has been married
twice, with several children from his second wife. The clergy
then pushed him, as head of state, to have a church wedding.
He is a radical leftist, although no longer a member of the PPS.
He resolutely organized the army in his way, with his friends
and helpers in the lead: he shoved the old Russian and Austrian
officers behind the fresh new ones. So that many younger men
have high military ranks here. He is a fascinating, deeply passionate man, a thorough antiparliamentarian. He calls parliament a chatter room. He refuses to be elected head of state
because he doesn't want just to open exhibitions. He is now on
the sidelines, but only for a while, no doubt.

One cannot, as I hear and believe, compare the Polish workers to the German ones. The former are still revolutionaries.
Many still have their "machine," the gun, in their pockets. They
have a different past from the imperial German past. They were
the people, and the current state was not created over their
heads. Many still do not grasp the "work" of the assemblies. In

1920 the Bolsheviks found no support in them; only the peasants hoped for a profit, voted for "councils" in the occupied territory, shared; the masters fled. Later, the approach to the peasants was intelligent, civil. The Bolsheviks do not know the Poles. It was wrong of them to invade the country.

A municipal politician orients me. Poland has a democratic constitution. But there are still executive statutes in the administration; for instance, the police don't need a court warrant to search a home. Some areas still have war regulations issued by the occupation authorities; in the eastern part, the provincial parliament can prohibit assemblies. The cooperative system is uniform, it answers only to the courts; it cannot be interfered with politically. The consumer cooperatives have over eight hundred thousand members; there are also agrarian cooperatives. The national minorities—Ukrainians, Jews, Germans, Byelorussians—are to develop fully in this country. The government is planning a university in Cracow for the large Ukrainian minority, the way Austria established a university for Italians: in Innsbruck, not Trieste. The Ukrainians want Lwów, which lies in the Ukrainian district. But the government fears that a university here would have a political tinge.

The chief political groups in Poland are as follows. The National Democrats, nicknamed Endeke because of their initials, represent the interests of large-scale farming as well as heavy industry; they have a petty-bourgeois following, and also a clerical one; they are, as one would say in Western Europe, conservative or reactionary. A Christian National agricultural group and a Christian Democratic labor group, which stick together. A farmers' group, called the Witos party after its leader, also Piasts with—mainly large-scale—farming interests, plus the recruiting rhetoric of the small farmers. The minorities, four parliamentary groups, some eighty representatives in the Sejm. Finally, Socialists and Communists. The Communists, poorly represented in parliament, have a large rural following. The minorities, elected en bloc, are free in parliamentary terms, but with different social and economic hues: Jews are capitalists and small tradesmen; Germans are Junkers and Socialists; Byelorussians have a radical farmers' club; Ukrainians belong to a spectrum of different clubs.

Poland's legislation is almost opaque. First of all, the country is made up of portions that are each governed differently, laws cannot be created equally. Some five civil codes are still in effect. Congress Poland initially observed the abolished regulations of the German occupation; in 1919 a neo-Polish legislation was established for the administration, on the modern Baden model. Now, unification commissions are at work.

All parties are afraid of a German war of retribution. They pin their hopes on the German democrats. The Poles hope and listen eagerly and half skeptically to what the latter say, to if and how they operate.

One man, who up to now has been listening, says: Sixty percent of Polish export goes via Gdansk (Danzig); thus, the port is vital to Poland. He gets upset when he talks about the "fantastically unperceptive" speech concerning the Polish Corridor, given in Geneva by a left-wing German politician. A third Pole joins us. He smiles a lot when the others speak. He's young; the remarks he throws in are sharp and witty. Meanwhile, the intelligent municipal politician continues outlining Poland's newspaper world. *Republic*, founded by the pianist and politician Paderewski, is the newspaper of large-scale farming and heavy industry. *Warszawska Gazetta* resembles the German *Kreuzzeitung*. The *Morning News* is fiercely anti-Semitic, a gutter rag. *The Echo* is the organ of the Witos party. The calm, democratic *Polish Courier* has few readers. Pilsudski's *Morning Courier* is very ideological. The workers have their *Robotnik* (Worker) in Warsaw, the *Forward* in Cracow. Then several other bland, but very widely circulated gazettes. Each newspaper has an average of ten or twelve thousand subscribers. I'm amazed: that's a very low number. Ah, the peasants, the illiterates. The clergy must be very powerful. How bizarre the form of a Western state thrust upon this country.

Now the young man puts in his two cents, and, amid the obvious reticence of the others, he comes out with all sorts of things. What he says has a strangely ironic tone. Although Polish, he speaks with a conspicuous detachment. There's Lloyd

George in England, he says. Lloyd George is utterly despised. He's considered a fool, an enemy of Poland. In 1919, when they were debating in Paris, he supposedly confused Silesia with Cilicia. They also hate the Italian Nitti because of his articles *Europe Without Peace*. MacDonald is a mystic, a muddled, unhappy idealist. Herriot is the consistent successor of Clemenceau. But the Poles are upset about the abolition of the Vatican legation. The Russians have an official mission in Warsaw. After all, not so long ago, Trotsky said: "Poland is our bridge to Europe." Which was not an off-the-cuff bon mot. During the chat about Russia, an interesting argument ensues between the sarcastic young Pole and the reticent others. He describes how many millions the Russians paid or had to pay after the peace treaty. Now the two others cut in: Russia still has nine-tenths of our artworks, and there are so many things it still hasn't paid for or delivered. "Yes," he says, "there you are: Who's angry and furious at Russia? The so-called leftists! They can't pick on Russia enough." His face twists as he starts tallking about the Jews. Fifty percent of the people in the right-wing press are baptized Jews, the bourgeois left wing has few Jews, the Socialistic left wing more. There are countless mixed marriages.

"Do you know what Frankism is? Frank was a Jewish sectarian in Poland several centuries ago. He fanaticized the Jews, got them to convert to Christianity. He was incredibly successful. The Polish king supported the action by giving the new converts patents of nobility. The baptized Jews automatically became Polish aristocrats. A contribution to the race issue. Just do a little investigating among those proud gentlemen today, but with kid gloves. You see, they are—anti-Semites."

The man who was talking about "Gdansk" can't get away from it. He repeats how wrong the Germans are to keep talking about Gdansk and the Corridor if they wish to achieve a peaceful relationship with Poland. Discussions about the Corridor are completely impractical and merely disruptive. I listen very thoughtfully; the boy nods at me, arch and scornful.

I sit in front of a very intelligent, very down-to-earth National Polish politician. "Like all other countries," he says, folding his hands in his lap, "Poland became very poor by stabilizing the farmers with the devalued currency. And the nationalities; national awareness is feeble among the Ukrainians; they alternately call themselves Poles, Russians, Ukrainians. The Germans here are well-to-do; a highly cultivated and privileged nation. Jews and Poles were on excellent terms until 1903. Then the Jewish Russians showed up, energetic, sly, the hated Litvaks; they aroused the opposition of the Poles and the local Jews. Now they have fused with them. The Jews are unilaterally merchants, but Poland's economic foundation is too narrow for so many merchants. That is the cause of their poverty. Incidentally, nowhere is the tension between very rich and very poor as great as among the Jews. While Germany, or rather a certain number of Germans, got something out of the inflation, Poland only lost. Now they're struggling to bring down the prices."

When he begins talking about the nationalities again, he is even calmer and more sedate than before. "We have to distinguish between everyday life and lofty goals. The parliamentarians and orators usually know nothing but lofty goals. At least, in parliament. They talk a blue streak about autonomy, independent culture, and whatever. But at home, in everyday life, everything looks different. No one even dreams of allowing the national life and cultural assets of a people to wither away. We Poles have learned well enough what that means. We know both what suppression is and what the effect of suppression is. We certainly want to let the nationalities develop. Understandably, the legal regulation of these things cannot be done overnight. Thus, one law permits bilinguality in the Ukrainian district. This and other things are not neglected. But think about everyday life: lowering prices, draining swamps, building roads, housing."

I stroll past the Museum of Fine Arts. This edifice was visited by the first president of the Polish Republic on a day of major domestic political tension. He first drove from his residence, the Belvedere, to the Sejm. En route, the agitated crowds threw dirt at his car. While viewing the paintings at the museum, he got the bullet in his back. It was an answer to the question of who

37

should rule Poland, a state nation or a consortium of nations. The shot opted for the state nation.

The representative Polish artists do not exhibit at the museum because of conflicts with the administration. Heinrich Sieinradski has a gigantic monstrosity, dated 1897: a black bull breathing its last, losing torrents of blood. A dead, all-too-white maiden is tied on its back. She is obviously a Christian; the men around her are Romans. A woman named Alexandra Lascenka has a room of her own; Egyptian motifs, palms, camels, tents, Arabs. Kopozynski is better: he has effectively captured the horror of a flight with weeping children. I wander through a room full of huge dreadful historic pictures after Makart; I am incapable of making my feet halt. History, history, and more history. I realize that these paintings do not demonstrate what the populace feels. Any more than our Avenue of Victory [in Berlin]. The populace is richer than all these painters know. Does "history" ever prove what a nation feels? How much of the nation participates in this kind of "history"? A stone girl sits on a pedestal, stretching leisurely.

In Warsaw, Lodz and the provinces, three thousand firms have allowed promissory notes to expire out of protest. In Warsaw, bankruptcies amount to two hundred thousand dollars. Poland is to be methodically transformed back into an agricultural country. An agrarian reform, smashing large-scale land ownership, is imminent. The dangers facing the young country: insecure borders, Ukrainian, Bolshevist menaces, an economic crisis, domestic poverty, national disintegration.

The population is forming cooperatives, collectives, everywhere in order to hold its own. Supposedly, beyond the big Vistula Bridge, in the area of the old citadel, there are new houses for officers, an entire settlement; they were built by a cooperative of Polish officers. On the main thoroughfare, opposite the university, I stumble upon a large scholarly bookstore; it belongs to the cooperative of middle-school teachers. The medical system has been tightly reorganized on a Socialist basis. A government decree of 1920 gave the medical-plan boards, consisting of employees and employers, the right to choose the medical system. In the provinces, the shortage of physicians makes a free choice necessary. The cities introduced a fixed system. All the earlier small-scale medical plans were liquidated; urban neighborhoods formed a medical group for every five thousand members; these neighborhood groups were assembled into units. Such units are: Cracow, Lwów, Poznan, Lodz, Warsaw, and others. Poznan has five and a half million members, Lwów a quarter million, Lodz a bit more. At first it was difficult introducing the fixed medical system. The physicians boycotted it. The medical groups had a very hard time finding doctors: refugees from Russia, from the outlying areas. But soon they had enough physicians, the medical revolt was quelled. In Warsaw, they now set up ten treatment centers, outpatient clinics, hired three hundred doctors, specialists and general practitioners. They gradually managed to replace the interim doctors with capable local ones. The physicians in a district have to make a certain number of house calls and perform a certain number of examinations at the treatment center.

The Poles know that they have to work very hard to raise the overall level in their country. Armaments devour a huge amount of money. They provide as intensively as they can for the spiritual and intellectual consolidation, the education of the country. Old Congress Poland had barely four thousand schools; now there are ten thousand. There are technical academies in Lwów, Warsaw, and Poznan; a mining school in Cracow. Professional schools have been set up, but they are poorly attended, and their number is dwindling for lack of a middle class.

An All-Polish Association of Student Self-Help has been formed for the universities. Pilsudski donates his salary as marshal to the University of Wilno. Universities were established in Warsaw during 1915, at the start of the occupation; the ones in Lwów and Cracow already existed, the ones in Poznan and Wilno are the most recent. Galicia had to contribute its Polish teaching assistants to the entire young state. These universities —at least, in theory—have no Jewish quotas, aside from Poznan, which is acutely Fascistic. I hear that at this strongly anti-

39

German, all-Polish university, there is also a tension between professors of Austrian and Prussian background. They are about to introduce a British innovation: the doctorate is to have a real value, and the master's degree will be awarded only for the elementary examinations. The philosophy faculty already prescribes such a master of arts.

I talk to a professor at the art school. He is in the midst of his work, in a meeting. White linen smock, mid-forties, salt-and-pepper mustache. Sanguine, a fine, likable man. This school was organized two years ago, it has a permanent faculty of ten, an enrollment of some three hundred students, including many women. He sees art and his own work in broad terms. It is not a mere painting of pictures, it also involves decoration, architecture, sculpture. I know this train of thought; he's a European.

"But what about Warsaw?"

He complains. "Warsaw doesn't appreciate art. It's a commercial city. Cracow is different."

They're planning a national museum near Poniatowski Bridge, which was blown up—the place where the fences have been erected; that's where the Sejm will be located, too.

"The war," he says, and I see it, "had a deep impact on the members of my generation." His face turns mournful and gray. Everyone's hopeful, he says, people are straining themselves to the utmost. But the construction, the tremendous construction isn't easy, he says. How heartily he enlightens me, how open he is.

I survey a gigantic, immensely difficult organizational chore. An entire nation has to put its shoulder to the wheel. They feel a proud delight in doing their job. A delight that I feel intensely.

Polish literature, I believe, is suffering a tragic fate. It used to be a pillar of the nation—so long as the nation was under the yoke. Now that Poland is free, its literature is becoming an ornament. Like everywhere else. Books are laid out in the shop windows, they are bought or not bought. And fewer are bought than in Germany; the editions are suspiciously small. The young authors themselves do not want the old one-track patriotic links to the nation. Since the establishment of the state, their vistas

40

have grown freer and broader. But few Poles go along with the young writers.

One book on display is by Reymont, a novel, *Variegated: The King of the New Israel* by Upajski: anti-Jewish, no doubt. Books by Ossendowski. Boy-Zelenski popularizes French literature. In general, a lot of French writers: Romain Rolland, Marcel Schwob, Claude Farrère, Poincaré. There's Henry Ford, Tagore. Heaps of Jack London. Pilsudski's war book *The Year 1920*. Older Polish literature, Slowacki, Kochanowski.

I ask a literary connoisseur about living writers. He tells me which German authors are known in Poland. Kellermann is appreciated; his *Tunnel* least of all; his *Ninth of November* had an enthusiastic press. The plays of Gerhart Hauptmann are seldom done; he's considered a Hakatist;[11] most recently, he acted offensively during the plebiscite on Upper Silesia. Hanns Heinz Ewers is widely read. He recently visited Warsaw, where he gave a lecture to a mainly Jewish audience. A monocle in his eye, he answered such questions as: "Are you Jewish?", "Are you a good kisser?", "What do you think of Lenin?" The Poles are deeply interested in exotic and French writing: Jack London's adventure novels are devoured, books by Ossendowski, Rolland, Anatole France, and Charles Louis Philippe.

What about the Polish authors? I've heard of few of them: language is as dreadful a barrier between nations as the political borders. Zeromski, a novelist, blossoms among them. *Ashes, The Struggle for Souls, Homeless People* are some of his titles. Reymont, the author of *Peasants*, is still alive. Wyspianski died not long ago, that full-blooded artist—a painter, playwright, stage director. *Wedding* and *Redemption* are his standard dramatic works. According to my connoisseur, they have symbolic and metaphysical traits. Wyspianski, he says, comes from the Greek drama; I can't visualize it, I can only listen. I hear about the younger authors: Rygier-Nalkowska, a woman; Kaden Bandrowski. I speak to him personally, a powerful, likable man who has the matter-of-factness of an expert. *The Arch*, his novel, is widely read; he gives me his latest book, *General Bartsch*. The youngest are the members of the Skamander group, a circle of talented poets; they are said to be growing less prolific. They oppose radicality of form and advocate radicality of content. They celebrate the street, women, Negroes. In other words, the great European wave, billowing into Poland. The essayist Brzozoski has a strong impact; he too is European.

And will their experiences be different from those of German writers? The intellect is a crane that flies away over the heads of the people. My impression is that Poland is far from having any time for lofty literature. What poverty, what huge masses of illiterates! For whom is high art being produced? I wouldn't give two hoots about the great European wave. I would look at the poor common people, not at the small random upper class.

The renovated City Theater in the long, sprawling edifice on Theater Square has been festively reopened. They are staging *Mazeppa* by Julius Slowacki. I enter a bright lobby; costumed guards with big pompous batons are stationed here. Coats are taken by women and girls in white aprons; a small white-and-red ribbon decorating their bosoms adds a nice national touch. The auditorium has two balconies, it's not deep; a rigorous and festive impact is made by the shiny white marble of the first balcony, which juts out into space. Seats made of warm yellow wood are everywhere; the walls are dark red; in the back, behind the white marble and the yellow wood is the powerful crimson that announces violence and death. Every seat has a blue cushion. A heavy cloth curtain drops, without any pattern on it. The performance starts at eight P.M.; it's over at twelve; the intermissions are short. Creaks and moans signal the revolving stage. When the play ends, it has grown more forceful from act to act.

It begins with impressive color and sumptuousness. The stage, with no perspective narrowing, is rectangular, enormously wide and deep. It represents a ducal hall, the set is royal. The ceilings have wooden panels, tapestries hang on walls, carpets lie on the floor—and what lovely tapestries and carpets! Beautiful old paintings, heavy candelabras. A solid balcony juts out in back; a stairway mounts up to it. In the room, people move about, wearing costly and courtly garb, as in paintings by Matejko. Murmuring and chattering, to and fro, of the court society, which is waiting for the king. Then he comes, the rickety man, a misanthrope, a genuinely Slavic face, small, wrinkled eyes, squinting, sober, a whiny, squeaky voice, which is very private—like that of a person accidentally straying into history. That's how a living author resurrects the dead past, a single living actor a dead play. The king is preceded by a candlestick held by a colossus, the duke, the lord of this castle, wearing a laced red garment; then, a blue brocade coat; and finally, when his son is dead, black silk. He behaves in a lordly fashion next to the puny worm, the king. But I don't believe a word the actor says. A handsome French youth is here, Mazeppa, a tenor from toque to buckle shoes, a page to King Jan Kazimierz. I know only the plot, I have to see all the pantomime, the words are mere tonal values. I am doomed to be an Expressionist of the strictest observance. There is also a very fine young lady: Amelia, the wife of the colossal duke. These Poles have a vast choice of attractive people among the actors, and they give them a higher priority than we do. How greatly this lady delights the old king, the misanthrope, under a tree. How well choreographed the dance of these two amid the courtiers. Tormented, she now sits next to him on the bench, flees. The duke's own son, the dark youth next to the laughing Mazeppa, secretly loves her, his stepmother; a Polish Don Carlos. But the duke rages with jealousy—over Mazeppa. The beautiful young duchess poisons herself, the dark youth kills himself. And we know what happens to Mazeppa: the duke ties him on the back of a wild horse.

So much nobility, moonlight, nightingale singing, and goriness. The verses overflow with azure feelings. That is life at sixteen. The Romantic grows no older. We others at twenty have our nightin-gallstones removed. In Germany, I've heard little about this Julius Slowacki, who supposedly died of consumption in Paris. A gushy Romantic; perhaps the actors could have performed his play courageously out of his soul, tenderly, lyrically, at times garishly, cruelly, chimerically, nebulously. The poets have treated Mazeppa no differently. A Polish nobleman really did tie him naked and alive on the back of a raging horse; but nothing happened to him. Nature wasn't gruesome. After his death, however, Franz Liszt drove him through an entire symphony. Mazeppa suffered worst of all in Germany. Here, he ran into Rudolf von Gottschall: the playwright worked him into a chamber drama.

Why, when I see the duchess, does Thekla, Schiller's noble-woman [in *Wallenstein*], enter my thoughts? No, milady, you are not of that family, weep though you may: "The oak forest roars, the clouds race."[12] You come from the theater school in Weimar.

I see the final cruelly adolescent scenes in Slowacki. The marshal, the colossus, has attended to everything, and now his son lies in the coffin, and he himself wears black silk. The duchess is dead, Mazeppa is flying on horseback. The marshal has a knife, and he puts it to his throat. It's good that the curtain drops. Once, in a hospital, I saw a man who had tried to cut his throat. They told me so, I innocently approached the man, who was lying on his stretcher and—he was still alive. They tilted his head back in order to show me the injury; they opened him; and then I saw the dreadful, horrifying sight: the throat cut from ear to ear, the breath coming out, the muscle stumps exposed; the blade hadn't yet reached his arteries. A gigantic bloody hole exuding air! And the man was still alive, trying to talk. The play releases me with that grisly memory.

The spectators applaud, get to their feet. The play has had an intense impact. The women have stood up, with their bare powdered arms, brilliants on their throats and ears. Their faces and the numerous men strike me as slightly rustic, coarse. Ah, the marvelous three chandeliers in the theater; they hang mighty in the room, a tremendous colorful glittering.

The Polish Theater is playing Romain Rolland's *Danton*. The author is a great pacifist and humane person, but his creative approach is very inhumane. I already encountered *Danton* in Berlin. "Hi, there," I think in dismay, it's going to be horribly tedious. I have to see what the Poles want from him. The play has three acts. If one is omitted, you're left with a boring intro-ductory act, and a third act. They ought to start with the third; it's not by Rolland, but by the given producer. In Berlin, Danton was a nonchalant epicurean. Here, he's a fat self-assured

Frenchman, bloated with pleasure, with joie de vivre, he's best at mocking and laughing. The mirth splits right through his sides. They certainly know how to put on a show. A member of the Revolutionary Committee glows in fat insolent naturalism, he's a thoroughgoing bastard, a swine, a beast, pulled from the gutter without benefit of washing. I'm delighted to see how much energy is unleashed by nastiness. They're big on details; they know how to transform all the extras into a Mob. And Robespierre is elemental, a perfect ass, unspeakably dismal; the moron as a force of nature. It's obvious from the very start that he will win. This is the shadow cast by Napoleon.

Thursday concert at the Philharmonic, a social event. My seat's in the balcony, right; I wind up left, get lost, am sent back and forth, I decide to leave, since they allegedly understand only Polish; suddenly, I'm at my seat. The Bechstein grand piano stands under me. The conductor's name is Fitelberg. Although he has a tonsure, I don't think he's Catholic. Artur Rubinstein at the piano. What can I say; I don't think I'll be hearing intrinsically Polish music. The director of this exemplary Polish theater is named Fischmann, even if he spells it Fiszmann. His stage director is a good Pole, but he studied in Berlin, with Reinhardt. I found the same hodgepodge in Berlin. The jazz band, a band of Negroes, is the most authentic music in Europe. May I be hanged if the god of the German bourgeoisie, Goethe, did not successfully read Sophocles. The latter lived in the Balkans, two thousand years ago. And the sweet terror in my bones: what's up with the Carolingians? They imported Near Eastern literature into Central Europe. The distribution center was Rome, the wholesaler; the kings took care of the retailing, with fire and sword; the books were the Old Testament and the New Testament. And wasn't that the organized murder and suicide of the nations? No; because nobody can invent something out of whole cloth. This Brahms concerto, played by Rubinstein on a Bechstein grand piano, is—Polish art! The pianist plays with his face toward me. He seems to be in his late thirties, looks pale, and sweats a lot. His beat is very sharp, his head and facial expressions meld in. Loud applause; masses of youth in the hall. In the balcony opposite me sits Grabski, the brand-new Polish prime minister and financial reformer.

The Philharmonic also screens a propaganda film, *Finland*; The Finnish envoy sent out invitations. Trees are chopped down in the snow. I can sympathize with the tree: as the laughing men come, grab axes, and strike its flanks. Then horses; and the trees are dragged down the mountain with ropes in their hair. The giant creatures are thrown on huge sleds; snowplows clear the way. In the valley, they lie on the watery surface, float to the place where they are driven together like cattle, hauled out, carried into a heating room. Their sap goes up in steam. Now the will-less trunks are cut up into huge chunks; the power saw chews and chews them. They're turned into bits and crumbs of wood that are thrown into pulp vats, into refined crushing apparatuses. Here, they are mashed into wet powder. And not much later, it becomes paper, bales as thick as trees, rolling off by railroad. And that's the fate of the tree trunk—which was produced in a lyrical pollination by a bee or butterfly, bore its leaves in sunshine, couples lay underneath; the tree itself was a colossal pumping and sucking machine, a chemical and physical wonderwork. Nor is the paper the final chapter. I know what becomes of paper. How it's printed, how it enlightens and bamboozles nations. The film merely shows how the avalanche begins to slide. Enlightenment through newspapers! Would the peasants be better off remaining illiterate?

The model farm that comes next is a cheerier sight. Milk is being churned into butter. Harbors are frozen; what ice breakers they have! Sports; a wrestling match, races, jumps. The discus thrower revolves in a circle. Man is a powerful animal; but what he does in a laboratory, without muscles, with his soft brain, is even more powerful. The Finnish army, troop trains, soldiers, soldiers. Very nice that they march so snappily. But here comes the monstrous creature, the tank. How it clambers uphill and down, as thick and shaky as a turtle. It doesn't handle trees gingerly, like men with clean axes. It dodders around them, clumsy, thick, and then it lops them, crushes them. The smashed corpse lies behind it; the monster keeps on creeping. Reels and topples. Dreadful the way it wanders through the forest. No one in the audience is not horrified. Yet it is our collective child.

A theater catering to popular taste; it has an earnest petty-bourgeois public. The orchestra and three balconies are filled. They're playing a local farce from the good old days, for the twentieth time: *The Trip to Warsaw*. Marriage and the distribution of power in marriage are evidently the same in Poland as in the other Europe: the henpecked husband is laughed at; the energetic wife rules the roost and is likewise laughed at; two daughters unceremoniously stupid. They come from a village with their birdcage: the caftan Jews play a good-natured part. The entire family gets lost at the Warsaw terminal, a couple of gallants abduct the daughters. They hunt one another all over Warsaw and are reunited in the end. Seven scenes, a total of four hours, singing, dancing. A humorous production: the shunting of the train onstage provokes as much laughter as a whole dozen ditties.

Fare for the solid middle class. A few off-color jokes, legs get barer, and you've got the big city. Panties are a barometer of culture; if they hang low, then the people are barbarians; if they rise, you get a vast view, and your mind soars. I discover that levels of civilization can be measured by the centimeter.

People gush over *Pat and Patachon*, a Danish movie. I attend a matinee. The jubilation of the people and many children. A short fat guy appears and a long skinny one. They dodder and muddle for hours on end. One of them opens a faucet, he can't shut it, the water shoots aloft. So, suffering, he sits upon the faucet. The audience splits its sides.

What—I wonder, sitting in the dark—do I find everywhere? Harmless fun. Movie music: "Where did you get those gorgeous blue eyes?" "Baby, you're the apple of my eye." A jazz band, at times bad, at times good. Arrogant military men, carrying their sabers. People sitting in a café, women gazing through the windows. Newsboys shouting. Loiterers at the railroad stations. Mailboxes, telephones, window clerks. In the evening, the moon, the sickle moon, soft in a blackish-blue mass, whitish clouds at its edge. I lie here in the laughter of the men, women and children, in the film wall, in the auditorium, in the usher

47

who sells me a program which I can't read, in the piano, in the bumpy playing. This is a Sunday afternoon, two hours of not thinking, of stretching out in this black restless room and relaxing.

At the Oaza, they dance. It's first class. At twelve midnight, the typical couples of the haute bourgeoisie appear. Two want to dance well; they execute their various pas with hard faces; they steal shy glances at the public. An elderly gentleman in a tuxedo, with his plump lady. A corpulent husband cutting a rug with his wife; they're tipsy. The music quacks marvelously; I'd give my life for this cacophony. The jazz band sits on a podium in front of a painted wall. I finally get to the bottom of this music: Dadaist Negroes. They make such terrifically sweet fun of old music. That's why I love them. They insult, scoff, and seduce. The people barely notice, but it sits. The clarinet plays with the baby grand, the violinist sings falsetto; the drum beats at the wrong time. They hammer away like stone breakers. Now the Chicago ascends. Two dismal people get up from their wine buckets, dance, remain dismal, never lose their misery. The man has black hair, stiffly combed, a kind of Herriot; he bends when dancing, stumbles. The saxophone begins to whine. The musicians step down from their podium; only the ones at the piano and the drum are bound. Now, all the flesh is shooed from the tables and revolves in the middle. The bourgeois elegance does not lose its balance. The leading dancer, spic-and-span, bows to a young slender woman in a yellow frock. They move in an ingenious tango step; there are rhythmic surprises; they hurry, then stand rooted. Glide with deep discreet steps; then he pulls her backward and rocks her over his pubic bone. He pushes his flexible partner ahead; one of his feet stands obscenely between her goldbug slippers. He turns, whirls, goes backward. The sax moos in accompaniment. Afterward, they sit at separate tables; she has slipped into a fur tippet; blonde, bobbed hair, pouting lips; he tugs at his necktie. Then they sway together for a sobbing Boston. The pianist swings back and bangs on the drum. A musician grabs a chair leg and whistles on it; the others join in a chorus, wheezing and bleating.

Women of good society broaden out below; they try to hide it with ribbons; but when they dance, the ribbons fly apart. Now a solo player sits in the middle of the room. He holds the metal blade of a saw between his knees, bending it with his left hand, rapping it with his right. Something magical ascends. He plays Puccini on the saw. It's more human than a human voice—an ethereal singing, drawling, breathing emerge from the metal. Hovering notes, immaterial spherical notes, from the blade of a buzz saw.

What do I find everywhere? Upper-class Europe. Some of me is at home here too.

# THE JEWISH DISTRICT
# OF WARSAW

*The Jews: their nation was silently imbued with the renunciation of land, country, and state. The return movement is taking place.*

Three hundred fifty thousand Jews live in Warsaw, half as many as in all Germany. A small number of them are strewn across the city, the bulk reside together in the northwestern sector. They are a nation. People who know only Western Europe fail to realize this. The Jews have their own costumes, their own language, religion, manners and mores, their ancient national feeling and national consciousness.

They were thrown out of Palestine, their motherland, two thousand years ago. Then they knocked about in many countries, partly wandering, partly driven, peddlers, merchants, moneymen, spiritually always in close contact with the host nation, yet keeping solidly to themselves. Parts kept crumbling off, but the nation remained whole. And now it is larger than it was two thousand years ago. Its members were shoved from south to north, out of Spain, where hundreds of thousands were settled, from France to Germany, into the lands of Poles and Russians. Economic hatred was repeatedly spewed upon them, dislike of the alien nation, repulsion, fear of their alien cult. Poland took them in during the thirteenth century.

50

They entered a country with almost no towns; between peasantry and gentry they assumed the functions of a middle class. They were protected by a privilege granted by Duke Boleslaw that allowed them their own jurisdiction and internal self-administration. The privilege was repeatedly confirmed by men such as Kazimierz the Great, and finally by Poland's King Stanislas Augustus in the eighteenth century. The Jews enjoyed a high degree of real autonomy. A proverb circulated early: "Poland, the heaven of the aristocracy, the paradise of the Jews, the hell of the peasants." Every century experienced its persecutions of Jews. The new age of nationalism wiped out their privileges. Minority and autonomy policies now appear in a different guise.

In this city of Warsaw, they settled on Abraham Street, in the center, were excluded from trade by the Magdeburg Rights, which Warsaw took over: only town dwellers and Christians could engage in trade. They were repeatedly driven from the cities, lived in villages under the aegis of the gentry. At the Great Parliament of 1788, the Warsaw municipal deputies demanded a sharpening of all anti-Jewish decrees. But the Jews remained under aristocratic protection. "There are certain economic necessities against which all other factors are useless." Numbering three and one half million, the Jewish nation is now growing in Poland.

In northwestern Warsaw, Nalewki Street runs parallel with Marshal Street and Cracow Suburb. Nalewki Street, a broad avenue, is the main artery of the Jewish district. To its right and left, long streets branch off, with new intersecting streets, large and small. And they are all filled and teeming with Jews. Trolleys run along Nalewki Street. The houses have the same façades as most of the houses in Warsaw, crumbling, unclean. Courtyards submerge into all the buildings. I enter a courtyard; it's rectangular and, like a marketplace, full of loud people, Jews, mostly in caftans. The back wings contain furniture shops, fur shops. And, after passing through a back wing, I stand in another swarming courtyard full of crates, teams of horses; Jewish porters loading and unloading. Nalewki Street has large stores. Dozens of variegated signs indicate: hides, furs, ladies' suits, hats, luggage. Stores are located on the ground floors and upper floors. Toward the city, in the southern part, along the Dluga, large, open, modern stores: cosmetics, stamps, textiles. I read strange names: Waiselfisch, Klopfherd, Blumenkranz, Brandwain, Farsztandig, Goldkopf, Gelbfisch, Gutbesztand. The members of the ostracized nation have been saddled with derisive nicknames. I read on: Goldluft, Goldwasser, Feldgras, Oksenberg. Jewish women pass through the crowd; they wear black wigs, small black veils on top, a kind of flower in front. Black shawls. A tall young man in modern clothes with his elegant sister looks strange; he walks proudly, with a skullcap on his head. Families converse in the street; two youngish men in clean caftans with their wives in modern garb and piquant Polish makeup. A boy in a sailor's suit is with them, his cap says "Torpedo." A Polish policeman directs vehicular traffic in the roadway. This contiguousness of two nations. Young girls stroll arm in arm, they don't look very Jewish, they laugh, speak Yiddish, their clothes are Polish down to the fine stockings. They amble erect. The shoulders of the men are slack, their backs crooked, they shuffle.

Morning. The conspicuous mass of old, white-bearded men. Lots of dirty, raggedy caftans. They gaze from pale, yellow, bearded faces. An intense commercial life on the sidewalk and the roadway; many also lean against the building walls, their expressions are very calm, muted. Five utterly shabby men sit in a row outside a house entrance, ropes tied around their waists: porters. Yiddish newspapers are hawked. Men emerge from the huge deep shops, toting sacks. How horribly tattered they are, boots with dangling soles, sleeves ripped out, seams bursting. A boy leads a man with white dead eyes; they beg. An old greasy woman accosts the passersby, holding out her hand. Three elderly Jews sit in front of a government *papierosi* shop, chatting, smoking. How many stand around, look around, waiting, waiting, waiting. A gust of wind blows frequently; then their long black coats fly open, exposing their white ritual fringes. A small fat man with a huge knotted rope around his waist stands in front of a shop window, his beard black, his face learned. His greasy caftan and his trousers are rags. Some people wander in small slow crews.

The enormous textile storehouses. I read the names: Seidenstrumpf, Butterfass, Tuchwarger, Spiegelglas. Then Jakob Natur, Israel Gesundheit. Every dozen houses, a Jewish fruit shop; fruit in a glass case. Through the crowd, a man carries a pack of sticks under one arm. The long, flowing beards, black and many reddish-blonde. The dominant type is skinny with a long nose. Several men usually sit in the dark background of each store, sometimes on tables, eating, debating. Carts loaded with bales of cloth are pushed along. I read the names: Amethyst, Diamant, Safir, Goldwasser, Mülstein. Now come crimson faces with carroty beards, broad-shouldered men. Gesia Street crosses Nalewki Street, it's narrow, very long, a trolley route. Jews wearing caftans in droshkies drive around the corner, elegant ladies next to them; droshkies transporting sacks.

And now, a big creature wanders amid the others: a very tall man in a long silk caftan, with a white, flowing, two-pronged beard. He wears a large round hat. His eyes peer straight ahead. His expression is strict, proud. A small clean man next to him. The tall man is a rabbi. He walks; ignored by the commercial crowd. And not far behind him, a Catholic funeral procession moves up the street. In front, right and left, lanterns with burning flames; behind the hearse, mourners, simple people, bareheaded; finally, a lone droshky carrying women. What wrinkled faces I see around me. They blow their noses on their hands, without handkerchiefs, wipe their hands on their caftans.

Dzika Street. The small goldware boutique: a radiant Jewish girl stands at the door, her sumptuous red hair is curly. At a goose slaughterhouse, a small coarse woman works in blood up to her elbows, drawing a goose. Paperhangers, bakers, butchers, junk shops. A book peddler hawking Yiddish publications. Gangs of kids: I notice their Slavic faces: the Jewish features emerge later on. Slowly someone shuffles down the middle of the roadway, a man: one chair in his right hand, one chair in his left, three piled on his head. An astonishing shop, very high and narrow, only one room, which is open to the street. Inside, an ancient man sits on a bench, smoking; his shop is stuffed from top to bottom, right up to his feet, chock-full of awful garbage, rusty scrap iron: keys, rings, wires, locks. The shop signs: Kleinfinger, Berlinerblau, Rotblut, Halbstrunk, Tuchband, Zweifuss, Alfabet, Silberklang. Painters, whitewashers, stroll along, in smocks, toting ladders; skullcaps on their heads. When talking, these people seldom move their arms and hands; what you see in Western Europe is disfigurement. A few old men have twirled earlocks; from behind, in their heavy, skirtlike caftans, they look like women. When they step across puddles, they lift their caftans like women. Very many of the ones standing here have dreamy expressions; they look somnolent.

All at once, an ancient, dirty manikin steals along the wall. When I view him from the front, he is waxen. His mouth is wide open, his left eye is small and red, the eyelid inverted, bare. However, his right eye gapes, it is whitish. He gropes out with the cane in his left hand. He thus fumbles his way along the decrepit wall in the bright afternoon. A little Jewish bootblack spots me, zooms toward me, pulls me from the street into a building entrance. He works my shoes lightning-fast with brush blows right and left; in the end, the cloth rips in the heat of his work. Eventually, my shoes sparkle like patent leather. Three other boys have gathered around us. The bootblack exchanges brief agitated hostile words with them. Then he's done, I ask how much. The three other boys go tense, and they draw closer. He asks for two zlotys; two whole zlotys! He is entitled to fifty groszy, one-fourth that sum. The boys wait to see how I respond to his impudence. And I—I pay two zlotys. Afterward, from the throng, I can observe my bootblack's radiant face, the other three communicating, greedy and hateful; then my bootblack suddenly whizzes right past me. Skedaddling—the others after him with a hue and cry.

The great synagogue on Tlomacki Street; a classical temple, narrow, lofty. Above it, the dome with the Star of David. A short beadle chats with a Polish policeman at the foot of the stairs. It's Saturday morning. They pour up the steps. Few of them wear caftans and skullcaps, this is the synagogue of the middle class, also the enlightened, the emancipated, and the assimilated. An empty vestibule with glass doors. And oddly: basins of dripping water to the right and left of the entrance; the arriving worshipers dip their fingers into the water: the vestige of a ritual ablution, and also how close to the Catholic stoup. Inside the temple, a swarming throng. The people converse, most of them softly, a few in an undertone. An elderly man tries to expel a boy from his seat. How the graybeard's eyes sparkle, and he finally summons the attendant. Shaking his head, coaxing gently, the attendant pushes the boy away; the graybeard glares venomously for a long time. On the back wall, next to Polish inscriptions, three rows of clocks with Hebrew letters.[13] Each tells a different time; I don't understand them. A man in front of me prays very loudly, his upper body swaying, a man in a hat.[14] Suddenly, he turns around, breaks off, pats the white-haired beadle on the back; they talk about a woman's illness. The attendant cries: "Don't stand in the middle, don't block traffic." Upstairs, women sit behind a high wide gate; I see fashionable modern hats. Not nearly as many women as in Christian churches. Most of the men wear prayer shawls, white with blue and black stripes. Some wear them like scarves, some wrap them around their arms, tightening them. Many young men walk about, including almost a dozen soldiers, and more join them afterward. On the whole, these are not elegant people, they unabashedly pick their noses while talking. A few respectable types wander slowly along the center aisle, the beadle makes room for them; they sit in front. Little boys in sailor caps stand on the bench; the adults accompanying them read books and hold on to the boys. These men have swift eyes. Many faces are full and broad. On either side of the room, I count seven windows, small, unadorned. Lofty columns rise from the gallery, partitioning off seven round arches. A small stairway leads to the altar. The red burning lamp, the central curtain. The liturgizing resembles the Catholic one. And it is amazingly similar to the Catholic one when the priest pulls up the curtain, produces a chinking clinking silver implement and holds it in his arm like an ostensory. Escorted by functionaries, the priest descends the steps, passes the altar while chanting, and remounts the steps. At the top two men stand, in normal clothes, reading

aloud. Here, there is a close rapport between parish and priest.
They read aloud, and every so often, the crowd and the choir
break in tumultuously. Now, boys appear up at the altar. I hear
that they are being confirmed. General whispering; a large number of excited people shove forward along the center aisle. The
temple has filled up, people are pushing in from the vestibule in
back. The white-bearded attendant fights with them. In a very
grandiloquent voice—which is changing, it keeps breaking—a
boy up there utters Hebrew words. People motion to one another familiarly, smiling. The men and women have all stood
up, craning their necks. People throng forward more and more
vehemently. The priest sings, and then another boy recites his
passages. Men are already leaving. Newcomers press in from
the vestibule. I also leave once I hear more of the same from
the altar. In the vestibule, they are debating in groups. They
stand at the foot of the staircase, eyeing the passersby.

Outside, the stores are closed. Men in caftans slowly amble
along the hushed street. As I approach Theater Square, the
tableau quickly changes. I am in Poland, in a surging Polish
metropolis.

The liquidation of the Jewish Middle Ages in Eastern Europe
commenced during the second half of the previous century.
The modern era appeared at the small Jewish towns with modern industry and capitalist economy. A chronic crisis began,
demanding a readjustment, which was only partly feasible in
this country. Emigration reached an enormous scale; in America, hindered by nothing, a swift economic restructuring of the
immigrants took place: seventy-eight percent of the American
Jews became workers. Among those who stayed on in Poland,
the crisis pushed many into productive and physical work.
Within three decades, one húndred seventy-five thousand Jews
became farmers. The Russian ukase: "Get away from the soil!"
throttled the movement.

The twentieth century has been exacerbating the uninterrupted crisis. The European war came: four hundred thousand
Jews, some eighty thousand families, were thrown out of their
homes, forced to abandon their houses, stores, workshops,

farms. In the aftermath, 1918–1921, civil war, epidemics, pogroms in Russian territory, claiming half a million Jewish victims.

A young Jewish politician, smiling imperturbably, tells me: the Polish constitution guarantees equal rights for the Jews. But in practice, a lot has remained the same as under the Russians. Anyone who registers as a Jewish national cannot advance in the Polish army. Article 10 in the Treaty of Versailles speaks about Jewish communities and article 11 about Jews; they are to enjoy the rights of minorities in language and religion. This is not, one must admit, a clear-cut legal recognition of the Jewish nationality. But the Jews count as a de facto nationality; in the Sejm, they are one of the minorities. The right-wing Poles want a national state, others a kind of federation. That was the goal of the Polish campaign of 1920, led by Pilsudski; he was in Kiev and he wanted the entire Ukraine; he was in the Lithuanian Vilnius (Wilno) and he wanted Lithuania. He wanted a Greater Poland, a federative structure inhabited by friends and surrounded by friends. The right wing opposed him, legions and youth were on his side. But the Bolsheviks drove him out of Kiev. What remains is the difficult, difficult partial solution of today, the patchwork of the Polish state of today. Incidentally, the young politician smiles, none of those issues is current. The immediate issues in Poland are: how to stabilize finances, how to ensure the survival of the economy.

How many Jews does Poland have? About three million. That's ten percent of the country's population. How many Jews are there in the whole world? Slightly less than fifteen million. I get a picture of the economic situation of the Jews here. The Polish state is going through a crisis of stabilization. The Jews are partly bearing the brunt of it. For large numbers of them live just by trading and, unhealthily, by speculating. Earlier, political measures prevented these masses from expanding economically and organizing normally. A property tax and a sales tax are imminent. Very few people have property or capital; the sales tax will affect the masses of shopkeepers. They will have to pay two and a half percent on every hand-to-hand transaction. As a result, Jews in Warsaw have applied for eight thousand fewer business licenses this year than last year. In Lodz, only a third as many as last year. The masses of shopkeepers are melting away. The government, itself poor, is looking for sources of revenue. It is resorting to state monopolies: tobacco, liquor, and matches have been nationalized. Thirty-two thousand Jewish families were involved in liquor and tobacco. The necessity is growing more and more urgent: "Leave business and switch to physical and productive work." However, for Poland, the official motto is: "One-third of industrial workers have to emigrate, one-third have to be reclassified, one-third will remain for domestic needs."

Emigration, especially to America, has been made very difficult at this time. A portion of the Jewish masses regards the establishment of a Jewish state in Palestine, the "homeland," as the only solution. I also hear about the Crimean project of the Russian government, and some people believe that Russia will eventually become a land for Jewish immigration. The purely economic transformation of the Jewish masses from shopkeepers into productive workers, farmers, and artisans is being energetically implemented by ORT, an organization that sets up workshops, supports settlements, and provides machines and seed. I am delighted by the poster of this intelligent and thoroughly useful agency: an enormous peasant wielding a scythe—a Ukrainian Jew; next to him, emaciated peddlers, loitering in a panel, gape up, astonished, at the giant.

I converse with a Zionist leader, a lively, bearded, thoroughly energetic man. He says:

"The Polish people mock and scorn the Jews; they also fear them a bit. The *szlachta* [Polish aristocracy] kept court Jews as jesters—something of that survives. Judaism no longer has a living religious and spiritual life, a religious and spiritual movement as in the days when Hasidism was growing. Jews are becoming increasingly secular. The old clericalism is being fought and must continue to be fought. Ways of life are gradually becoming freer. Many Jews now travel on the Sabbath, smoke in the Saxon Garden. The Sabbath is rigorously observed only in Jewish neighborhoods. The caftan and the capote don't tell you much. There are Communists who wear caftans. The old Jewish schools, the kheders, are vanishing. It is a sign of the decrease of clericalism that Orthodox Jews have had to form a party."

I learn that the distribution of votes among minorities in the Polish parliament was decided by way of a deal; the minorities formed a bloc. There are thirty-four Jewish deputies. The Zionists, although not in the majority, are the political leaders. The Jewish minority demands the abolition of Sunday blue laws. They want to keep their stores open on Sundays; now, they are not even allowed to work at home on Sundays. Two days of rest are detrimental to them, forcing them to work on the Sabbath. They want subsidies for their schools. I hear from another side that the government cannot fund these schools, since the Jews themselves are at loggerheads about the language of instruction: Yiddish or Hebrew. They also demand the elimination of Jewish quotas at institutions of higher learning, in ministerial offices; the possibility of promotion in the military.

A Jewish club, the left-wing workers' group Poale Zion:[15] large rooms, a vast dining hall. The meal is eaten ritually. Young people play chess. A library of two thousand books. They have a cooperative, they pay unemployment insurance.

I am taken to a modern Jewish school. Across a courtyard, into a wretched back wing, up an appalling staircase. Two intelligent young teachers. The language of instruction is Yiddish; Polish and Hebrew are important subjects. I walk through a charming school museum with clay sculptures, I sit in on a class. Small boys and girls. They paste, draw patterns, figures. They come and show them to me radiantly. A higher class: well-dressed young girls sing; the singing teacher at the piano. A recess, during which one class sings a boisterous ditty, its exuberance smashing through all the walls, shattering all ears. This is a secular school of the Jewish people. In the academic year 1924, one hundred three of these schools exist in sixty-nine Polish towns, with an overall enrollment of thirteen thousand students. Then there are secular high schools and teachers' academies for Jews. All in all, over two hundred such institutions with twenty thousand students. This is an autonomous emancipation of the working masses of the Jewish people. They are not Zionists, they reject the clergy; and, as Socialists, they condemn the entire bad social system of today. Thus, they are waging a struggle on two fronts: for political and for economic liberation. It is similar to the action of the old Polish Socialist Party. A pamphlet quotes the playwright Sholem Asch [chiefly a novelist]: "Our schools, more than any other, must avoid a biased education. A child's soul belongs to no one. Our road to humanity is the Jewish road." Another essay is entitled: "The School of the Awakened Masses."

I visit two major Jewish publishing houses, I get a picture of the impact of the language quarrel. This mountain of good European literature is translated once into Yiddish and once into Hebrew. Excellent textbooks appear twofold, in two languages, Hebrew and Yiddish. Hebrew is promoted by the bourgeois, purely national Zionists. Yiddish, the true vernacular of the masses, is cultivated by the supporters of the working class, the Socialists, the secular.

I peruse their newspapers, a Zionist one, a Socialist one, a nonpartisan one—all in Yiddish. They have interesting articles. One mocks an edict by a Galician rebbe: Women are not allowed to wear their own hair in public. Women are to ignore the custom of wearing transparent dresses, to avoid sinning. Otherwise they will be considered whores. In a home, the married couple's beds should stand far apart; double beds are prohibited.

The merry war of the Jews of Radom with their rebbe: Before the war, a son of Radom's morkh-hauro (the rebbe's deputy, without a teaching post) could be seen around the town—a young man like all young men. No one paid him any heed, and no one dreamed that this youth, who wore European clothing, would cast an eye on the Radom rabbinate. In 1912 the office became vacant, and the man who was elected was Zirelsohn, well known and now the rebbe of Kishen.

Zirelsohn was already en route to Radom. But he received a threatening letter from Radom, warning him not to go there: a Lithuanian rebbe should not take office in a Polish town. The writer of the threatening letter turned out to be Yekhiel Kestenberg, the young man in Radom, and he knew what he was doing. A short time later, the provincial government appointed him deputy of a government rebbe. That was the first step.

Radom seethed, but it was no use. After a while, Kestenberg showed up, dressed in an elegant capote, and he acted as if he were the rebbe of Radom. During the war, he shored up his rabbinical position, going to any lengths to do so. When the Austrians came, he sucked up to them. When the Austrians were gone and the Russians came, and black days began for the Jews of Radom, Kestenberg went up to the podium and sermonized: I warned you not to get cozy with the Austrians. But in the end, the Austrians established themselves solidly in Radom, and the rebbe waited on them hand and foot. The Austrians thanked him for his efforts by appointing him rebbe.

The war ended, and Kestenberg began to feel that it was time for him to be confirmed by the actual Polish powers that be. In late 1920 he submitted a petition in Warsaw, asking to be nominated *rov* [rabbi] of Radom.[16] But a Polish minister of state understood what a Jewish rebbe did not understand. The answer was that according to Jewish law, a rebbe has to be elected by the community and not appointed by the government. And the government ordered that the Jews of Radom should convene to elect a rebbe. An electoral committee was formed, and they were ready to start the vote.

But several weeks later, Warsaw ordered them to table the election. A Jewish delegation from Radom went to Warsaw, presented itself to the minister, and asked why the government had rescinded the election order. They received the following reply: A well-known National Democratic parliamentary deputy from Radom had contacted the minister and informed him that Rabbi Kestenberg was a very reliable person, who served the government loyally. The rabbinical election in Radom, he said, was a camouflage for Jewish revolutionary activities, which the Jews of Radom wanted to begin, and because of other unrest in the country—there were strikes in Czestochowa—the minister had been forced to call off the election in Radom. Kestenberg had worked hand in glove with the deputy to prevent it.

Radom Jews of all stripes promptly got together and dispatched a memorandum to the government, pointing out the abnormal situation that Radom had no elected *rov*, and also decrying the false information and suspicions about the Jewish community of Radom. The minister thereupon notified them that the rabbinical election had not been canceled, but merely delayed, and that it would take place along with the next municipal election. God helped, and the election came to the community. Rabbi Kestenberg began to work on all sides. He drew up his own slate of candidates, which was roundly defeated: of the twenty-two men voted into office, only three were on Kestenberg's list. The community board was constituted, an administration was picked, and at its first meeting, the administration unanimously resolved to hold a rabbinical election in Radom. The administration's decision was accepted by the community board with sixteen ayes, two nays, and four absentees. On September 21, the community board ordered an election for the rabbinical office. But on September 26, the newspaper published a different statement by three members of the board: it said that Radom already had a *rov*, the brilliant Yekhiel Kestenberg. In order to convince oneself as to who was right, one only had to read the second report, which was published by newspapers on October 3 and signed by thirty members of the administration and the board: Radom demanded an elected rabbi, and the election absolutely had to take place. Furthermore, it went on, before the Radom community board had published the second announcement, a community delegation had approached the minister, informing him precisely about the Kestenberg matter and the Radom election. The minister had thereupon confirmed that the election could not be canceled and that Radom can and must elect a rabbi. However, the Gaon[17] Kestenberg has not held his tongue. And just as he found protection under the National Democratic deputy, he has now tried to get the Association of Rabbis to take him under its wing. The association is to place a fiat on all the Polish rabbis in regard to their candidacy. He is losing no time and sparing no effort to carry out his plan for preventing the election of a rabbi, even though the entire population has explicitly demanded an elected and not an appointed rabbi. We hope that the Association of Rabbis will be intelligent enough not to interfere.

# Journey to Poland

The eve of the Jewish Day of Atonement.[18] In the morning, I wander down Gesia Street, a long thoroughfare. A few stores are still open, the majority are already closing. A tremendous human surging fills the street, the trolley is mobbed. I walk past an old, long building, a military prison; red iron crates are attached to the windows; the light enters the cells only from above. One shop is called Kirschensaft, a barber's name is Nordwind. Many men coming my way—only Jews—have a slip of paper on their lapel. I don't understand; is this a demonstration? The side streets teem incredibly. A graveyard announces itself with stonecutters' yards. This is the eve of the Day of Atonement; the Jewish Day of Judgment is imminent, people have to repent, cleanse themselves. But first they have to appease their dead. Now they are going to the cemetery, to their dead, begging them for forgiveness, pleading with them to plead with God on their behalf. A human torrent is surging toward Okopawa Street. That's where the big cemetery is located; it's surrounded by a low red wall; the iron gate is open. Inside, a forecourt with benches occupied by men, mostly in caftans and skullcaps or vizored caps; a few are smoking cigarettes. Along the wall, at the tree trunks, between the trees, men stand, alone or in groups, each man holding a book, murmuring, humming, rocking, shifting from foot to foot. Here, I already notice the grumbling noise that comes from my right, from the cemetery: individual cries, very loud, disjointed talking, also chanting. There must be a large crowd, a very large crowd here; I don't see it as yet. It's like being near a large assembly. Sometimes the singing, calling, the general confused din are so intense that the place sounds like a county fair. The human torrent veers right along the wall. The main current flows between the graves, a broad triumphal avenue. Rich monuments, marble plaques, black and white, loom up here, Hebrew and Polish inscriptions, many only Hebrew, long texts. One high plaque is covered with a scaffolding; the visitors surround the grave, reading, pointing: "Peretz, Peretz."[19] I see another strange monument: a serpent twisting around a tree trunk, plus a broken wheel, a broken wagon shaft. Another gigantic plaque with a long Hebrew text;

above it, the gold image of a crowned stag and a hand holding a knife.

I am startled by a woman's fierce, piercing shriek. It begins and ends, often renewed, with a long painful chant. No one pays it any heed. And as I thread my way through the rows of graves, I find a headstone; but on the ground—everything in the cemetery is covered with green grass, with lovely, leveling grass, with rampant meadow flowers, white, red, blue—on the ground lies an elegantly dressed young woman next to an elderly one. The older woman, curled, clinging tight to the bottom of the headstone (I can't see her face, her head and shoulders are covered by a large black shawl), she screams, calls, calls, moans. She calls, in Yiddish:

"Father, our beloved father, you were such a good man, you sat next to me in the room, all these years, in the shop. I've stayed here. I'm here. Help me to get the children to study so that they'll be well off. Life is hard. Life is so hard, Sarah is here. We're not well off. Why did you die, for us. I didn't do anything bad to you."

Now and then, the younger woman sits up, blows her nose, wipes her eyes, lies down again.

And when I follow the bend of the wall, when I leave the row of marble graves, the boulevard of the notables, I can no longer see anything of the burial mounds. I find a large agitated meadow, with small rocks, sunken into the earth and edged with larger ones. It looks wild, churned up. Men with prayer books stand here and there, behind the gravestones. And from all over the meadow, even from where I see no people, I hear chanting, shrieking, wailing, moaning. Like single plumes of smoke rising up and turning into a dense cloud. Now and again, something emerges from the green, a back, a head, a face. Always women, girls, in shawls, plumed hats, under the old flowery wigs. They lie on the graves, weeping, lamenting, accusing themselves, calling, appeasing the dead. Many call in a simple tone of pain and lament. Many women use a liturgical singsong, similar to the chanting in temple. This is the place where they pray aloud; the divine service of the women is over the graves. The men with the prayer books stand upright, murmuring, bowing earnestly and solemnly; at their feet, the women and the girls huddle in the grass, lamenting, moaning, emitting the shrill singsong.

More have now arrived, in hired carriages, automobiles, private vehicles, the elegant men, the women. The women walk next to the men. With reddened eyes, twitching lips, they stand at the graves, staring at the plaques. A dreadful staccato moaning comes from one side. At a column, a broken one, stands a woman in modern dress. She clutches the smooth column with hands gloved in fine yellow leather. The moans emerge from her, staccato, helpless. Sometimes, gasping for air, she removes the handkerchief from her face; her face is all puffed up. She can't hold back her moans. Now, her hands slide away, down the column, she drops to the grass, over the grave, her face down, wailing. From elsewhere comes a female voice, virtually scolding at intervals. An old wrinkled woman kneels and lies there; she screams loud, barking, always with brief pauses. She embraces the headstone with both arms. A group of men in a circle around a grave; rocking with their books; one man reads aloud, resonant. The graves are all set up in one direction, overgrown, overrun with thick grass. Raw broken bricks, sometimes heavy pebbles, lie on many headstones, sometimes even on the marble monuments; they hem in sheaves of grass that have been placed there as tokens. White tissue paper has been put around one grave; the paper bears black letters, carrying its plea across the grave. Many people walk about, seeking, pushing apart the grass that already completely shrouds the graves.

By the time I pull myself out of the sea of murmuring, moaning, female shrieking, and push my way toward the exit—it is almost eleven A.M.—all the beggars in town have gathered along the main cemetery road, and so have the adolescent representatives of the Jewish welfare organizations. Today, people give, as if hoping to redeem themselves from punishments for the wicked things they once did to the people who are now dead and for all their sinning of the past year. The day of the dead and the poor. Scores of beggars, blind people, deaf people now lie in front of the rows of graves. They stand in the center of the thoroughfare, dividing the human torrent. They push their way

65

in between the people. Calling, lamenting, grabbing, seizing the hands of passersby; they are relentless—like the self-reproaches of these people. There are mutes, who babble as they stretch out their hands. One of them babbles a powerful litany. From everywhere, you hear: "Jews, *rakhmones* [pity]! Jewish children, give!" Dreadfully, dreadfully ragged women carry children swathed in shawls; yellow crones stand in their hard wigs. A large circle of people has formed around a marble grave: a young man lies in front of it, blowing foam. His arms and legs jerk rhythmically, his hands follow slackly. His cap lies next to him. I glanced at him on the way in; he is still lying there. His cap is filled with banknotes; money keeps flying down to him amid words of pity. His thick foam moves with his breathing; it's soapsuds, the man is a professional, a swindler.

Wallets and breast pockets are opened everywhere, bills and coins fall, some beggars have whole piles of paper. The male and female helpers of Jewish organizations stand under the trees, holding cans. They have pins and blue, red, white slips of paper in readiness; the slips that I saw out on the street. The helpers call, head toward the passersby, plunge the pins into coat collars.

At the exit, the mob of people is dreadful. A hazardous thronging. The shrieks are tremendous; the young helpers follow the passersby into the street. A car park has accumulated outside. The trolleys run more often, but without reducing the huge crowd.

Cold shivers run up and down my spine when I see and hear these things. I ride back on the trolley, climb the hotel stairs, sit in my room; it takes me awhile to collect my thoughts. This is something horrible. It is something primordial, atavistic. Does this have anything to do with Judaism? These are living vestiges of ancient notions! These are vestiges of the fear of the dead, the fear of wandering souls. A feeling handed down to the members of this nation with their religion. It is the remnant of a different religion, animism, a cult of the dead.

In the evening, I go to a *shul*. Across the courtyard of an apartment house into a long narrow room with electric lighting.

It is crowded with people. The women's gallery runs upstairs. At the entrance, there are posters by a Palestinian rabbi and his portrait: an appeal for donations to a fund; this *shul* belongs to a Zionist congregation. My guide and I have a hard time pushing our way through the wall of men, squeezing past the *bimah*, the enclosed platform in the front third of the room, where they read aloud from the Torah; until I arrive at the front wall next to the cantor and his small choir.

Amid the utter hush of the assembly, the cantor intones the ancient Kol Nidre prayer.[20] He is squat, has a white beard, a white coat, a prayer shawl over it. He wears a skullcap, it is made of velvet, embroidered with gold threads. The prayer shawls of the other men are simple and plain. A few wear elaborate ones with silver embroidery. The cantor has begun very softly. He chants the same prayer once again, louder. And now, for a third time, in a full lamenting voice.

This chant ushers in the evening, intensely and powerfully. The people do not seem consistently anxious and agitated. Here and there, I see them chatting. The small choir gets into gear; the teenagers and young men sing from memory. The cantor conducts them himself; during the singing, he caresses this boy or that, nodding to them. Then comes a passage that forms the climax of the evening. The white-bearded man, as a preparation, has drawn his prayer shawl all the way over his head. Others in the room do likewise. The cloth drops down over his forehead; he squeezes the cloth together under his chin. And what I then hear, what he then sings is an echo of the wailing and yammering that I heard at the cemetery this morning. But now it's in the chant. In this ardor, the man sucks himself in just as he has drawn himself into his shawl, in an ardor that moves everyone. He truly weeps, he truly sobs. Sobbing has become singing. Singing borne by sobbing. The song sinks into its primal element. He trills; his voice drawls down level by level. Then, desperate and pleading, he throws it high again, it sinks back, woeful. And again he throws it high. The weeping overflows into the women's gallery. Like the man, who never yields in his yammering and urging, who intensifies them, the women, overhead, give in completely. Their weeping grows louder, stronger, drowning out his weeping. Ultimately, a truly anxious universal weeping has spread out, reverberating through the room. The men rocking in their prayer shawls sing, deep and dismal. The head of the bearded old man is still bent back, his eyes are shut. His tears flow visibly down his cheeks. Then he grows stiller. Solemn chants come, also strange and joyous songs. And in the end, when everything is over and they are leaving, someone launches into a song. And old and young, male and female join in: the proud, hopeful "Hatikvah," the Zionist anthem.

In the courtyard, I see bright windows; lights burning in them. I look through a window; men in prayer shawls are sitting there on a bench: a Hasidic *shtibl* [prayer room]. They sit there praying all night long. The next morning, I reenter the Zionist prayer room. Here too, many have remained overnight. Horribly stuffy air; some lie with their heads on the benches; the white-bearded man leads the prayers. On Nalewki Street, I walk through a house lobby. The vast courtyards are lifeless. A boy jumps around, wearing a round black skullcap, a long black belted coat. He's pale, scrofulous, dirty. With my companion, I walk across the second empty gigantic courtyard; an elegant young Jewish woman shows us the way. The rear wing contains a large prayer room of the Gura people, followers of the great, the mightiest rebbe, the one from Gura Kalwarja. A couple of boys run in front of a door, dressed like the scrofulous one, but in nice white woolen stockings, and they wear slippers.

And, as we begin to climb up the dark stairs, along worn steps between crumbling masonry, this is a very special place. Loud, indeed shrill singing, no, not singing, already resonated across the courtyard. It resonated from here. Now, down the steps, comes a wild confused shouting, then a murmuring with individual cries, a sonorous tangle that sometimes fuses into a single noise and roar. The men stand and sit on the stairs; we have to step gingerly across legs. The entrance is two flights up. There is an awful thronging and almost no possibility of penetrating it. But my companion is bold; I'm embarrassed because our clothes stand out, West European; here, everyone wears a skullcap and a caftan. Then, when I stand among them in a large room, which opens into an even larger one, I recognize how festively earnest, profoundly earnest—no, agitated—these people are. Now, I also realize what their beards mean. You understand the beard when you see these men standing there in their big wide prayer shawls, which they have drawn over their heads. These are Arabian heads, these are men of the great sandy desert. I can picture the huge mounted camels next to them. Their sharp richly expressive overly lively faces. Something mighty, lordly, heroic lies upon them. I can see them as warriors; these are not men on Nalewki Street in Warsaw. So many old men, dour men loom here, facing the large adjacent room, which sometimes emits an especially loud lone voice, the cantor's, no doubt. Innumerable boys read next to the adults; everyone is tensely, intensely concentrated. The men all read the same passage, but each on his own, a priest to himself; you can tell by how tremendously serious they are. The worshipers here rock in a peculiarly sharp and expansive way. At one point in the prayers, one man suddenly kneels, then, tumultuously, all the others; they get back on their feet, slowly and chaotically. The simple brown-bearded man next to me prays strong and loud. Now his voice changes: I can't follow what he reads: he weeps. The others also have broken voices. Now their voices rise in a chorus, an ecstatic tangle begins, a shrill chaos. Mute rocking, then sudden shrieks. And now, what's this; a singing, in unison, a joyous song. The place livens up, it's like a dance, an exuberant rejoicing. It starts with words, then, like laughter, ends as "lalala."

The people surge and billow. Men keep pushing from front to back, from the neighboring room into this one. They push all the way back to the back wall. A faucet is running there; they return with dripping hands, which they hold aloft, shaking them dry. They have to wash after every contamination of their hands, even if they have only touched their head. They all wear white coats, with prayer shawls over them; I see their caps and coats hanging on the wall in the large room. How dignified they stand. The black glow in the eyes of these simple men. How proud and self-assured the boy next to them prays with his full round beardless face.

The terrible stairs going down. In the courtyard, through a

ground-floor window, I see absorbed men sitting in prayer shawls. They are followers of a different, not so powerful rebbe. Down the streets to a different rear wing, as woeful and decrepit as the first. And how densely beleaguered the stone stairs are here. The whole Jewish nation is praying, they all lie down before their god. They pray on the stairs. We climb up between them. In the corridor upstairs, older boys punch and fight one another, trying to push into the *shtibl*. An old man intervenes with terse words and ominous glares. At the doorway to this apartment, the men sit on the floor. In the wide vestibule, they huddle along the wall, their heads wrapped up in their prayer shawls. Inside, in the small room, they stand cheek by jowl, holding their books. No one prevents us from entering; but every so often we receive an astonished, unfriendly scowl. And now an old man sitting on the floor gapes at me for a long time, especially at my feet: "Shoes are not worn here." We quietly push our way downstairs.

On this eve of the Day of Atonement, the Polish air force scheduled a recruitment concert at the Philharmonic. I'm told that only eleven people showed up; this is told not without pleasure. In the morning, a Communist scandal: outside the prayer rooms, Jewish Communists hawk gazettes with caricatures attacking "clericalism." The news vendors are driven away; they yell, "Religion is the opium of the people," fistfights break out. At a workers' kitchen, Jews have eaten and smoked on this high holiday; a brawl here too. Jews emerging from pastry shops were harassed by pious Jews.

The mighty festival is over. The Feast of Tabernacles is right around the corner. Planks are already being carried to the courtyards of Jewish streets, ordinary boxboards, raw, to be hammered and trimmed into shape. A door is inserted; the roof is covered with verdure. Hut by hut grows in the courtyards. Every family has a table and benches, they push them inside. In many courtyards, they shunt wire from the electric system, over to the roof of the tabernacle, to light the interior. Some do not build their huts on the ground, they prefer balconies, the highest, which are not surmounted by others. A strange feast

70

for this nation. Do they realize what they're preparing here? These are remnants of a nature festival. What a drab memory for a nation of peddlers and thinkers. No soil, no country, no state. No sowing, no harvest, no nature. They move in with wretched wooden crates, next to garbage cans in the dark court-yards, or on narrow roof-high balconies. On top of the crates—how lamentable—they strew some foliage. Along with their state, their country, they have lost sight of nature, the whole tremendous world of colorful things, of singing, flying, growing things. Their children no longer learn about crystals, plants, animals. How little the adults get to feel of those things. They go about, dressed up in the robe of metaphysics, from dawn to dusk, in rapport with their supernatural god. In some nations, this condition developed into pessimism and asceticism. The Jews have remained strong, earthly; they even have, as I see, the optimism of striving people. Their metaphysics is that of active people whose active energy has been blocked and who have therefore turned inward. They are: Arabs. Supranational religions have derived from them, but they themselves have remained the Jewish people and their religion has remained their religion. They have remained as such, even when they were ultimately driven entirely into spirituality and only seemed to be a religious community. They are now going to celebrate a feast of nature in the dark courtyards of the metropolis, next to garbage cans, on roof-high balconies. It looks like a gesture of the indestructible masses: despite everything!

I can't help it: as I walk through the building lobbies and view hut upon hut, I feel amazement, awe. And also joy: the mind lives, the mind creates in nature. Mind, spirit, willpower hold them together. No so-called disaster has shattered them, be-cause they wouldn't let it. Wandering through the millennia, reeling, driven, they are a symbol of the one thing that carries the future, carries the birth and creation—of the spirit and strength of the self. It made me happy among the Poles: they now are dwelling in their very own homes. The Jews cannot miss out on it. Even if they have ripened for a greater mission. For such a tremendous experiment cannot really end in the normal way, with some cozy fireside happiness.

71

I walk along Krolewki Street, past the Stock Exchange, reaching Grzybow Square, which sends Granizna Street northward to Nalewki Street. This triangular plaza with All Saints' Church has the usual swarming of pedestrians and peddlers, stick and cane peddlers, cloth peddlers.

Men carry long green bundles, reeds and twigs, in their right hand; a small cardboard box in their left hand; the box contains an apple. Preparations for the holiday. Lots of little boys in black skullcaps scurry about. They wave colorful paper flags with green and red staffs. The stiff paper sports harsh red pictures with Hebrew letters and the face of Moses. In the middle, the paper opens like a small shrine, exposing a new inscription. The children place an apple with a candle on top of it. That's the joy of their Feast of Tabernacles.

One morning, before seven o'clock, I set out from Warsaw with my companion; we are traveling to see the great rebbe of Gura Kalwarja. The church portals are open, beggars huddle outside, people sing inside. In the cool gray morning, we drive through the silent Sunday city; the car fills up with men in long black coats and black skullcaps. They all carry and lift packages, pouches, whole sacks, crates. We don't know where the railroad station is, but all we have to do is follow the black procession of men, the young, old, black-bearded, red-bearded Jews, whole scores of whom are now trotting along the street.

In the shabby, wretched ticket hall, they form a line, two abreast; very few Gentiles. Intense agitation; it's already late, this is the last train; a holiday is starting this afternoon, and they will not be allowed to use a vehicle. They walk around, bribing those at the front of the line to buy tickets for them. They offer five, ten zlotys. Finally, they all dash through the barrier, up to the lamentable railroad cars with shattered windows. They stand and crouch on the train platforms; all the corridors are crammed; the bearded faces, skullcap by skullcap. Someone stands right in front of me, his back toward me, his face toward the car window. He has a white prayer shawl on, he winds a phylactery around his arm. A lone peasant woman in a white kerchief huddles outside, on a gray sack. She was nursing her baby in the waiting room, still nursing it as she passed through the barricade. Then, as she ran, the baby lost her breast; it bawled; the other child, a little girl in peasant cloth, ran alongside the mother. Now the mother is sitting on the train platform. A Jew has offered her his gray sack to sit on; she puts the baby back on her breast. Its little feet, in blue stockings, stick into the air. The train passes a devastated farm, a war ruin. Lively debates in the cars.

The trolley passengers gaped at the Jews, whispered, smiled: "Gura!" Now, coarse, sturdy Poles sit in the railroad carriage, with dogs and hunting rifles. At a few stations, they joke around, yell: "Gura!" but the Jews ignore them. Some Jews even pet the dogs, and a discussion evolves among them whether they too will ever go hunting. In Palestine, someone says, Mount Carmel is being reforested; but they don't know what's happening to the wild game there. And then the Poles join in: they say that the many religions have not brought happiness to mankind. Basically, everyone thinks and believes the same thing: people really ought to be able to get along. These Poles act enlightened, they want to be decent, conciliatory. The Jews understand, concur; both sides sound phony. People curiously eye me and my companion, we are both wearing European clothes; he addresses them in Yiddish, and the Jews become friendly. But will I, I get to see the rebbe: their heads sway, they whisper, they're very skeptical. These people come from far away; one of them—with a fine intelligent face—wears a round black velvet hat. He's from East Galicia; the rebbe of Gura has a large following there.

The Galician starts conversing with a Zionist: the mistake that the Zionists make, he says, is that they want to set up a dictatorship everywhere. Palestine is already practically Communist.

The Zionist: That comes automatically. You would have to set up a dictatorship to prevent it.

The Galician: The Zionists don't care about the Orthodox Jews, the pious ones. Yet it was the Orthodox Jews, not the Zionists, who established Palestine. Palestine lives on their thoughts and yearnings. Their donations also operate there.

73

With their constant voyages to Palestine and with their thoughts, the pious Jews prepared Zion just as the occupation prepared today's Poland.

An old man—with his white sailor beard, the heavy bags under his eyes, the smoking pipe, he looks just like a Boer—says: He was in Palestine five years ago. He enjoyed seeing the country and seeing the people work there. But work and soil are not enough. People have to be devout. There, people only act as if they were. They celebrate the Sabbath, in stores and on the street; but they don't observe it at home, as is appropriate. They neglect the religious laws. There are people who claim to be Jews, yet they never keep the Sabbath.

The Zionist whispers to me: "When the Messiah comes, the laws will be abolished." But he doesn't have the nerve to say this out loud.

At a small station, the hunters and the dogs leave the train; the weather is gray; they march valiantly through puddles and pools.

Three Jews with sacks have been traveling for long days in passenger cars, all the way from northeastern Poland, on a pilgrimage to Gura Kalwarja. They are distressed, I see, they have prayer books in their hand; they want help; the rebbe is a saint. He is, they say, more than the other rebbes, more than the rebbe of Chortkow, of Bels; he is the greatest, the greatest of them all.

When the little train has swum along for two hours, it stops in Gura, emptying out completely. And, once again, we don't have to ask the way to the village. As we turn into the broad main street, a fantastic unsettling tableau heaves into view. This swarm of pilgrims in black—those who came with us and others —with bag and baggage, teeming along the lengthy street. These black skullcaps bobbing up and down. The yellow trees stand on either side, the sky above is pale gray, the soil tawny— between them, an almost frightening, bustling black throng moves along, hundreds of heads, shoulders serried together, an army of ants plods along, inches along. And from the other side, people trudge toward them, look down from the windows of the cottages, wave.

But the men and boys who await the travelers and come to meet them are a very special breed. They have long hair, their curls shake; the curls, twisted as tight as corkscrews, drop sideways from under the skullcaps and dangle in front of their ears, next to their cheeks, on their throats. I get a picture of what earlocks are; what a proud adornment. How proudly these men, youths, boys stride along in clean black caftans, in high shiny black caps; they look romantic, rapturous, medieval. Their faces have an extraordinary look, an earnest stillness. Some of them boast free, proud expressions. The handsome boys are festive in white stockings and beautiful slippers.

"Where is the rebbe's court?" At every step we take, we are surrounded by men (no woman walks here) who gape at us, talk among themselves. Their eyes are distrustful, chilly. It doesn't help that my companion speaks Yiddish to them nonstop. New ones keep sizing us up. I feel as if I've come upon an exotic tribe; they do not want me, me or my companion, they regard us as intruders. At the left, amid the small houses, a huge wooden gate is open. We go over there with the others, find ourselves in a vast crowded rectangular courtyard. It is closed off by a clean, simple, sprawling wooden house, one floor.

We are in the vestibule of the house. Men with raised arms emerge from the left-hand door; some men swirl towels: beyond the door lies a room for prayer and assembly.

In the middle of the vestibule, six or eight men keep watch; they eye us with open hostility. My companion addresses them. I notice their scornful expressions. They shrug, smile, cross their arms, leave us standing. My companion tells me that they said the rebbe is receiving all and sundry; no, there are no special appointments, no exceptions are made. If we absolutely insist on seeing him and even speaking to him—which they do not believe will happen—we have to line up with the others. My companion says—and I already see—that these people are nasty; they'd much rather kick us out. When further parleying proves useless, we decide to line up at a door, where a dozen young men are waiting. More and more keep pouring into the room. We are the butt of universal attention. People keep coming over to me. Since I cautiously hold my tongue, my companion instantly steps in. This doesn't go on for long. Because soon we are completely wedged in, and it's every man for himself. A dreadful, incredible mobbing has begun at the door. Silently, they push, squeeze. Silently, they all press against the narrow door, which opens from time to time and closes again. This is much worse, much worse than any urban crowd that I have ever experienced. I can say nothing. I keep wishing they'd let me out. But when I see the way they cling to one another, this fierce mute doggedness, I give up. I do not jam along, I hang between the others, who pant into the back of my neck, into my ears. I let my feet hang loose, I draw up my knees, and I am carried.

Slowly—I'm almost done for—I see the crack in the door coming nearer. The door now remains open; the man inside, the doorman, is no longer able to shut it. The big bearded men in skullcaps have reached over the heads of the others, and their hairy hands have grabbed the door hinges, the doorjambs; with red faces, they wordlessly pull themselves over to the door. And no one complains, no one curses. They moan. My companion, the powerful man, has separated from me. With an intense thrust, he extricates himself from the mob, walks around it, pushes, shoves, storms over to the other side of the door, which is not so beleaguered. And suddenly, I lose sight of him. He has vanished inside. What now? What should I do now, how can I hitch up with him again? No sooner has he been inside for several minutes while I remain alone in the terrifying muscle mass than a long arm strikes out at the men ahead of me. I see the big doorman pushing against the mass. With his left shoulder, he pushes the first few back, his long right arm beats, bangs on the fingers thrust into the door hinges, on the shoulders, on the black skullcaps. The hands let go. I cringe, he's about to reach me. But instead, he punches the chest of the man next to me, reaches out, grabs my arm. He yanks me inside. I'm at the head of the line, I see my companion standing inside, he waves me over. Another step, I'm inside the room. I shake myself, breathe.

An enormous, completely empty room, wooden floor, wooden walls. My companion stands in front of me with an elderly man, who points toward the window, at the right. I look there, walk over. There is a table at the window. And at the table, with his back to the light, sits a stocky, pudgy man. He keeps rocking to and fro, incessantly, now less, now more. A round black skullcap perches on the crown of his head. His head is completely wreathed in a tremendous mass of curls, dark brown, with touches of gray. Thick sheaves of curls tumble over his ears, over his cheeks, along the sides of his face all the way down to the shoulders. A full fleshy face surges out from the curls. I can't see his eyes; he doesn't look at me, doesn't look at my companion, as we stand next to the plain wooden table. The rabbi's thick hands burrow through a heap of small papers lying in front of him; slips of paper with writing on them. He and my companion are conversing. The rabbi stops rocking, he keeps rummaging through the papers. His expression is ungracious, he never looks up for even an instant. He shakes his head. All at once, my companion says: "He says you can ask him something." I think to myself: Impossible, that's not what I'm after; I want to speak to him, not question him. But the rebbe is already speaking again, softly; I can't understand a single word of this very special Yiddish. Then, suddenly, I have his hand, a small slack fleshy hand, on mine. I am astonished. No pressure from his hand; it moves over to mine. I hear a quiet *"Sholem,"* my companion says: "We're leaving." And slowly, we leave. Someone else has already come in, he puts down a slip of paper, says a few words, goes out, backward, facing the small rocking figure at the window.

What happened? My companion tells me that the elderly man at the door thanked my companion for our coming to speak to the saint. He wanted to push my companion back out the instant he entered, but the doorman pulled me in after all. The tsadik, the stupendous man, was, I hear, quite inaccessible from the very start. He asked about me: "What does he want? Who is he anyhow? He wants to ask me something? He wants to talk to me? I don't know who he is. Is he a lawyer, someone from the court? Why does he want to interrogate me? I won't be interrogated. He has nothing to ask me and I have nothing to answer." In conclusion, he was gracious, said *"Sholem,"* a blessing.

77

We steal out through the back door of the house. We are received by a host of beggars. They pester us insolently, criticize the amount that we give them. Others whisper curiously: "What did he say to you? Did it turn out all right?"

We circle the house; eyed with amazement and revulsion, we enter the wide-open *bes-medresh* [synagogue], a huge, airy, square hall with the *bimah* [platform] at its center. Benches and bookcases along the walls. They contain tomes that have been read ragged. The oldsters on the benches, with or without prayer shawls, sit poring over voluminous works, singly, jointly, speaking, reading, rocking.

The cool autumnal street. I am scared, flabbergasted, embarrassed. We talk to people, enter a Yiddish tavern. An old tavern keeper lets us in. Inside, we are inspected by his stooped wife and his daughter—in her thirties, with a squinting, obviously blind eye. There is no cognac, no beer. Cold roast goose, jars of pickles, jars of herring and onions are gathered on the table. At the next table, two young fish vendors, loudly smacking their lips on a piece of sausage, join our conversation, in which we calm down. The people come here, they say, to be near him, to pray in the home of the saint, and to have him wish them *sholem*. Many write their names, wishes, requests for advice on slips of paper. Those are the slips that we saw. As many as eight share a room in the village, always two in a bed. Some five thousand followers of the rebbe were here at the New Year. They were lively, they drained many barrels of beer. They wish the tsadik happy New Year. They have to pay a lot for their rooms.

In the afternoon, they mob the tsadik's banquet. A big crowd, like the audience that morning, even bigger. A huge table is carried into the hall. Several men crawl under the table very early, to make sure they'll be near the saint. The tsadik sits down with his sons and the important guests. Everyone else stands around. At the table, the tsadik speaks, provides exegeses on the Talmud[21] and the Torah, new interpretations. The pious observe him and his guests, his movements, seize upon every word, elucidate it to one another. The biggest prize is eating *shirayim*, leftovers from the tsadik's plate. They fight over them.

78

Occasionally, the tsadik himself hands someone a scrap from his plate.

The villagers pay scant attention to the tsadik and his followers; they earn money off them. The father of the present rebbe was a very pious man; this one is too worldly for them. He is very rich, by birth, through heavy contributions, shrewd investments. He owns property in Palestine, where he recently settled religious disputes. He never takes a penny from the pious who consult him. Fantastic stories circulate about him. I find a printed pamphlet with a picture of him, this spiritual prince of the Jewish people.

In the village, I feel virtually expelled, I can't stand the obtrusive and derisive looks of the rubberneckers in the street. I want to leave, I am delighted to see the railroad station. On the train, they tell me a story about the rebbe of Gura and the railroad. Some time ago, the rebbe of Gura wanted to take the train to Warsaw. A stone was hurled from the platform at the carriage he was sitting in. Although hesitating at first, he stayed on the train after all. But upon returning, he told his followers about the incident. These men were deeply upset: a stone had been thrown at the rebbe, from inside the platform barricade; furious at the railroad administration, they decided—to stop traveling by train. They boycotted the railroad. They left Gura on wagons, on boats. Distant followers were notified, newcomers used only carriages and boats. The main customers on this railroad line are the pilgrims to Gura. After the Jews kept up their boycott for a while, the railroad officials in Warsaw, who had already received a complaint from the pilgrims, grew thoughtful. The administration tried to put things right, come around. The Jews insisted that the stone had been hurled from inside the barricade, which, they said, was not sufficiently protected. Now a high railroad executive personally traveled to Gura and offered a sum of money as compensation. When the authorities expressed their regret about the incident, the Gura pilgrims laid down their weapons and started using the railroad again.

My companion knows Yiddish ditties that mock the rebbes. They parody Hasidic songs; he says they're well known everywhere. One ditty gibes at the "philosophers" of the big city; they would be better off "at the rebbe's table," letting him teach them how to think. Another ditty carps at the modern problem of the railroad; the rebbe has an easier time of it; he spreads out his cloth and sails across the ocean. Other ditties are obscene, they sound just like anticlerical products of the Lutheran and pre-Lutheran era.

But the next morning, when my companion and I go to a courtyard in Warsaw and stroll amid huts, a Hasid, a follower of the rebbe, invites me into his hut. We sit in the semidark room. Two of his sons join us. Wine and all sorts of covered dishes are on the table. He says he has eight children, three from his first wife, five from his second.

"Yes," he smiles, "you people in Germany don't have so many kids. But God doesn't like what you do. Man shouldn't interfere with God's works. That's what we believe."

I recount what I saw in Gura, I ask him about the meaning of eating *shirayim*. His sixteen-year-old boy speaks up: in that crush, some people faint and they could catch TB; they have to be carried out. His father ignores him:

"Eating and drinking: our attitude toward them is different from yours. You believe that you eat for the sake of your bodies. We do not believe that. We see eating and drinking as something spiritual, something that contributes to the mind. Bread and wine may be nothing, or nothing much. But when they reach the tsadik, they change and become something special. The tsadik is not like just anyone. He is holy, because of his learning and because of his father and grandfather, from whom he is-sues. He is closer to God than other people. When the tsadik touches the fish or merely looks at it on his table, something of his spirit goes over to the fish. And if someone else partakes of that fish, then he absorbs something of the rebbe's spirit. People crowd and shove around the tsadik, but they gain something. Merely being at his table. . . . The things he says during the meal are completely new things, which come to him from God as he eats."

The man talking to me is warm, his eyes are gentle. He speaks very tenderly. Often he smiles compassionately and a bit ironi-cally past his son and me.

How does a democratic nation come up with saints? An old vestige: the kingdom collapsed; the structure that people cling to is religion, cult, and its chief carrier is the rabbi. He can be understood in national terms: rabbis are the leaders, kings, dukes, princes. And they actually ruled until the past century. But that's not all. The Jews brought the Middle Ages along. They have their Torah, a single book, but it is accompanied, namelessly, by magic and by faith in witchcraft. In this respect, Judaism resembles Buddhism, which has its own teachings but tolerates the survival of ancient deities. Behind the backs of the rabbis, the populace attributed these illegitimate magic powers to these Jewish leaders, these spiritual rulers. Especially once the mystical Hasidic movement brought back magic. The magicians became rulers, became rebbes; the worm turned. And the rabbinical dynasties still exist—although their great era is past—and they hand down a mysterious chosenness.

I ask them to translate the booklet for me, the one with the portrait of the rebbe of Gura on its cover. These are fine melancholy speeches that this rebbe's father gave at the table.

"A *kohen* [priest] who buys a slave may feed him from the tithe. But he may not do the same for an Israelite. Why is that so?

"The more profound answer is: The body is together with the soul. The soul is fed by heaven, the body by the earth. When the body binds itself to the soul, then the body too is fed by heaven. Thus the children of Israel were fed by God for forty years in the desert. And if the body does not bind itself, then it must get along on its own. The same thing is true of the Jews. All Jews belong to God as his slaves by virtue of an everlasting purchase. According to the Law, they should all be fed by heaven. But because we sin, God cannot accept us as real slaves, and we have to get along on our own."

Another speech:

"The sages say: This world is merely a hallway or vestibule leading to the real house, the afterworld. But there is a verse that says: 'An hour of good deeds is better than the whole afterlife.' What does this mean, what is its sense? That was what the

81

rebbe asked. His Hasidim were unable to reply. Whereupon he continued: In reality, this world too is the afterworld. But we do not realize it. To do so, we must be free of sin, cast off all our desires, approach the glory of God. Then the world will not be merely a vestibule, a hallway leading to the actual house. The transitory, surface pleasures of human beings are mere illusions. A man eats: what does he get out of it? While eating, he says: It is sweet, it is rich; afterward, it is nothing. And other pleasures: the instant one believes they are significant, they vanish like smoke. An hour later, the next day, one forgets them—and wants them again. But the man who has repented forgets the pleasures of this world. He joins with God. He feels spiritual joy, which is greater than all the joy in the world. That explains why this world is only a vestibule. If you repent, and the hidden light is revealed to you, you have to leave this world early, and you will discover the endless glory of God, and you will eventually arrive in the next world."

# WILNO/VILNIUS

*The church has a horrible hole in its dome. It was left by a
Bolshevik cannonball in 1920.*

The huge waiting room of the terminal in Warsaw is surrounded by a wooden fence, rectangular, wide; inside, black
swarms of people squat, lie, sit beneath the unsteady light. A
wonderful tableau. They sleep, leaning back against the wooden
benches, lie on sacks in the room, side by side, facedown. They
snore, sigh. A few eat, smacking their lips, using penknives to
cut slices off the big round loaves. I push my way through to
the train to Wilno; in this central station, none of the station
officials, ticket sellers appear to know German. I climb up into
the train. In the dim lighting, I see no sleeping car. I have to
hurry, I get in. Now come hours of useless struggle to find the
sleeper. A struggle without language, for I am struck mute.
First, I spend a quarter of an hour sitting next to a gentleman,
who absentmindedly reads a newspaper; then the conductor
comes in, and comes back several times that same night. I am
aroused from my light sleep another three or four times in order
to show my ticket. Each time, I also show him my sleeping car
reservation, I ask him in German and French where, where,
where the sleeper is, whether the train even has one. Before
resigning and lying down, I wander through the train, but find

no sleeping car. Each time, the conductor returns my ticket and sleeping car reservation; he ignores my gestures and questions, he simply shoves the tickets back into my hand.

Then, in my compartment, a change occurs, something I have never seen before. Two conductors walk in, climb on the seat cushions, tug on the wide wall; lo and behold, from the top of the walls they pull beds out, left and right. The beds have no cushions. The newspaper reader stretches out horizontally on his cushion down below, I do the same opposite him. Above us, on the shiny cloth, which is supported by metal braces, two strangers lie down after yanking open all the doors in their quest. One is a conductor on this train. I marvel at these bizarre goings-on. To think that men wearing filthy boots are lying down in first class. And what sleeping cars they have in Poland, not a shred of linen. I rock along until morning, annoyed, amazed. And then, in Wilno, I see the lovely shiny sleeper. It came along quite peacefully. I stopped presenting my sleeping car reservation; I was fed up.

Starting at dawn, I gazed out the train window. I was interrupted only once, when my fellow dozer above me lowered his fat legs in white woolen stockings full of holes and, moaning, pulled on his muddy jackboots right in front of my face. At seven A.M., the landscape changes. It becomes hilly, undulating. Earlier, it stretched along evenly, like a steppe, sometimes with meadows and farmland. Now it becomes undulating, hilly. Woods, firs, and deciduous forests recur frequently. A castlelike building shoots past on the left, a ruin. The entrances and outlets of tunnels are guarded by sentries with rifles; the country is in a state of unrest. The newspapers report attacks by Bolshevist and anonymous gangs; I suddenly feel that these are more than attacks by gangs, these are war movements. We lumber very slowly across a high narrow bridge. How wonderfully lively the landscape. The hills turn into mountains. The flaming red and yellow of the withering trees; in between, the hushed dark green of the tall firs. Long rows of railroad cars on the tracks, movement inside the train. Outside, small houses, individuals, groups, on streets. Wilno Station.

In the frosty morning, I stroll along an avenue. It is flanked by low houses, most of them old and wretched. Then, from the left, a street runs into the avenue, a rather narrow street without a real sidewalk. I keep looking about for the main thoroughfare, I assume there has to be one. Then the arch of a tall, sizable gateway looms over the street; I hear singing, I pass, seeking, through the old structure. A crowd of people is lying on the right: peasants, townsfolk, male and female, on the ground, kneeling, bowing their heads all the way down. But these are not the singers, the singing comes from somewhere else, from above. And when I turn around, I see a chapel up on the arch. And, open to the street, an altar stands there, with many burning candles and a tangle of things that I cannot distinguish. The people coming up the street are holding their hats or caps. I too doffed my hat under the archway. A miracle-working effigy of God's mother is up there. The Madonna looks very lovely. She appears over a tremendous half-moon, which resembles the huge curling horn of an animal. She is visible from the chest up. Her sacerdotal clothes are richly ornamental. Her crowned head leans to the right. Her two hands lie crossed on her chest. Her narrow throat emerges from splendid and very colorful garments and cloaks. Then comes a high narrow face, her eyes are open only a crack, her lips are shut. Sharp golden rays surround her entire head. She prays, or is entranced, or listens, mild and melancholy, or is absorbed in her sorrow, trying to transcend it: I cannot pinpoint her expression. The image looks suggestive, touched. The seekers here tend to fuse their pain with that of the celestial being and to withdraw more calmly. It is a great achievement of art that it can make such an image and that a painted image can serve as an example.

The street is named Ostra-brama. It lies almost mute, the worshipers barely emitting a sound. At the corner, men are burying drainpipes in the ground. I amble up the street with its small houses, woeful paving. It is ten A.M. But the shops are still closed. A few are open. And then I look at the names on the signs and realize it is the Jewish stores that do not open. The Feast of Tabernacles is still in progress.[22]

The street widens like a square. On the other side, an ancient stone box: it's the old theater, with carriages in front. Upon passing a movie house, I notice that the posters come in two languages: there are Polish posters and Yiddish ones. The signs of many shops are likewise in the Hebrew alphabet, in Yiddish. I often encountered this in Warsaw, in the Nalewki district; but here, it's spread throughout the city. There seems to be a very large or very courageous Jewish population here. Yet I don't see any Jews, and that's the second thing. Individual Jews must be standing around, even if it's a holiday. And now I notice that I do see them but don't notice them. They stand next to me outside the movie house, walk about in white caps, young men and girls; older ones slowly cross the bumpy square, conversing in their language. No one wears a caftan! I see no one in a black "capote." They all wear European clothes—and yet do not speak Polish. This is a different breed of Jews than in Warsaw.

The narrow street that I turn into on the left has many large old buildings. One looks like a very ancient church. The building next to it could be a monastery. However, young men and girls wearing white caps, carrying books and leather briefcases, are going in through the low entrances. This must be an institution of learning. And upon stepping into one of the low warm vaults, I see posters; the doors are marked. This is the university with its classrooms. I keep asking: Where is the main thoroughfare? Slowly I realize that my standards are skewed. This *is* a main thoroughfare. The streets are almost alleys, twisting, with small plain houses. I walk along a high pavement, and it drops off steeply into a really splendid gutter. A nice dirty little brook flows at either side of the roadway. In some places, the brook is covered with thick boards, flows underground, underboard, so that walking is less hazardous. Men and women in small-town, medium-town garb. Here and there, light-colored and flesh-colored stockings on women and girls, a little powder, mostly crude housedresses, heavy practical boots. Outside the store windows and doors: thick planks painted red and brown, locks, heavy poles upon them. A policeman stands at a corner of this street. I enter the hotel. My room is large, shabby, without curtains.

In a small square in the western part of the city, not far from the Zakret Woods, stands a house of worship, lighting the adjacent streets with its big gold cupolas: a Greek Catholic church. Its surroundings are neglected, poor and sparsely constructed; a graveyard across the way. It's noon, I enter the church. A whole row of old beggarwomen lined up inside the door, opening it the instant somebody pushes it, bowing. Monotonous liturgizing, a feeble choir. A wide foyer painted in washed-out colors, windowless. A few men and women kneeling and standing. Gazing into the circular church, which is illuminated by daylight from above. There are no chairs or pews on the stone floor of the church; in the round, however, several small, altarlike structures, tables, covered with all kinds of things, flowers in receptacles, loads of big and small burning candles, pictures and slips of paper. A woman with two small children heads toward one of the decorated altars, which holds a basin of water. She dabs some water on herself, then lifts up each of the children in turn, and they emulate her. I have the impression that all these things stand on the altars and have been or are being consecrated by some kind of procedure. A gold altar panel closes off the entire space. The panel is wooden, not as high as the ceiling. Another room is behind it. The wall is covered with big murals, all of them on grounds of solemn Byzantine gold. They depict old men with halos, also Christ. Perhaps these are the apostles. I have to keep looking to the right, into the circular space—for I cannot go there; more and more people keep coming, some fifty by now, all of them standing and kneeling in the anteroom and densely spreading out just beyond it, in the circular church, little people, mostly women, very few workers. To the right, a bizarre structure stands at the wall. White cloths and red and white artificial flowers hang over something. Bright fabrics hang in front. The fabrics also deck out the small rooflike superstructure. I gradually recognize it: a wooden crucifix with Christ colorfully painted on it. At his side stand two holy women, festooned with cloths and flowers, just like him. A male voice sings deep; I don't know where it's coming from, the circular space is empty. The worshipers in front of me cross themselves in a very urgent manner, kneeling from time to time, putting their foreheads on the stone floor while propping their arms upon it.

Now, the gold altar panel opens in the middle: it is a perforated door. Deep inside the opened room, large tables with structures, implements, become visible. High, gaudy things also stand on them, perhaps flowers; way in the back, more gold pictures. And a marvelous azure moves in between them and in front of them. It lies with silver on a mantle worn by a white-bearded, white-haired priest, who steps from behind through the aperture of the altar door, singing in his deep voice, making the sign of the cross over the congregation. He turns, walks back to the large oblong table with the structures and implements, liturgizes, spelled by the invisible choir. Steps lead up to the altar. Several boys, accompanied by men and women, have come up, stationing themselves on either side of the central door in the gold panel. The priest approaches them, singing, holding a vessel that he brings from behind. He seems to stroke their foreheads. Then he returns, descending into the circular room amid the men and women, who crowd around him more densely. Under the marvelously bright azure with silver stripes, he wears a rose-colored garment. It can be seen when he manipulates things with his open arms. Broad blue strips fall forward.

His assistant is a simple elderly man in coarse street clothes. He drags a table over from the side, places it in front of a small mensa in the center of the church walls. From above, he brings a brightly flaming censer on chains. The old priest takes it, chants, swings it back and forth. Clouds of bluish smoke rise aloft. The fragrance of incense. The white-haired priest chants, responding to the choir, walks with the swinging censer past all the tables in the circular room, lets the fumes waft across them. He turns around, toward the kneeling people, hurls the vapors over them. He heads toward the big gold altar panel, constantly chanting, pours smoke over the paintings. A consecration, a benediction. Fire and smoke: a reminiscence of ancient immolation. He mounts the steps into the rear altar room, moves along the tables, fills this room too with the vapors. Then he does something at the large, heavily laden oblong tables, taking hold of now this, now that implement. What can he be doing? His motions look like sacred gestures. I see that mysterious acts of magic are being performed, witchcraft. How indomitably these things survive despite the bad name they are given. In the end, the whitebeard, with his good sound face, dragging clodhoppers under his celestial robe, is standing down below again, in the round space. The congregants change; they come and go. The door is always opened and closed by the beggar women.

Outside, the gold cupola of the church has a dreadful hole. The metal is ripped open, you peer into a horrifying blackness. It was caused by a Bolshevik cannonball in 1920.

Many people I speak to know Russian. Not a trace of hatred for Russia. If you ask whether they know Russian, they smile as if caught in flagrante delicto. This is true of the locals; the Poles who have moved here from other places hate and fear the Russians like the Poles in Warsaw. I have a map of Wilno from the Russian period and a more recent map. Nearly all the streets and squares have been renamed. In Warsaw, this renaming delighted me, elated me; strange: here, I don't really care for it. It seems to have been inflicted upon this city from above. It did not issue from within, as in Warsaw. The main thoroughfare in the center used to be called Bolshaya, the one in the northwest Georgievsky Prospekt; now Bolshaya is called Wielka and Zamkowa, and Georgievsky Prospekt is renamed after Adam Mickiewicz. Then there is Slowacki Avenue, a Pilsudski, a Sigmund, a Kosciuszko Avenue.

An educated woman whispers to me: the Pole is polite, sentimental, and deceitful; the Russian has a free nature, he is honest and charming. Oh, she misunderstands me. I am a friend of the Polish people. The Poles had bad luck for centuries, they were forced to hide their feelings, they couldn't be open—under those very Russians, the honest, charming ones. Suppression makes you crooked and feeble. And Poland does not lie free like Russia, not vast like Russia; it is wedged in between east and west, between north and south. This produces anything but simple people. A bridge: is that land or water? I feel distressed.

The Wilno territory is a burning issue. The Lithuanians claim

Vilnius as their capital. The Poles have occupied it. The Polish-Lithuanian border is closed. A permanent state of war exists between the two young states.

Along Dominican Street in the drizzle. A dirty yellow stream flows along the gutter. The sidewalk is made of stone and then suddenly of boards. Countless windowpanes are patched. A shop window contains hats, kerchiefs, ribbons; another contains apples, cookies. The cab horses gallop in wooden yokes. Posters advertising Aircraft Week are on the pillars. Wyspianski's portrait hangs in the window of a stationery store: a Slavic face, sideburns, elongated mustache, consumptive cheeks. Underneath, there is a female painter and poet, a very fine soft face despite its fat; she gazes down with compressed lips. She is a human being, he a sick artist. The street sinks to the left, broadening. A huge soldier in a rose-colored busby strides toward me. A bookshop contains German Reclam volumes, Springer's *History of Art*, Lehmann's medical atlases, Rauber's *Anatomy*. All the shops tend to become cheap. A hotel across the street is named Versailles; why the fuss?

The university is an old sprawling edifice. It was founded by Stefan Bathory, a Polish King, whom the aristocratic voters summoned from Transylvania. His Polish remained mediocre until the end of his life, but he ruled the country well. He had to put up with an elderly princess, a Jagiello. The university, which used to be a secondary school under the Russians, has huge, thick vaults. You walk through long corridors, up and down stairways. An ancient, fabulously solid, very relaxing edifice. It must be bombproof in wartime. The building strikes me as organically grown rather than built. Electric light doesn't fit in with the dense eeriness. These reading rooms, lecture halls with their old worn wooden desks; everything is used, everything has become humanly familiarized, adapted, round. Iron doors everywhere; you dive into depths, cellars; suddenly, you're back in a tremendous warm room, a catalog room. People have lived here for ages, putting things aright.

A small elderly gentleman guides me. The archivist is the man for all seasons here. He leads me through countless stairs and corridors marked "Caution" and "Attention." Then he takes me into the government archive. I've never laid eyes on tomes like these. Some are centuries old, some younger, from the Russian period; a single volume is often thousands of pages thick, and it holds out, it's bound in unbelievably solid well-thumbed brown leather. Normally, book spines are narrow; the ones here are much wider than the covers. These monsters are tied up in strings. One series is entitled *Codex diplomaticus*; the author, of German extraction, is named Dögel. Many tomes are handwritten. The little man says: if the archive files were lined up end to end, they'd be nine miles long. These are court records; a curious linguistic chaos. The titles are in Russian, but the contents are in Polish. I glance through a trial record that he shows me: the beginning and the end—rituals—are in Russian; in between there is a long Polish text. Bizarre Ruthenian texts. Collections of material from the German occupation, magazines with pictures of German generals. Nothing can escape immortality.

The old gentleman gingerly places a document in front of me: Julius Slowacki's high school certificate. It is written in solemn Latin like a university diploma. This was where Slowacki and Mickiewicz attended high school; they lived on Zamkowa Street. Slowacki got mostly B's, a few A's. He signed his name on the other side: an artistically fine calligraphy, the characteristic penmanship of an aesthete.

Down below, in the penumbra of the corridor, there is a torso of stone or plaster, like a medieval figure from the Cathedral of Naumburg. If only they don't set it up and sketch it; this is the only way it can live: on the floor, under the vault. Behind this door (these doors alone, these warm lecture halls would have to make this a university, so that these young people can go around here, sit on the benches; learning here is different from elsewhere)—a fifth faculty resides beyond this iron door. Wilno has five faculties. And the fifth is not a dismembered philosophical faculty, nor is it a second theological one; it is the faculty of fine arts. Who knows why it was made into a separate faculty. I don't mind in the least, I even gloat. Its head professor is a renowned Polish landscape painter. I don't get to see him, his assistant guides me. But there's nothing much to look at: one or two rooms in which two women stand in front of portfolios. They look art historical—both the women and the portfolios. The other things standing and lying around here are scholarly, artistic, seemingly incompatible with one another: stones found in the Wilno area, prehistoric items, fabulously beautiful decks of cards, plaster casts. Then, bizarre human shanks; with chains and rings attached. They could be criminals; perhaps they were monks, penitents, who punished themselves and were buried like that. I feel as if these rooms were haunted by a ghost—the professor and landscapist who feeds on all this. This is not so much a faculty as his fruitful fluctuating state of mind. It's nice of them to give him space. I see that this is a young state.

Outside, the beautiful rectangular courtyard is named after the first president of this university, Peter Skarga. Below there are arcades; there were some upstairs too, but they were walled up by the Russians. The Russians cared more for warm rooms than for beauty and architecture. You mustn't, of course, tie your boots with Cleopatra's necklace; but should the need arise, then I think you can. There's a niche over the arcades; the Madonna is gone, you can still see the inscription.

The university also has a church; it must be as old as the university itself. I've seen a lot of churches, a lot still lie ahead; I have to measure out my church consumption carefully, so as not to shoot my load too soon. First, I approve of the vestry with its brown wooden wainscotting, its Flemish columns. The paneling looks like a decoration; then comes the surprise. The caretaker pulls on a panel, and there are boxes everywhere. They are empty; perhaps they once contained the secret sciences. The church has wonderful windows, carpet-blue and yellow. A bust gazes down from the gallery: Moniuszko, an opera composer, whose name I have first heard in Poland; he was an organist here in this church. There are memorial tablets and the proud personal chapel of the Ogynskis, a family of counts;

92

they even have their own organ. When the doctoral students graduate, they are taken to this church. This is a very medieval custom. What does a young state do with antiquated "braids"? It wears them: partly for pomp, partly in earnest, partly to annoy others.

Pilsudski, who attended high school here, opened the university himself. One evening, when I am speaking to a Polish officer, he tells me I could see Pilsudski on his train; he is heading toward his nearby country estate. But I don't go. I'm not much good at joining a guard of honor. I'm too small.

In the morning, I hear a roaring of trumpets. There's a firehouse facing the hotel. An open-framed wagon bursts out of the entranceway. It carries a small number of slack-looking, nonchalant firemen in gray-green uniforms and flashing metal helmets, which they are in the process of adjusting. There's something Roman about their helmets. In the midst of the men, on the rickety vehicle, stands the trumpeter, straddle-legged, clutching the trumpet and blasting away, so that all the people halt in the street and listen to his wonderful blasting. Two valiant brown horses are hitched to the wagon. They jog along courageously through the streets and alleys, hauling the wagon toward the fire. A second wagon, with a strange apparatus, reels after the first; it also contains flashing helmets. That must be the pump wagon. Next, two azure barrel wagons. They contain the water, which they carry through the streets to the fire. Finally, another open-framed wagon with doughty warriors, including several civilians. They zoom stupendously into the town. No doubt about it: they will conquer the blaze. Half an hour later, another trumpet blare. They are coming back. The fire is out. Or else it never burned.

How gladly I would see more Polish, more Lithuanian, more Russian culture. But I'm hindered by language. And almost no one guides me. Outside of Warsaw, I am poorly assisted.

The center of the city is old, antiquated, cramped. Northward, it turns into a different district with a different, a more

modern face. The large commercial thoroughfare, Adam Mickiewicz Street, veers along from east to west. The cathedral
square and the castle hill lie at its eastern end.

Mickiewicz Street, lined with dense rows of trees, has large
lovely stores. Fruit shops, wide and deep, splendidly stocked. A
couple of bookstores; whole windows containing only Russian
books. A Hotel Bristol, which doesn't look bad. The best restaurant in town, two cafés with fabulous, genuinely Russian cakes
and candy. They have a whole roomful; I wonder who'll eat it
all up. Somewhat withdrawn, a Polish theater; I honor it by
timidly slogging past. "Jackie Coogan," *Long Live the King*;
maybe this Jackie has some talent; but I abhor trained animals
and child prodigies. I find them embarrassing.

Farm wagons in the street, some in convoys; the farmers have
come a long way, they fear being attacked. The drivers walk
alongside. Some wagons are tiny; the farmers wear top boots,
black fur coats and white ones, high fur and lambskin caps.

But looming autumnally, in a blaze of yellow and brown foliage, the castle hill stands there, with the oldest of old Wilno.
There once lived a Lithuanian grand prince, Gedymin, who
built his castle up there. Down below, a fire burned in a pagan
temple. The man whom the beautiful, delicate Jadwiga of Poland had to marry, the first Polish-Lithuanian Jagiello, became
a Christian—by contract, I believe—and destroyed the temple.
He replaced it with the Cathedral of St. Stanislaw, to wreak
vengeance on Christianity. When a Christian sees this dreadful
edifice, he reverts to paganism. Nothing comes of these shotgun
marriages. The church looks like a Greek temple or a Polish
municipal theater. Vistula antiquity. The marriage was dis-
solved by death, Poland and Lithuania are asunder again, the
cathedral could not be rescinded. Supposedly, St. Kazimierz
has a silver coffin here, weighing two thousand five hundred
pounds; eight silver statues of Polish kings stand here, but all
the perfumes of Araby . . . A campanile stands free, next to this
Greek temple or municipal theater. I walk by at noon, a blare
comes from the top. The man up there blares in all four directions. I hear it: he's a soldier, and this is a Polish custom in the

garrisons. The Russians took along the monument to their Pushkin from the park at the foot of the castle hill. They must have been after the metal. German headquarters were housed here after Rennenkampf's retreat; German music was played at the town park in the afternoon. Rows of benches are lined up as in a resort park.

On the hill. Red brickwork; legend has it that a tunnel runs from here to Troki, the neighboring village. Red barracks below, yellow bushes down the slope, the shiny black surface of the river: the Wilja. Masses of small red-roofed houses down below, a rolling of wagons, a hammering. Behind me, to the side, stand —oddly enough—three adjacent tall white crosses: Poles, I hear, who were killed by General Muraviev in 1863. During the occupation, the Poles, forgetting nothing, already got to work putting up these crosses. A cannon: the Russians used to fire it at twelve noon as a midday signal. So many old customs: doctoral graduation in the church, the blowing of trumpets, the shooting of cannon. Clocks have been circulating recently, but how slowly do such things come to the notice of the authorities. I delight for a long time in the shiny water of the Wilja; behind it, the wreath of forests.

After looking down at what is known as Castle Square, with a small old church next to it, and the castle itself, I am down below again, unable to make up my mind about entering. After all, it's only for the old breed of tourists, and I belong to the new breed. My companion would love to see it; he's from Wilno; so I've decided to show him the castle.

"The Russian governor-general lived here?"

"Yes."

"I knew it; it was obvious. Later on, the Germans turned it into either an officers' mess or an army hospital—the general command was over there, wasn't it?"

"A hospital."

"The marble plaque with the gold inscription says that Napoleon stayed here during his retreat from Russia. He had to leave town in disguise during the night of November 24, 1812."

A gypsy woman passes the entrance, she's holding a child by

the hand. The gypsies have a camp outside town; lots of them are coming from Russia. My companion says they're fleeing the Bolsheviks.

"They're not fleeing the Bolsheviks, my son. When poor people come to power, they strike only at the rich. The gypsies always flee, or rather, they do not flee, they wander."

I impress the word "wander" on my companion. Then we enter the courtyard of the castle. It's almost one P.M. We can walk about undisturbed. Napoleon has fled, the Russians have left, the Germans are gone. Now we are here. My companion and I ponder whether we should hoist a flag, issue a proclamation in Polish and Yiddish, explaining that we have come as friends and that the inhabitants should assist us and our troops in every way. But he first wants to ask the caretaker, and I have no objections. The caretaker already noticed us, and he was so startled that he instantly took off for lunch. My companion catches up with him. They speak—what do they speak? Russian. They admire Napoleon and speak Russian or Polish. I do not admire him and I speak French. When I address the porter in French, he replies that he doesn't know Yiddish. Crestfallen, I wander along, climb stairs. A waiting room comes my way; its carpet has vanished in the course of centuries. We work our way through to a ballroom; raggedy rococo furniture mourns for Napoleon. There are rooms that are whitewashed, and they contain the usual tiled stoves. They ask themselves and me what they are doing in a castle. Muraviev, the dreadful man, lived in a very horrible room. It has no windows, not a single window. A mere cubbyhole. Muraviev was so afraid that he never slept in a room with a window. And now I notice a smell that cuts me to the quick, a smell that I have never encountered in a castle. But I do not regret coming here; this is an unusual castle. Muraviev must still be alive, there is an upsetting smell of his fear. I myself get scared, I want to flee; through my companion, I ask the caretaker whether Muraviev is still here. Muraviev has to be here; I smell his presence, you can smell him here. The caretaker answers calmly: First of all, he doesn't know Yiddish; secondly, Muraviev is not here. What I smell is the sewage system, which isn't here. He says it hasn't been here since Napoleon's

time, and ever since, it's been making itself felt with an intensifying smell. This condition is preserved, for this is a castle, a
historic sight and smell. I am relieved, the dreadful Muraviev is
not here. The caretaker shows me a real vestige of the Russians:
a winding staircase to which several stairways lead. The secret
stairways that the great tyrant used for his emergency escape.

The barracks run along the river. Masses of soldiers are exer-
cising; a permanent war footing. A hospital is located way outside; it belongs to the university; it was dedicated just recently.
The hospital is small; the surgical ward is downstairs, the ward
for internal diseases upstairs. The view of the garden is utterly
beautiful: a very piebald cow is grazing there.

The weather has turned very cold: in the streets, people's
breath is steaming. I am taken to a number of churches; I follow
obediently, but cautiously shut my eyes and ears inside. At one
church, I see a chubby Polish peasant face hewn in a stone
pillar. At another church, I am told, Napoleon stood in front of
it and said he'd like to take this church to Paris. I can't stand
these goddamned old artworks. A small carpet-weaving school
at a bridge is more interesting. During the Russian period, the
house was a brothel; a cottage on the other side of the wooden
bridge belongs to it. The war terminated the idyll. Now, the
place is filled with clappering and clattering, banging and booming. Nothing but young girls sitting at looms, sitting like the
organist at his organ, stepping on pedals, reaching up to the
yarns.

I hear pleasant things about the German occupation. The
Germans, I'm told, left three cemeteries behind: one for civilians, one for officers, one for rank and file. The Good German
Lord holds court according to civil and military laws. Then, out
in the Zakret Woods, I see their graves in long, long rows; simple
wooden crosses, as well as the strange Greek Orthodox crosses
of Russians: the horizontal beams slant. The hush is profound.
Below lie countless dead men who left this world amid the roaring of cannon, amid the moans in a hospital. Poor creatures;
not one of them could have left this dreadful life without complaint. I feel tormented and abashed as I walk along these rows.

I sense that I must ask forgiveness. Because they lie there and I live. I do not want to ask, I must not ask how they are. I would like to: they feel as good, as snug and comfy as the long green grass that rises from their graves.

I wander along Dominican Street, past students in white caps. And when I reach the corner, where the policeman and the hackneys are standing, I find German Avenue, the Jewish street. Here, I understand the language. Store by store, countless people, Jews, hauling, lugging, standing in groups. A rare caftan, usually European provincial garb. Very narrow side lanes, street peddlers all the way into the courtyards. The shops are open, often windowless, rows of meat and poultry stores cheek by jowl. Arches span a few streets. They mark the boundaries of the old ghetto. This is an energetic life, here and at the castle hill, on the water, where the soldiers exercise.

I enter the "Jewish Courtyard." Under the arch, boys distribute Yiddish leaflets, publicity, and an invitation to a meeting. A medium-size courtyard with small plain houses. Steps lead up to some of them. Prayer room next to prayer room. At one point, steps lead down; to my amazement, I find myself in a huge, very dilapidated temple. Inside, there are galleries for women, the windows are closed. The temple itself is filled with men praying, walking to and fro, chatting. In the middle, they set up a wooden stage, the *bimah*, surrounded by columns, fenced off. It is very wide; steps lead up to it. Rows of benches surround it. There are also individual lecterns on which books lie. Unadorned men in prayer shawls move on the *bimah*. I see no women. A man sings. Agitation in the room. In back, two canopies; a group of clocks on the wall.

The prayer room of the great Gaon. I hear his name often—the great learned Jew of Wilno a century ago. Stairs leading from the courtyard up to a large warm wooden room. The *bimah* is at the center; men in street clothes and prayer shawls bustling on it. One clutches the Torah scrolls, which are wrapped around two wooden sticks; he lifts them up toward the room. Another steps up, takes hold of the Torah, rolls it up solidly, ties it up. Meanwhile, liturgizing. Elderly men with very sharp, brooding expressions sit at wide tables, propping their heads over their books. Others converse softly, leaning back, scratching their white beards. Small groups read a single book together. Here, there are more individual lecterns than in that large hall. Few people walk about. Their eyes are glued to the books.

Who was the Gaon? My Jewish guides are well informed. His name was Eliyahu ben Shloime. He was known as Eli Shloime, "he of perfect judgment." He was born in the first quarter of the eighteenth century, and was nearly eighty when he died. At the age of seven, he already gave a lecture at the great synagogue of Wilno; by nine, he had memorized the entire Bible; by ten, most of the Babylonian Talmud.

Upon hearing and seeing how precisely they know all these facts, I am amazed. The only thing I learned about was the Battle of Marathon. So there are any number of other important issues. (Why was Marathon of all things sliced from the cake for me? I haven't eaten it for a long time.) The Gaon studied mathematics and astronomy, but became important because of something else. A Jewish "heresy" cropped up in the Ukraine. It was spread by a lone man, poorly acquainted with Talmud and Torah. He began to say all kinds of things to the poor Jewish masses in the flat Russian countryside, in the hamlets and small towns. The faulty Talmudist was Rabbi Israel Baal-Shem-Tov. He didn't go inside the *bes-medresh*, the synagogue, he remained outdoors, studying, people said, the voices of the birds and the speech of the trees. "Ah," he said, "the world is full of light and wonderful secrets. And the small hand blocks the eyes, preventing them from seeing the great lights." Then: "What else is the Torah but a guide for serving God and a go-between for a union with God. However, the rabbis do not pursue this goal, they flaunt their learning. Anyone can be great and righteous without knowing the Talmud." The uneducated ran to him. He must have been an imposing, elemental person. This wonderful man taught the vast power of the soul, the omnipotence of the soul. They made him a tsadik, a superhuman, a mysterious being who saves others, works miracles. Even rabbis followed him. He taught joy and merriment, ardent prayer;

sorrow struck him as reprehensible. Pure thought, feeling were everything for him; praying in the forest and amid the sheaves of grain was also good. These people called themselves the pious, the Hasidim.

For a while, the Gaon went into exile to purge himself of his sins; he wandered through Poland, Germany, praying, struggling to do his duty toward God. He settled in Wilno, castigating himself, studying Talmud, Cabbala.[23] He didn't even want to see his family. He was a fanatic of knowledge, a severe critic. He rebuked Maimonides for pursuing philosophy, an execrable thing; he rejected the great Rabbi Isserles. And now, in the Ukraine, a fantast stood up, an ignoramus, confusing the Jewish people, under the Gaon's very eyes, during his lifetime. The Gaon had papal sovereignty. When things got too wild for him, he anathematized the Hasidim and their leader. He refused any contact with them, and left Wilno when he was urged to listen to the renewer. He anathematized the Hasidim first at fifty-two, then again nine years later:

"Crush them and let them perish like chaff in the wind. Eject them from the camp where they dwell, like the leprous and the pustulant. Let no one wend his way to their gang, or join them, or belong to their congregation, or partake of their meat, or marry any of them."

At seventy-seven, he cursed them one last time. Meanwhile, the new doctrine, which was hardly new, hardly a doctrine, had spread. The Baal-Shem-Tov lived in the small Volhynian town of Miedziborz. "God's teachings are perfect: they refresh the soul." And he died. Burnings of books (Hasidic writings) and persecutions increased. The great Gaon of Wilno could not stop the movement, which struck roots even in his residence. *Misnagdim*, protesters, was what the old believers called themselves. The fighting stopped. Even the rebbe of Apt, an early Hasidic leader, declared:

"The Shulkhan-Orukh is our royal highway.[24] When swamps formed on this road during the long duration of our exile, and the highway grew impassable, the Baal-Shem came and found a detour, which, although it ran through mountains and forests, was dry and led to the destination. Now, gigantic boulders are blocking this narrow path, so that it is no longer usable. Newcomers are beginning to seek byroads and walk along new, hazardous chasms. But the spirit of the Baal-Shem stands there, raising his hands, urging us to come to our senses, and to lead the people not along crooked paths, but back to the royal highway."

The Gaon was not defeated. His city, Wilno, the Jerusalem of Lithuania, remained the center of the rationalists.

The historian Eduard Meyer characterizes the Semites: "The intimacy of emotional life and the warmth of feeling that distinguish the Indo-Europeans are alien to the Semites. This is an intrinsic reason why the Semites lack the creative formative power of the imagination." Perhaps he included the Jews among the Semites. In regard to present-day Jews in Russia, Poland, Western Europe, it is hard to determine their Semitic percentage. Nor do I know whether the black skin makes the Negro superior to the Caucasian, or the light skin the Caucasian superior to the Negro. Meyer, however, would probably lapse into utter silence when faced with the Baal-Shem and his Hasidim.

In the Gaon's library, I again hear about the mighty man. The old librarian spreads tomes out in front of me. The tattered volumes are the Talmud. At the top center, the yellowish paper shows the texts of the Mishnah [25] and the Gemorah [the exegesis of the Mishnah], which are surrounded, in smaller print, by the commentaries, especially Rashi's. A huge tome beautifully bound in white leather provides photographs of the Venetian text of the Babylonian Talmud, two volumes. The name of Strack, the German Judaist, comes up. This is where the Gaon lived; a small thick book that he penned lies there: commentaries on the Talmud. A Russian encyclopedia contains a portrait of the Gaon himself: a fanatical face, burning eyes, solid mouth. His beard blazes around his face. The faces of the wise men along the wall of the reading room are milder, warmer, but today they pale next to the Gaon's face. The way wisdom, gentleness pale next to a mighty person. Today. But the mighty person is also gone the next day.

I can't help thinking as I go out: What an impressive nation Jews are. I didn't know this nation; I believed what I saw in Germany, I believed that the Jews are the industrious people, the shopkeepers, who stew in their sense of family and slowly go to fat, the agile intellectuals, the countless insecure unhappy refined people. Now I see that those are isolated examples, degenerating, remote from the core of the nation that lives here and maintains itself. And what an extraordinary core is this, producing such people as the rich, inundating Baal-Shem, the dark flame of the Gaon of Wilno. What events occurred in these seemingly uncultured Eastern areas. How everything flows around the spiritual! What tremendous importance is placed on spirituality, on religion! Not a minor stratum, an entire mass of people—spiritually united. Few other nations are as centered in religion and spirituality as this one. Jews had an easier time of this than others, they didn't have to tussle with polities, revolutions, wars, border improvements, kings, parliaments. They were relieved of such concerns two thousand years ago, by the Romans. And the Jews didn't really complain. It didn't make them sit by the waters of Babylon and weep. Their focus was always on the temple. They needed the state only for the temple. The proper temple stands only on Zion. When the state didn't emerge, that idea gradually transformed the entire nation. The Jews were soundlessly imbued with the renunciation of land and state. And they made themselves into the nation of the temple. The nation that carries the temple within itself. An unparalleled process. It was possible only under such prolonged, artificial conditions.

What if history were turned backward and the Jews were really given Zion? And this is becoming an urgent issue. The old artificial conditions can no longer be maintained, their rigor is slackening. The modern age, economic necessities, are driving the Jews out of their seclusion. The backward movement is rolling. The tragedy of fulfillment is rolling. The temple that they will find when and if they seek it will not be the Temple. The religious ones, the spiritual ones know it. They say: Only the Messiah can give us the Temple. The most genuine Jews stopped waiting for the "state" long ago. One can preserve oneself only in the spiritual; that's why one must remain in the spiritual. Politics cannot bring about heaven, politics produces nothing but politics. The "modern" era presents no problems for those Jews.

However, today's external circumstances, political, economic, and the plight of the masses are facts. The old organism will put up a strong resistance to all change. "State," "Parliament" loom on the horizon—against the Gaon and the Baal-Shem.

I get to see the changing, loosening forces. In Eastern Europe, the emancipation of the masses is taking place within a national framework—indeed, the strongest accent is on nationalism.

I am briefed by a highly educated man, and lo and behold: he was born in Germany, he has taught at a German university. He's got three doctorates (Rabbi Israel Baal-Shem-Tov didn't even know his Talmud), he's a physician, a highly prestigious one, as well as principal of the Hebrew Secondary School. While he speaks in front of me at the table, patients hobble by en route to the electrostatic machine. This middle-aged man came to Wilno during the war. The city, he reports, has two Hebrew secondary schools, one classical and one emphasizing modern languages; the former has some five hundred students, the latter two hundred. There are also two Hebrew elementary schools and a kindergarten; they are developing an evening university similar to the Humboldt Academy. There are Hebrew elementary schools in the Wilno district and several middle schools. The secondary schools, modeled after West European ones, use Hebrew as their language of instruction and, along with West European subjects, they also teach Hebraica and Judaica, ancient, medieval, and modern Hebrew literature, and the Talmud. These secondary schools are supported purely by tuition fees, which are enormous.

The Hebraist movement, the Tarbut movement, he explains, is not identical with Zionism. Hebrew has to become the vernacular of the Jews. Yiddish is a borrowed language, a sort of German dialect. You can borrow a top hat, but not a language.

Language is the essential characteristic of a nation. The Hebrew students are supposed to Hebraicize their environment everywhere. Yiddish is demanded by people who are left-wing, nonreligious or antireligious. Admittedly, a kind of class stratification exists in the Yiddish vs. Hebrew fight: the lower classes want Yiddish, the middle classes Hebrew; the primary schools are marked by Jewish nationalism and Zionism. Tarbut is not antireligious, as shown by the study of the Bible, the Talmud. They want a Hebraist cultural movement. For the Zionist, Zion is an end in itself; for the Tarbut follower, Zion is a means of achieving a Hebrew culture.

I step into the Hebrew teachers' college. A strange building; it also contains the Jewish community headquarters and the Yiddish teachers' college. For some reason, no classes are being held this morning. They're awaiting a Zionist deputy. I'm introduced to a young man with a commonplace face, who addresses me in Hebrew; upon realizing that I don't understand him, he snubs me. Then, a teacher, a moron, he stands, blithely talking and smoking, with a group of young men and girls, all between seventeen and twenty. Fresh young creatures, they speak Hebrew. I can't help it: it sounds like Germans speaking French in Germany. These people deploy their linguistic knowledge vivaciously, no doubt quite nicely. I'm guided by a young girl instead of the silly teacher. The course of study, she says, takes four years here, one hundred thirty students are enrolled, sixty percent girls. They study ancient Hebrew literature, Bible, exegesis, Talmud, medieval culture, philosophical literature. They study those subjects, I believe her. They are not antireligious, they are simply indifferent to religion. Gymnastics is also a subject, so are sculpting, drawing, singing.

I sneak away without much ado, over to the other wing, to the enemy brethren. Classes have been canceled for the Yiddishists, too. But I do find a teacher. They have a student body of one hundred twelve here. The parents are workers, artisans, shopkeepers. The man says: No Hebraist truly believes in the Hebrew language in the Diaspora. There's no need to debate the use of Hebrew in Palestine. It's an artificial action. Most of the Hebraists are bourgeois, assimilated Jews concealing their assimilation. When they're off duty, they speak Polish.

A newspaperman is here, he has a very fine mind; a philologist, a passionate Yiddishist. He explains: Zionism is a national resurgence for the Western European Jews, a throwback for the Eastern Europeans. It does not solve the Jewish question, spiritually or economically. For an unforeseeable length of time, Palestine will be only for a chosen few. It's politically incorrect to let Polish Jews sacrifice everything for such a goal. Hebraism is fruitless, hopeless. It weakens Jews in regard to more important things. It's not uninteresting, he says, to note that, contrary to the Yiddish movement, Zionism is very popular with the Poles. Yes, I should merely observe, and I'll see that the educated people, the people of quality are Zionists. Zionism simply involves no obligations. A Zionist donates money and remains a fine man in Poland. Here, in the Wilno district, the Folkists and the Bundists [26] really have the upper hand. Three thousand children are enrolled in their elementary schools. The Central Yiddish Education Committee is headquartered in Wilno. They have a humanistic secondary school, a secondary school concentrating on modern languages, eight elementary schools, two Fröbel kindergartens, evening schools for workers, the teachers' college.

A Yiddish girls' school. Girls, twelve, thirteen years old, mostly brown hair, some black hair, neat, nice clothing, some twenty very cute creatures, sit there politely. The girls discuss the situation of women on the basis of some opus, they ferociously criticize the female inferiority of the earlier Jewish era. A smart pretty girl stands in front, next to the teacher, facing the class, speaking slowly. In back, one girl pulls her neighbor's hair. In the last row, two girls first shake hands, then quickly embrace. They talk about the Jewish heroic epic and whether there is such a thing. Now, one girl with large blackish-brown braids, in a black skirt, stands in front; developed breasts stick out in the taut blue woolen blouse. The instruction is clear, lively. They laugh a lot with the teacher.

In another room, little girls are in their Polish class. Funny how they answer chaotically, writhing, raising their hands. They have Polish books in front of them, excerpts from Polish authors. One little girl's black hair is shorn just like a boy's. At first I mistake her for a boy. Then she steps forth, and a pair of long white underpants peer out from under her skirt.

In a lower class, boys and girls sit together, reciting charming Yiddish poems. A book contains many of them. One goes like this:

*Feygele, feygele!*
*Pip-pip-pi!*
*Vu iz der tate?*
*Nit do hi!*
*Van vet er kumen?*
*Morgn fri!*

*Vos vet er brengn?*
*A glezl bir!*
*Vu vet er shteln?*
*Unter tir!*
*Mit vos vet er tsudekn!*
*Mit a shtikl papir!*
*Ver vet trinken?*
*Ikh mit dir!*

*Birdie, birdie!*
*Pip-pip-pi!*
*Where is Daddy?*
*He's not here!*
*When will he come?*
*Tomorrow morning!*
*What will he bring?*
*A glass of beer!*
*Where will he put it?*
*By the door!*
*What will he cover it with?*
*A scrap of paper!*

*Who will drink it?*
*You and me!*

And another:

*Afm heykhen barg,*
*Afm grinem groz,*
*Shten a por Taitshn*
*Mit di lange baitshn.*
*Heykhe mener zain zi,*
*Kurtse kleyder trogn zi.*
*Ovine-meylekh,*
*'S harts iz mir freylekh.*
*Freylekh veln mir zain,*
*Trinkn veln mir vain.*
*Kreplakh veln mir esn,*
*On dem lebedikn got*
*Veln mir nit vargesn!*

*On the high hill,*
*On the green grass,*
*A couple of Germans*
*Stand with long whips.*
*They are tall men,*
*They wear short tunics.*
*Oh Good Lord!*
*My heart is merry.*
*We'll be merry,*
*We'll drink wine.*
*We'll eat dumplings.*
*We won't forget*
*The living God!*

And then:

*Daine bekelekh—*
*Vi rozane blumen.*
*Daine lipelekh—*
*Vi tsuker zis.*

*Daine eygelekh—*
*Vi shvartse karshn,*
*Tsu bakumen fun zey*
*A zisiken kush!*
*Daine horelekh—*
*Vi der gegroiste zamet*
*Daine hentelekh—*
*Vi ribelekh.*
*Dain harts mit mainem*
*Tsuzamengebundn,*
*Un keyner veys nit*
*Fun unzere wundn!*


*Your cheeks—*
*Like rosy flowers.*
*Your lips—*
*Sweet as sugar.*
*Your eyes—*
*Like black cherries,*
*To get a sweet kiss*
*From them!*
*Your hair—*
*Like ribbed velvet,*
*Your hands—*
*Like radishes.*
*Your heart bound up*
*With mine,*
*And no one knows*
*About our wounds!*

These verses have an ancient German tone, but they grew in the Jewish nation. The Yiddishists do not want to give up these riches, the Hebraists do not want to give up others.

A student of Greece says:

The exaggerated cultivation of the written legacy of remote forefathers is altogether Oriental, and indeed, the Greeks are essentially Oriental. Most of the Eastern nations all the way to

China possess, aside from their vernacular, a more or less secret hieratic language, in which the ancient sages wrote. Arabic, too, has an old, sacred literary language, which is both written and understood from Mosul to Mecca and as far as Mogador; on the other hand, within the individual countries of this vast area, numerous younger and extremely divergent popular dialects are in use.

Thus, not just the Baal-Shem vs. the state, but also Orient vs. Occident. The first rift in the Jewish nation: Gaon, Baal-Shem vs. secular politics.

The second rift among the emancipated Jews: supporters of the bourgeois state vs. Socialists. The Socialists—universal, humanistic, international—are better at holding the old Gaon line, the great supranational idea.

The Yiddish school, the Yiddish teachers' college look like the Hebrew school, the Hebrew teachers' college. The respective assets—Hebrew literature and Talmud on one side, humanities and natural sciences on the other—change nothing. Each is a Western institute with national insignia. A glance at their classrooms, their curricula, would show them that they speak Yiddish or Hebrew, but are Western. Both are modern, national, Western. Civilizers.

The economics and politics of the countries that the Jews live in are driving them full force into the arms of civilization. That's what they mean by "secularization of Judaism." In the process, the Jewish millions are developing a new sense of a free European nation, throwing off the weight of the old bondage and contempt. They want to be national minorities or else have the old Asiatic homeland borrowed from their religion.

The masses—an old world is collapsing—are taking a prescribed, necessary route. They should, however, be sure not to put on clothes that the Western nations have discarded.

In the afternoon, a children's performance at a Yiddish theater. A big beautiful room at the theater square; it used to be a movie house. The entire orchestra and all the galleries are filled with small and big children, boys and girls, all of them clean, lively. I can recognize only a few as Jewish. The nonsense of "race" is blatant; there are several types here, and yet they all are Jews and want to be Jews. The admixture of various races is obvious, as are the effects of the Slavic, the Polish milieu. They are staging Sholem Asch's *Motke Ganef*,[27] in Yiddish. The play, performed hundreds of times in America, began as a story. In the first act, Motke, a boy, a thief, leaves home. His father drives him out, his mother comforts him, unable to let him go. The boy threatens; he promises her: "I'll come back with a coach and two horses." In the second act, he's a groom in a circus, where he falls prey to a shady lady. She robs a rich suitor so that she and Motke can flee together, she hands him a knife so that he can get the suitor's ID card. In the third act, Motke runs a brothel, he's a pimp, a strong violent man. And then—he sees the "pure girl." The catastrophe is heralded. He's fed up with his life. He wants to marry this girl, he kicks out the joy girls, the circus woman who helped him and followed him. But it's too late. The fourth act is already here. Motke triggers his own doom. He feels an urgent need to confess everything to the girl, the family maid. He has to reveal his past, thinking that confession will liberate him, absolve him. And he has to confess, for she addresses him with the terrible name of the man whose ID card he carries. He does not want to bear the dead man's name. She listens in horror, silence. Although she finds him ghastly. However, the girl's parents have also been listening. And just as his own mother shows up and his happiness is complete—he hugs the women: "Two mammas"—the whistles shriek. Cops burst in. He can't save himself, he leaps out the window.

This gripping play—penned by a good technician, with a poetic heart—is mounted with noteworthy bravura. The director aims at effects and thinks he can achieve them by overdoing everything. Overvehement gestures, overemphases; from the stage to the audience. Only the mother is discreet; she's a dilettante. This mass of intelligent lively children's faces. A bright festive company. I walk about enchanted.

A lyric poet guides me; she's a fine sensitive creature. No city, no landscape is as heartwarming as an exquisite person.

On Sunday, two young men accompany me to the old Jewish cemetery on the outskirts of the city. En route they tell me that it will probably be closed. And it *is* closed when we stand at the large wooden gates. The caretaker lives in a different neighborhood. The more cunning of my two companions instantly tells me I shouldn't worry, they have an idea. He triumphantly repeats the word "idea" several times; the other man agrees. I'm eager to see what happens. The wooden gate, bolted on the inside, constitutes the entrance to the graveyard. The terrain is surrounded by a wooden fence and a wire fence with large holes. One man shinnies up the second man, gets on top, climbs down the other side—and that's what they call an "idea." Half a minute later, he opens the gate, and—it's a terrible thing to say—we laugh, laugh as we step into the cemetery, bolt the gate behind us.

Here, we find a vast lawn with several trees and, irregularly, here and there, alone and in clusters, low stone slabs. Withered leaves lie everywhere, even piled up in a few hollows. A fine drizzle is coming down. The stone tablets bear long inscriptions, red and yellow square Hebrew script. Lions are often depicted on the slabs. Shards, stone fragments, bricks lie about. Terrible the neglect of this cemetery. Bits of brick, small stones on many headstones. Straw under the small stones, also slips of paper with Hebrew writing. These are memorial tokens of pious Jews who have prayed here. For they travel from far away to pray at the graves of famous men, holy men. That deep and dark feeling drives them to come here. Somehow—they think, they feel— the holy man is still by his grave, by his body, and they can approach him as their forebears did during his lifetime. The dead man is tied to his grave, his vanished soul to his corpse, and his soul can be evoked by prayer. And the pious man, the rebbe, the saint stands closer to God and can obtain more than a normal man from God, perhaps by way of God. How dilapidated everything is here. I hear shouts, orders, soldiers singing, and, all at once, a mooing. I climb over a small rise on which shattered stone plaques are strewn. When I stand on top, I see a cow grazing below. Pasturing on the graves. Its pats lie around.

A large tomb off to the side: the Ger Tsedek. My companions tell me his story; I already know it. He was a young Polish count, Valentin Potocki; he was studying with a friend, they went to Rome and to Paris. And one day, when he was strolling through Paris, he saw an old Jew sitting there, praying, poring over his books. The count spoke to him. They agreed that the count and his friend would come often; the old man would show them everything contained in the writings of the Jews. They came for months on end. And eventually, both friends had lost their Catholic faith and wanted to become Jews like the old man. They sought admission into Judaism. They succeeded in the free city of Amsterdam. The two friends grew beards, donned caftans, returned to Poland as poor Jews. I don't know the details. The parents of young Valentin Potocki looked for him in Rome and Paris. They couldn't find him. It was only after many years that they had some news: they were told about a pious man living near Wilno, venerated by the Jews. He was known as the Ger Tsedek. And this man, they learned, was Count Valentin Potocki. It was a dreadful blow for the aristocratic family. They tracked him down, he didn't deny it. They made useless efforts to win back the apostate. A court of law convened, sentenced him to death in this Wilno: death by fire. It was the end of the eighteenth century. One day after his execution, they were informed that the sentence had been reversed. The family provided no grave for him. A pious Jew, a follower of the dead man, Rabbi Lezer Ziski, bribed the guards, charged over to the site of the burning, and gathered ashes and remnants. He buried them on this very spot, where I am now standing. The site did not remain a secret for long. A tree grew from that very spot, its trunk bent strangely across the grave, the branches dangling over it. Potocki's friend remained undetected, he married and moved to Palestine.

I see the grave, the stone fence, the bizarre tree. Stone fragments are tossed helter-skelter across the grave. Logs molder among them. Those are pieces of the tree growing from the Ger Tsedek's grave; parts of it have been sawn off. Who sawed them off? The singing of the soldiers draws nearer. And now a whole squad of soldiers in loose formation comes in through a broad gap in the wire fence. A mounted junior officer in their midst, cursing. They are lugging food buckets, leading horses by their bridles. Thus they march across the cemetery, noisy, shouting, singing, from one barracks to another. They climb over the stone rubble with their horses, swerving around well-maintained graves. Just recently, soldiers demolished the grave of the Ger Tsedek, sawed up the tree. The culprits were apprehended and punished. They were ordered not to take this route. But—it's a shortcut from one barracks to the other, and the fence is defective. The Jews of Wilno, I find, are proud, but only partially and in a very Eastern manner. The grass runs wild and high. On the mounds, you keep stepping on shattered headstones. They often bear the beautiful, tail-lashing lions, the ancient symbol of strength. The tomb of the Gaon of Wilno. A low stone house with a fence of iron bars, it's locked. It contains his grave and the graves of his kith and kin. He lies here together with these people, whom he didn't know so well during his lifetime. When his wife died, he said: "I had to go hungry very often, but I did it for the sake of Torah and God. But you went hungry because of me, a human being." Whole piles of small written notes lie on his stone plaque and on the adjacent ground. They even hang outside, on the iron fence, tied to the bars with straw and tussocks. . . .

There's a community of Karaites here; Troki supposedly has a large one, and so do Halicz in Galicia and Lodz. The Karaites are a splinter group of Judaism. First, the Jews, landless, stateless, templeless, developed the Talmud in Babylon; the work was completed in the fourth century A.D. Then, as described by a historian: "Talmudic study degenerated into a matter of dry memorizing, lacking all power of spiritual stimulation." The son of a Jewish prince in ancient Babylon launched an anti-Talmudic movement, urging a return to Scripture: a Luther of Judaism. He sharpened the rules that he believed he found in the Bible, and he abolished others. The old Jewish group and the new one denounced one another as heretics. Karaism still lives today, a vehement enemy of Talmudist Judaism. They've built themselves a new temple on the outskirts of Wilno; I want to see it.

On the way, one of my companions tells me that the Karaites used to be very powerful in Wilno. The main temple was in their hands. One day, a violent conflict erupted. A great Polish king, Kazimierz, wanted to endow the Jews with privileges, but the question was: Who were the real Jews, and in which hand was he to place the power, the Karaite or the Rabbanite hand? All power was at stake—cult, school, self-administration. The king invited representatives of both groups. A Rabbanite and a Karaite appeared before Kazimierz. The Karaite, upon entering the room, took off his dirty shoes. The Rabbanite similarly took his off. Then he wedged them under his arm and stationed himself in front of the king on his throne. The great Kazimierz was surprised:

"What are you doing, rabbi? Carrying your shoes under your arm? Why don't you leave them outside like the others?"

The Rabbanite answered:

"Your Majesty, I know that we do not complain about shoes. But I did not dare leave them outside. I did not dare. I would like to reply to you by quoting our Holy Scripture. It is written: 'Moses kept the flock of Jethro, his father-in-law, the priest of Midian . . . and came to the mountain of God, to Horeb. And the angel of the Lord appeared unto him in a flame of fire out of the midst of the bush. . . . And when the Lord saw that Moses turned aside to see . . . he said, Put off thy shoes from off thy feet, for the place whereon thou standest is holy ground.' Moses, our leader, blessed be his memory, did as the Lord ordered him to do. Let me tell you what else the Bible says: When Moses returned from the burning bush, Your Majesty, and looked for his shoes, he couldn't find them. Someone had followed him, a Karaite—and he had stolen them."

The Karaite, cut to the quick, yelled at the rabbi:

"What are you saying? What do you dare say to the great King Kazimierz? How dare you tell lies to the great king. Lies, yes, lies, Your Majesty! A Karaite stole Moses' shoes! A Karaite! You're only hurting yourself, rabbi. Moses was alone at the burning bush! All alone. Did the Karaites even exist when Moses was at Horeb?"

The rabbi laughed, bowed to the king, bowed to the Karaite, and tenderly hugged his shoes: "Listen to him, Your Majesty. Listen to what he himself is saying and not I, and judge. He said: No Karaites existed when Moses, our leader, God bless his memory, stood at Horeb. He said so himself. The only people there were the people of Jethro, the priest of Midian. He knows our Scripture very well. And here he comes forward, the Karaite, and tries to speak against me. He wants to receive the privileges from you. Because he is nobler, more genuine. Who is nobler? Is a child nobler than a father? Where is a child nobler, more genuine then a father? A child, I tell you; did I say a child? Who knows, who can determine what sort of child this is, a legitimate one or, heaven protect me, an illegitimate one, a substitute, whom the father refuses to acknowledge." The great Kazimierz raised his hands. He laughed with the rabbi and the courtiers. The Karaite snarled. But the rebbe received the Jewish privileges.

It's a long drive down Mickiewicza Street to their temple, at a huge marketplace, past a new court of law. Then comes the river. A thin drizzle is ruffling its surface. Beyond the bridge, out in the open, on the undulating bosky terrain, stands a large, sprawling, exotic church, a Russian church with gold domes. And not too far away, out in the green—the small temple of the Karaites. Byzantine domes, a brand-new building. I enter through the side, find myself in a very bright plain church interior: truly, a puristic Protestant coolness and austerity. A row of pews to the right and the left. Some fifty, sixty people, men and women, standing along the benches, facing the front. The men keep their hats on, some wear a short white narrow prayer "scarf" over their shoulders, the remnant of a prayer shawl. They gaze forward, at the wall, where golden Hebrew letters form the Ten Commandments. There is an altar platform; a simple table with a blue tablecloth stands in the middle at the front; a runner embroidered in red has been placed across it. A very thick book with red binding lies on the table; it must be the Bible. Way in the back, a curtain with gold threads closes off the wall. And in front, a man is singing, liturgizing. A tall man; I see him from behind. He stands beneath the altar, wearing a black-and-blue robe and, over it, a white shirt in the style of the Catholic surplice. Now he turns around; to the right, in the front row, two men in ordinary clothes spell him in singing. Now and then, the congregation joins in, singing "Amen." No organ, no choir. The books that the men and women read are in square Hebrew script; the shelves of most of the pews contain other books as well. The worshipers stand very quietly, no one moves his upper body, a few have their hands folded on their chests. Now a man steps forward from his pew, kneels down at the mensa, bows all the way to the floor, rises, and picks the thick red book up from the table. Amid the singing of the congregation, he carries it deeper into the background, places it in a closet. Then the service ends. They slowly pack up their books, insert their prayer scarves into small sackcloth or leather pouches. As they wander past me along the aisle, I can scrutinize them. Many wear caps, they look like craftsmen, workers, shopkeepers. They speak Russian to one another, a few speak Polish. I hear no Yiddish. Their backgrounds vary. Barely half these people have Jewish features or expressions; the rest are Russians or Poles, with high Slavic cheekbones, short wide noses, all kinds of Mongoloid touches. As the temple empties out, the preacher or cantor wanders among the people in the middle aisle. He wears a flat round cap as dark as his coat but circled with a white stripe. His beard is white; a typical Slavic face.

As they leave, a heated debate ensues. In the back courtyard of the temple, there is a spacious tabernacle made of boards and covered with verdure, in the usual way. A number of outsiders want to join the Karaites going across the courtyard and into the tabernacle. But the Karaites won't hear of it. One Karaite, a simple man, snaps at somebody in Russian, telling him he doesn't belong here; you don't lie down in someone else's bed. Other Karaites, especially one woman, join in. The outsiders have to retreat. From the door, I watch the entire congregation cross the green courtyard and slowly vanish with the priest inside the large communal tabernacle.

My companions are upset, stunned by the torrent of hatred. As we leave, they tell me that the Karaites here speak Russian almost exclusively. Among themselves, however, they speak some kind of "Tötör"—Tartar. They have no idea where they got this language from.

# LUBLIN

*People in such houses. And someone dares to speak of the beauty of the archway.*

Someone is snoring in the train: this is no sawing, it's a gurgling, crackling, until he swallows; the valve is shut. Now he starts in again. The faces; the people sagging in and out in the lamplight. Sometimes they bob on their cushions. There are two brawny men, one with a dark mustache, a full Polish face. When he sleeps, his face gets puffy, his mouth slackening completely, his lips drooping away. His sleep is so dull and dense. He doesn't sleep, he is slept. Devoted and dark, he performs his duty, suffers the constraint. The other man's head, with its dangling mustache and grayish-white Vandyke, is thrown against the back cushion. Lying and sitting there, he sleeps like a seer. He's busy watching, seeing. He eagerly follows the images unrolling before him; he looks at them; his head is held fast.

I am the waking predator loping among them. I am reapproaching Warsaw; it is already dawn. The landscape is swampy, marshy, with isolated grass islands. Fog is brewing on the flat meadows; suddenly, whole clouds of fog roll up on the edges of the forest, settling all across the countryside; people are up to their hips in fog, their torsos are visible. Trees loom out, cut off.

Near the villages, the steam evaporates. A brownish-green meadow carpet stretches out. Warsaw drifts toward us. And past us. We are heading toward Lublin. I have to go south. Lublin is supposedly a lovely old city.

I am frozen stiff in my compartment throughout the long bright day; my legs ache, they're almost dead. In the evening, I leap up in the darkness. The small, harshly flashing railroad station in Lublin. My heart jumps for joy.

And as my droshky rolls into town, the whole big night sky appears for the first time in months, the immense black night sky with tremendous constellations. Fiery handwriting, fiery handwriting. The sky arches overhead as deep as the ocean, as deep as the abyss, with glittering stars. To think that I don't leap up, go under in the swarm, zoom upward. At the same time, I am filled with tremendous pride as I stretch out in the droshky and keep looking at the sky. As if the heavens were a sign—I don't know of what.

For a long time, I roll through unlit streets; then all at once, it gets light out. And I pass through a street that is thronged with people. And I hear something that haunts me throughout my days in Lublin: laughter, chatting, loud laughter in the street. It all comes from people, from men strolling in crowds. I never saw such crowds in Wilno. How bizarre. You travel for miles and miles, across sand, mute steppes, bogs, and all at once (the cities are separated) this laughter. People again walking under bright streetlights, shops are open with candy and cakes. I feel it profoundly, it makes me happy. Gratitude shoots through me, moves my hands.

How warm I lay in the hotel last night, dreaming, until five A.M. I dreamed about many figures, I couldn't grab them. I dozed for a couple of hours in order to fully swallow the taste of my dreams.

This main thoroughfare is called Cracow Suburb as in Warsaw; it's lined with trees, small two- or three-story houses, medium-sized shops. Short side lanes, the town peters out right behind them. A black obelisk stands over there; two tasteless gold women shake hands; the numbers 1569–1825 appear on the stone: the union between Poland and Lithuania was consum-

119

mated here. And behind the column, a huge building is being torn down; men with pickaxes stand on top; a lamentable rubble field. This was the Russian cathedral, the Greek Catholic one; it's being razed like the cathedral in Warsaw. I feel sorrow. All at once, I'm alone and gloomy. In Warsaw, I could accept the demolition: it's the capital. But why this systematic destruction of churches? They should let them stand. What's being offered in exchange? Stupidity, hatred, and blather. It gives me the creeps.

An old officer strides across the roadway; he wears an old Russian coat. Peasants trudge by in high lambskin caps, ladies in light-colored stockings. Beggars bow in entranceways. I peer into houses: deep courtyards, rear wings, wooden, with galleries, which are filled with crates, with laundry. One house is collapsing; rubble lies on the ground; the structure is propped up with wooden beams. The town hall is garishly whitewashed; unemployed Polish workers sit on its porch, dangling their legs. I scrutinize an old gate with a tower; colorful icons are suspended on it.

And few people; few well-dressed burghers, Polish workers, peasants, Jews in costumes. A medium-size town, a small town. Only it's not sleepy like a small town in Germany; poverty is too blatant in its face, hounding it, hot on its heels, behind it, in front. They all have to keep moving. And a great past crumbles in the houses among them; diluvium in broad daylight. I walk back along the street, past the small hotels, where people were laughing and strolling, and where there are now faces of frozen people going to work. The foreheads of these men are high and broad, receding. Their type is Russian blonde and brown, shaggy. White-blonde children scurry about. I encounter robust men, their bony or fleshy faces are square-shaped. Dangling bushy mustaches, some twirled.

And the houses are already thinning out. Small lilac petals fall on the street, fall in whole masses. I'm almost out in the countryside. An old splendid park comes, then come barracks; recruits yawn in the windows. Small farm wagons creak into town. On a side street, an empty sports arena; the Catholic graveyard. Another sprawling edifice: the Catholic University.

This has been the major portion of Polish Lublin. But everything is mute for me; no one walks at my side.

Low rooms, white tablecloths; a high flowerpot blossoms on one table: I've entered a restaurant. If a customer walks in, the waiter moves the flowerpot to an adjacent table. If someone sits down at that table, the waiter moves the pot to the next table. Eventually, he has to carry it outside. Very powerful notabilities sit at the wall behind me; I can't see them, I only hear them smacking their lips and clicking their tongues. An old short fat man comes; his left leg is lame; he bows deeply to the table behind me. A young man in top boots slowly saunters in. He has already taken some bread from a table by the entrance, and chews it as he struts in. Then he sits down across from me, twirls up his mustache, and cunningly starts to seek something in his mouth. He doesn't find it. He pokes his right and left grinders and then ogles his finger. Finally, he wipes it on the tablecloth. Two girls, one in a blue cap, eat their soup. A whole bevy of earnest white-capped high school girls peer through the window. Two officers walk between the tables. A pleasure to see the spruce uniforms, the straight figures. They sit there with medals, silently waiting to be served.

I sit in what I'm told is a good hotel, on the Bystrzyca, in Lublin. The city was founded way back in the tenth century; my hotel bears witness. When I enter this hotel in the evening, I find a desk clerk; he lies like a sarcophagus figure in a small room in the back, his cap pulled down over his face, and he understands nothing. If he signals, he's merely responding to a dream image, he has grasped only what the dream allows. I mount the stairs. The banister is made of almost genuine marble, for the time being of wood painted white. I live two flights up. The walls were whitewashed, oiled—in the tenth century. Eventually, they turned gray, following a natural drive. Later on, the hotel frequently found itself in a war zone; machine guns were fired inside the building; several walls and doors are riddled with holes, cracks. The hotel administration, trained in history, treats the traces like landmarks. Military customs have also been handed down in the hotel: in the corridor, at the crack of dawn, they whoop as if for an attack, terrifying conversations are held through the door. And below me, in the courtyard, an engine has been set up; it operates from six in the evening till about four in the morning and it snarls like a locomotive. You go to bed, it puffs in measure, and you soon feel as if you were in the thick of a war or riding in a sleeper; a gratuitous illusion.

One of the most astonishing things in this hotel is my door. Wandering through the corridors, I already noticed that there's something special about the door handles. We are no longer quite used to tenth-century craftsmanship. The Main Street, Cracow Suburb, contains the monument, the obelisk, commemorating the union of Poland and Lithuania. A far more ancient monument, of an archeological kidney, is the typical door handle in the hotel where I am now writing—sitting on the bed because the wire of the electric lamp does not reach all the way to the table (people didn't write here during the Jagiellonic period, or under King Sigismund August). From the outside, the doors in the hotel look unassuming, somewhat fossilized and worm-eaten, yet like normal doors. It's only when dealing, or trying to deal, with them that you realize what or whom you're coping with. Things have a sort of character here. Normal beings die in the course of time; others, when aging, become extremely frisky.

When I enter my room, I at first do not enter my room. For I have no key. The key has its place, to which it has grown accustomed, in a room on my floor, halfway around the building; in any case, not with the desk clerk. It returns to its place obstinately and instinctively, like a horse or a dog, even if I've mentally left it at the desk. Once I have the key, I have two. There are always two on an iron ring, a pair of twins, which I cannot separate. I can't determine which of them is mine, the right one. I have to reestablish its identity every time, physically, hit or miss, since I cannot put a knot in the iron. And an ink mark that I put on the correct key was wiped off by the barefoot boy servant. I again tried to make it clear to him what the mark signified; he spoke Polish, I German. I talked, gesticulated. He eyed me with interest, then called over a second boy, who also took interest in me. The two of them perused the mark—that fruit of my long reflections—shook their heads, laughed. They then obviously assumed that I was complaining about the mark as an uncleanliness on the key. For suddenly, one boy spat on the key, wiped it off on his sleeve and handed it back to me with a brightened face. They waited for my reaction. Now I tried to remove the correct key from the ring—whereupon both of them intervened, broke into a long litany of protest, and pushed the hopelessly inseparable objects back into my hand. I retreated. There I stood in the corridor, which was fairly dark, or rather pitch-black. I stood with the twins, pondering what would happen this time. I was already acquainted with the temperament of the key and this door. The door handle dangled, but with luck (and luck, to my chagrin, was always with the barefoot boy), it functioned. The lock, on the other hand, was thoroughly obdurate and enormously deep, penetrating the entire massive door. The key bored all the way through the door, stabbing it right in the heart—and emerged on the inside. That was the rub. You had to stay inside. The door calmly allowed the attacker the pleasure of lunging in—and the key got stuck. You were supposed to halt at a certain depth. At which? That was the mystery. There was one thing I never understood: the other key, the wrong one, somehow also fitted. But if I twisted this key, the notoriously wrong one—which obviously belonged to a different lock, perhaps the one on my wardrobe, which was always keyless (this strikes me now, and it's probably the solution of the enigma, as the reason for the bellboy's reluctance)— if I twisted the notoriously wrong key for a while, say, a quarter to half an hour, at a certain depth of the lock, then so much for that. I had to say, *"Pater peccavi,"* and get the boy, who instantly began rattling the door amid enigmatic procedures and entreaties, calling it to order, then taking one of the two inseparables and gently unlocking the door. It opened. I myself sometimes managed to catch the right key. I then turned it in an extremely civilized way. I palpated the interior of the lock, gingerly, tenderly. For it made no sense acting crude here. Like an animal, the lock put up with anything. I hunted, anxiously, very cordially, sanctimoniously. At last, I found the questionable depth, turned the key, once, twice—sometimes (my heart froze), thrice, four times, five times. I could go on forever; I would never determine when I had to stop. Now I realized the meaning of the bullet traces on certain walls and doors: they were signs of the shots used to kill guests who had refused to let go of the doors, ultimately holding up progress in the hotel. I work fearfully, and I had luck! The door wasn't very nasty; old age makes you feeble and kind. After a number of back twists, it worked.

But, you see, the door did not open up. It *was* open, but it did not open up. Now it was up to the handle.

The handle dangled in a rather loose condition, which also guaranteed a sinister solidity of the door. Usually, the door didn't close all the way; it instantly sprang open. But once it snapped to, it did so resolutely, pigheadedly. I had the task of coaxing the handle after my assault on the lock, softening it, performing certain actions in order to maneuver it out of its state of inertia. This too was possible only with love plus energy. You had to be gentle when pressing, pulling, rocking; then suddenly, after lulling the handle into security, as it were, you had to give it a powerful thrust. The surprise, the sneak attack, the coup de main did the trick. The door flew open, flew against the washstand, which the hotel administration had, with military foresight, provided with only two massive wash implements, but no tumblers or carafes whatsoever. Only the uninformed could be irked at finding nothing to rinse their mouths or brush their teeth with; they had no inkling of the soul of this house.

I, already accustomed to such things, put up with it all. I was familiar with the door in a magical, cabbalistic way. If it opened easily when I left in the morning, then the coast was clear. If it resisted, I made no effort. I fasted , petitioning it every hour on the hour, until it let me out. The door showed great understanding, complete sympathy with my affairs.

In the evening, I sit alone in a big empty movie theater, the Coliseum. It can hold a thousand people; not even a hundred are here. An icy floor. A small orchestra begins. Who can resist when the violins start singing and come to you, speak to you immediately and quite personally? Ah, to couch it all in words: the weeping and sweet urging of the violins, the relaxing moans of the cello. They are filled with warmth, resonant warmth. How greatly a movie image is changed by music; that's a beautiful movie up there: Barbara is very beautiful. I sit through part of the movie twice, although the theater is dreadfully cold. A Russian convent: nuns bow deeply; their high wimples resemble medieval ones. They ardently cross themselves. Then the painter comes to decorate the convent ceiling, and he sees Sister Irene. This is the actress Barbara; I don't know her last name. Refined, slender, beautiful Barbara. I understand every image without the title cards. The way she is half-forced to model for him, then grows confused. Barbara renders it so delicately, she's so wonderfully refined. The prioress, striding about with her crosier, has found out something; the painter has to leave. And at the same time, Irene loses her pious strength bit by bit. Helpless, shining with love, she lets him carry her into his automobile. Then, in the big city, she becomes the most beautiful society lady. But her power of resistance is gone. Intoxicated with champagne, she embraces a new friend, a new love burgeons in her. Her husband receives an anonymous letter. These things have been depicted a thousand times, and they mesmerize you again, a thousand times. Jealousy eats its way into the poor painter—that infernal torment, which makes a man lonely, turns him into a murderous beast. He crumples up the anonymous letter, playacts, yet cannot deceive himself, waits until his misfortune is certain. No, not his misfortune; this has already struck him. He waits for the remedy, for the victims on whom he wishes to shatter himself. The two of them, Irene and her lover, are lost in the delirium of saying good-bye, embracing, kissing—O, unhappy painter. The young lover dies; the duel decides against him. The painter dreams: now everything is fine again. He approaches her, begging. Her disgust, dismay. She lucidly sees the beast, which has sated itself! She is his prey, which he has won, on which he intends to feast. She feels nothing but hatred. She weeps for the dead man. And so back to the convent.

A church niche contains a marble statue, which is unbelievably, excitingly alive. The church is dark, but the statue in the niche receives white sidelight, daylight; the illumination wakes it up, so dim, an unearthly white-gray. Why do the peasant women lie in front of it, staring at it? They know it's a column. But they think and feel in images. The world, nature also think in images, in forms, shapes. The column is no symbol, as the down-to-earth believe. It is—really Mary! In all churches, the columns are truly God; Mary. In Wilno, in front of the beautiful miracle-working Madonna, I felt it with the throngs. Nothing is more natural than the feelings of these naive people; I share their piety.

After passing Archediakonska Street with its crumbling ancient houses, the avenue opens out, an airplane buzzes overhead, and I stand on a hill. A lower part of town lies at its foot. The hill slopes down, green; chimneys smoke in the background. But to the left, a splendid, powerful, imposing edifice rises over the low, confused streets. It is shielded with merlons. Some of its windows are walled up. From the interior of the building, from its center, a strong round tower looms, carrying a repulsive iron superstructure. Dirty streets run alongside it, I can peer into a garret. This mighty structure is the old fortress, now a prison. I can't run down the slope like the boys.

A street, Grodska Street, leads me downward. Children play all around. The area becomes lively, very animated; I have wandered into a Jewish district. Houses are painted yellow and pink. An arch bends over the street, garish red; people live upstairs. Men, women, and children move to and fro. This is a gate that was talked up as beautiful. Oh, I know your game, you apostles of beauty, you woeful ones. I also see the dwelling on top of the arch, the people gazing out the window, the people in the neighboring houses! Shame upon shame. And someone dares to speak about the architectural beauty of the gate. Someday, I would like to visit Italy and Greece in order to see and expose the things that are loved by the infamous art lovers, the tender brutes, whose eyes must be opened. I feel a bitter joy upon seeing the dirty garish red, the whitewash on the artwork. Yes, that's what life looks like. The street runs down, narrow and arched, with dark cheap stores. An old water-carrier trots by, a crossbeam over his stooped shoulders; the buckets hang left and right. The neighborhood obviously has no water system. Men skulk along in rags; you can see the white skin of their legs and shoulders. Crooked streets run into the square below, by the fountain; the square is surrounded by fragile wooden houses, small grouty stone houses. Jews in dirty caftans wander back and forth, shrieking women; a scissors grinder is working. I enter one of the alleys. The tiny houses have only two floors or just one; some houses are painted red. Two high, mighty stone axes at the castle threaten all of them. I'm in back of the castle. The street becomes a dead end. I take another street. Once again, those shacklike houses: this street is named Krawiecka Street. Masses of kids. The ground is muddy. Ragged women lug babies. Another airplane roars overhead.

I circle toward the fortress, the castle, the prison. It stands on a hill, which carries brown stubble. Little boys play soccer on it with a small piece of a branch; they wear pants made of thin variegated calico. And now come loud shrieks of women. A cluster of people is approaching, people make way for them. A number of children dash ahead, an old earnest Jew in a caftan and skullcap powerfully strides ahead of the shrieking women. He doesn't look back at them, no one helps the women. Why don't they call the people; after all, the prison is nearby. Why do they let the women shriek helplessly, the old man must have done something to them. And now, the entire swarm trudges past me, the children like flies, the women shrieking horribly, helplessly. The man walks unconcerned. And now I see: the man has a rope, a strap backward over his shoulders. And on his back, he lugs—I see the man from behind—a long black box, a lightweight box. Ah, a coffin. That's what it is. This is a funeral. And this is a corpse, a child's corpse, a funeral of the poorest of the poor. The man lugs the coffin by a strap on his back. That's why the women are shrieking behind him, yelping, tearing their hair: the mother, the relatives, the keeners. Right behind them, a peasant woman, walking along the muddy sidewalk, enters an open gateway. She stations herself there, legs astraddle, pulls up the front of her skirt: a steaming jet of water

127

hits the stones between her feet, which instantly move further apart. The jet of urine shoots thickly from her skirts, as if from a robust horse.

The street gradually slopes up. Business in every dark vestibule. Many men smoke on the pavement. The gutter is limewashed; the air smells of disinfectants.

I come to a marketplace. Bright sunshine. Geese and chickens are in cages and wooden crates, they hiss and cackle. A throng of tattered men loaf about. A few have tied sacks to their bodies. A few have trousers that expose whole parts of their upper and lower thighs. Men in better clothes peddle, hawking old things, which they hold in their hands; one looks at the other. This is Duska Street. Patched top boots are for sale. The way a peasant woman carries a goose: the animal's head peers out from under her arm, its neck is wedged between her arms, she grips the yellow feet in her hand. Scores of children come running from the school: loosely swinging their books and notebooks on strings.

I scrutinize these children, and they scrutinize me; they are very anemic. Pale adult Jews go in their national costume, red beards, hollow, emaciated faces. Some people look enigmatic, terrifying. What rags the little girls wear. One girl, perhaps ten years old, wears a small white lambskin; a big red ribbon in her hair. But when she stands at the gutter, the wind comes, blows open her fur, and all she has on is a shirt and short panties. The big Jewish street running from the market is named Lubartowska Street. The Polish streets are moderately full, but this area is teeming. A wooden bridge crosses the water. Affluent merchants live on Lubartowska Street, which contains mediumsized and small shops. There is a dense heedless chaos of people running about; only a few focus sharply on the passersby. Men stand outside their stores; they and many others look very tough and strong. These are coldly calculating men, ruthlessly determined. But I also see the redheads, anemically pale and bright red; under their hair, they have bleak, woefully pleading eyes without brows.

The walls of the houses gape, have niches, recesses: these contain wooden booths and vendors. Many wagons rattle up the street into the village of Lubartow; they are driven by Jews huddling on top of crates and straw.

They drive past the crucifix that stands at the end of this street; I am told that German soldiers who died in combat lie underneath.

It's afternoon. Sleet begins falling. To the left, on the street, a huge wagon factory looms; the industrial building in the middle of the throng of peddlers. It used to be owned by a German; it burned down, was rebuilt. Poor women, with steaming pails in their hands, gather in the sleet outside this extensive structure: they are getting the hot waste water that runs out of pipes. Behind a green forecourt, the Jewish hospital. I go in, glance down the corridors, into the rooms. A red enamel plaque in the hallway offers thanks for "American aid." Someone has died: a woman's songlike wail resonates across the vestibule. The sleet becomes snow. The peddlers wait drearily in the dark shops, wait outside their doors. Toward the end of the street, they are building the great Jewish college, that of the Orthodox, a world yeshiva. The Catholic university is located on the other side of town, this Jewish one is here. It is meant for a thousand people, students and teachers.

Such are the provinces. The big city engages in politics; religion, a laggard, follows in the provinces.

I'm helpless; I look for someone who can supply explanations. On Lubartowska Street, I see a sign with Yiddish and Polish writing. I can tell it indicates an exhibit of paintings. And since several young men are standing around, I address them in German; they understand. I let them guide me about, and then they give me a young man to show me through Lublin. The paintings are part of a traveling show. Many have national subjects: old men, worshipers, prayer rooms; there are also sculptures. But only the subjects are national; the technique assimilates Western methods. My young guide is a Bundist, a Socialist; otherwise, he is horribly innocent. He's almost completely out of touch with realities; his only source of enlightenment is the daily newspaper. Smiling, he stands in front of the yeshiva:

"The Orthodox Jews are going to construct it. And once it's

done, we'll move in and turn it into a modern school or hold meetings."

I keep silent, I don't believe it. We walk to town. At the market, a peasant woman drives her little wagon up a precipitous street; it slides back on the wet ground. She whips; now it moves.

My young foolish companion picks me up and shows me what he knows. He takes me past the theater: they're playing Fall's operetta *Madame Pompadour*. Across the street, the Cistercian church is closed; my companion explains: "It's unusually high and it's according to the old system." I don't know what that means; but when I ask him, he comes out with more enigmas. The bishop lives near the cathedral, in a small house. I notice a beautiful modern building near Archediakonska Street; my companion says it's a school; before the war, it belonged to a French woman. He presents the hills that we pass: "Various big battles and wars took place on these hills, with gangs." An old house up there is caving in; only half is left. People were living there shortly before its collapse, and, the remaining half, lo and behold, is still inhabited. The corner house, whose timbering I peered into from above, used to be a church; then it sheltered the homeless; now, the clergy are constructing a residence for clergymen there. What do the axes on the fortress signify? "That was done as advertising for the city, hey."

He wants to take me to the old Jewish cemetery, which is world-famous. We walk through the slums. Huts sinking into the ground are homes for families. I can't believe that people live in some of these houses. But he laughs at me and demonstrates that they do. The area borders on open fields, quagmire. To the right, at the bridge, I see the meadows and the chimney: "Here you can get an overall vista."

The old cemetery. Two women shriek and clamor together when we are announced. They yell because the old groundskeeper, one woman's husband, isn't here, and now she scolds because he's not here, the jackass, and the other man is getting the money. Then a younger Jew in a caftan and skullcap guides us. We walk over mounds that rise strong and undulating. We are already walking across graves.

Much is sunken, overgrown; stone plaques emerge from the graves. The last funeral took place ninety-six years ago. At a spot where the hill sinks, the naive pious man points his stick: here, long ago, twelve pious Jews buried themselves rather than be forcibly baptized. Everywhere the thick high grass, the bushes, hiding the grass. A few headstones are isolated, most are in groups. Some stones, as in Wilno, have recesses: for supplicatory notes.

The guide, while frequently blowing his nose in his hand, earnestly tells us: "Here lie men who made the whole world tremble." Beautiful, richly ornamented stones loom here, animal pictures, symbols. He points at a grave that's off to the side: "Here lies a *kohen*. Every day that the sun shines, a little bird comes and sings its song. If it's driven away, it comes back."

A group of sages lie together, a rich man is among them: "He gave them money to study." The great Marshal Luria of Lublin has been lying here for three hundred fifty years: vicious hands knocked over his tombstone and dirtied it. The ancient fragments lie in the grass; a new stone was put up; it praises the dead man overexuberantly: he was a light of Israel, penned numerous Talmudic exegeses, was a saint. Colored stag ornaments. Grave plaques were removed to cover boggy spots on roads. On one very beautiful plaque, a bookcase containing books is opened, hewn very vividly into stone: Here lies an intelligent woman. A man named Rebbe Avrom Kashe was very holy. When he died and was being carried to his grave, someone yelled an insult at him along the way. The corpse thereupon sat up and asked for warm water to wash his hands. He was given some; he splashed it toward the house from which the shout had come, and the house fell to pieces.

We approach a high isolated grave. But the guide holds us back, places his stick on the ground: "The law requires that we remain at a distance of four cubits." This is Rebbe Jakob Pollack, he's been lying here for four hundred fifty years. The Jewish king-for-a-day of Poland rests amid a gaggle of graves; a crown carved into the stone, a naked human figure shooting an arrow. I stand before a new heap of rubble: "A rabbi gathers his ten disciples here." Two plaques touch; they are very beautiful: a mother and her daughter; the daughter has an eagle; two little birds perch with the mother.

The caretaker greets one tombstone very solemnly; this is a saint, who could see everything within a radius of four hundred leagues. But ultimately he saw so much filth that he asked God to let him see for only ten leagues around. And it came to pass. His name was Horwitz; he died over a century ago. Then there's the man who was nicknamed Ironmind. Why? When he looked at a tree, he could see precisely how many leaves it had. Another headstone is inscribed on both sides: the front is colorfully painted, the letters on the back look like Hebrew mirror writing. Initially, the stone had only one inscription, the colorful one in front. But one night, the other letters came forth from the stone of their own accord. They emerged overnight by themselves.

No one in this town has any time for me. One man spares a couple of minutes. A rich Volhynian sugar manufacturer named Jaroszynski was the donor of the university. It is supervised by the episcopate, which hires the professors, chooses the president. They've got three faculties. And no money. They're trying to become a public institution, but the other universities are opposed because the government would then have to subsidize this one too. The university is Catholic; but its statutes require only a Christian baptism.

As for the coexistence of the Polish and the Jewish people: During the Russian period, these two nations were on good terms. Then the Russians used the Jews against the Poles; that was the start of Polish anti-Semitism. In this city, social intercourse between the two nations is virtually nonexistent. The Orthodox Jews are powerful. They received the majority vote in the municipal elections. But the town council actually fell apart; it got into a conflict with the government because over half the councilmen spoke only Yiddish. The government demanded that at least the chairman speak Polish. But when he tried, all hell broke loose; and that was the last session.

132

I forge ahead to the railroad station. The street leading there is very long and flanked by small, mostly filthy houses, lots of shabby stores. I also find a factory. A modern bridge crosses a narrow muddy rivulet; I believe that this is the Bystrzyca, on which Lublin is located. An embankment is being built on one side of the rivulet; a trolley car is to take a shortcut into town. Big Polish peasants and workers: next to them, the dreadfully ragged Jews. The Poles in their fur caps and workers' caps, broad, calm, imperturbable, slow, often with sluggish, mournful faces. Some have a sly attentive, a shrewd jocular look; observant earnestness is preponderant. The Jews in this neighborhood are usually lively, attentive, bustling. They yell a lot; I often stumble upon quarreling groups. Often, I also run into special types. While dark color predominated in the Polish population of Warsaw (I think they have assimilated with the Jews), many Jews here have a very light skin, short pug noses with flaring nostrils, wide flat foreheads, short faces. If not for their costumes, I would take them for Polish peasants. I address an eighteen-year-old with mortar on his hat and shoulders, he tries to do business with me. He attended the old schools; his ignorance is horrifying. He asks me whether Belgium is near Vienna. But he is crafty. He wants to hear what I think about the whole world. He himself feels:

"God made the world, that's certain. Man made a house, that we know. A man has a father, his father also had a father, but ultimately? And what about the whole earth? I go by what my father and grandfather believed—may they rest in peace."

He is an utter rustic, curious—about everything at once, yet conservative and distrustful. Intelligence is ethnological; nations have different kinds of intelligence. The way of life dictates a few things that are part of intelligence. The Jews are generally said to be intelligent. The East European Jews are really sharp, you have to keep on your toes when you're with them, they delight in being polemical and superlogical. Formality is their element. But they intensely reject all outside things, and this is due to their seclusion. They reject, nor can they accept; they are blind; they lack insight into many things, many connections. This is something ungainly and quite rustic, rural. It sticks to them even after their "emancipation."

My foolish companion wants to show me the city again. He takes me to a small municipal museum. One room has lovely watercolors by Maryan Mokwa. A painting is titled "Sea Tempest"; my Parsifal nods: "You can see it." Another section of the museum has a nice natural-history collection: stuffed birds, fish, snails. Suddenly, Parsifal cries: "Oh, look, just look here, those are the bones of a dog." A skeleton. In regard to a human skeleton, he muses: "Was that a living person? . . . Really! . . . You don't say." He stands in front of flax: "This is extraordinarily worthwhile."

I wander into a meeting. The Polish speaker is a strong, thickset man; his brightly colored handkerchief hangs from his jacket pocket like a rooster's comb. Standing there, he puffs out his chest; it's very resonant. As he talks, his head tilts back slightly. His eyes are open, he speaks blindly across the tables. He hurls the words from his mouth with the tip of his tongue, with the muscles of his glottis and pharynx. His words explode. He relishes their sound-taste with his lips, with his ears, as he stands there, listening to himself: his hands, which are spread and propped on the table, his head with its open and nonseeing eyes lowered during the pauses, then tilting back proudly. His words—they tell me—are the words of a cautious, comfortable man.

That evening, at the hotel restaurant, some people from the theater sit at the next table. Two young women, a pale quiet one and a merry redhead. A big fat young man dotes on the merry one, they look good together. Then a blonde man with hair currycombed back; and behind the flowers, on the table, another man: I can only sense him. The currycombed blond leaves by himself. The couple remains, as do the invisible man behind the flowers and the pale elegiacal woman, who soon says goodnight. The easygoing man with prospects of embonpoint and his merry partner laugh and drink together. In the end, the young Falstaff jokes mirthfully with the waiter, and stands up with the red-cheeked woman, who looks as if she gets coquettish onstage. Plump and tired, she takes off with him. The invisible man remains behind the flowers.

It makes no sense waiting in this town. I take leave of my East European Parsifal. He tells me about a Polish man at a newspaper, he may know German or French. Just as I'm done packing, I receive a card from this man: "My dear sir! Will you give us his questions and we tomorrow give you answers." The last straw.

Once again, the sky, the vast heavens. But so nearby today, unhindered by anything, surging toward me from the cool night with a hurly-burly of stars. The nearness of these hosts of stars. They surge forward colossally; my face, my entire body feels them in the flesh.

# LWÓW/LEMBERG

*Today's states are the graves of the nations. States are col-
lective beasts.*

From provincial Lublin (it welcomed me with a tremendous
starry sky, it sees me off with a tremendous twinkling) to the
south, to East Galicia. Vast meadows and farm areas come
along. It's blissful sitting alone in the railroad car, with the
plains around me. Everything is mowed, haystacks stand there,
yellow-green piles. Small whitewashed houses with black gable
roofs emerge, bevies of houses with green moss roofs in the
sunshine. What friendly pictures. A clump of trees, tall, se-
cluded, shielding two wooden houses; dogs leap around between
the trunks. At times, the landscape is interspersed with lakes
and sloughs. One hour later, I ride through a dense deciduous
forest; it stands greenish-yellow, brown, and full. Dusky pines,
very young leaves nestle in the underbrush. These large forests
appear more and more often, dark massifs, interrupted by vast
stretches that contain only a few lone pines. The rare fields (the
forest is being cleared) are filled with red flames and blue smoke,
with weeds, roots, and branches. The train pounds loudly, the
noise of a horse galloping across stones.

How mysterious the countryside becomes. I travel across gigantic stretches, and the red flames jab out from all the fields,

which are haunted by the blue haze. Fairy-tale farm wagons
drive through the woods, loading up tree trunks. How wildly the
train sways. It slenderly zooms forward, sliding and shooting
from right to left. Hills, variegated heather. Nothing can stop
me from mistaking this for a German landscape. This is the
province of Saxony. I am traveling northward, going home. And
it arouses a joyous feeling in me, and I stare hard at the landscape for a long time, I recognize it. Oh, how good it feels. I'm
going home. Do I want to? Yes, I do. Soon I walk through my
streets, sit in my room. I see everything again. What a confused
landscape lies back there.

It's growing dark outside. My compartment is hot. Yesterday
at this time, I was walking through the streets of Lublin in a
frothy sleet, sitting in a school among cute chattering children.
And now I've got hold of the illusion: this is earth, this is earth;
where is there such a thing as Polish, Russian, German earth!
This is truly the same earth on which I grew up. Why should I
feel like a foreigner! When night comes, I will zoom in the train
through the darkness, and this will be the earth; and the air that
will whoosh by is the same as everywhere else. Moscow, New
York, Hindustan, Berlin, and we all have the same parents. The
sparks of the locomotives glow and whirl in the twilight. I can
see only the nearby verdure on the trees. The forests, near and
far, have turned black, the fields submerge in brownish black.
The light of my compartment lamp, its reflection dazzling in
the windowpane, hovers brighter and brighter over the whitish
sky with its murky streaks. We ride across a gigantic dark pla-
teau, we slice through roads. All colors, all colors have been
covered by the twilight. Something gray, an increasingly denser
gray, stretches outside, coalesces, vaguely brightened from
above. Now, black rows of leafy trees stride through the gray.
The glowing reflection of my compartment lamp shoots over
them. Next: lights, chimneys across the landscape. The train
creaks, cracks. Harsh arc lamps, wild wafting locomotive steam.
Freight trains carrying timber on the tracks; children shouting.
The fields are gone. When will I see them again? What will the
darkness do with them? The train grinds to a halt. Five minutes.
The train starts slowly, bounces, trembles, rolls. What has be-

come of my landscape, the fields? The reflection of the incandescent lamp thrones high, whitish yellow. And under it, behind it, outside, a steady grayish-black mass.

And now and now. My lamp reflection grows brighter and brighter in the window. The broad light-mass of my train carriage falls, flits outside across the fields; the transverse line of the window post runs across like a finger touching the fields. And now, as I stand up, an enormous shadow looms outside with a head and a cap. That's me. The shadow lies outside on the roads, flying brokenly over a bridge railing. I in the train and I outside. I recognize myself. My mood becomes mysterious, cheerful. Oh, the bright fiery sparks, marvelous. Deep-black field. And toward the sides, the large rectangles of shining train compartments break like spotlights into the darkness, rip them up momentarily, burrow tirelessly forward through the air and over the earth—a whoosh, a sinister being, a superstealthy being. The sparks shoot by horizontally. A maternally pregnant darkness lies far away, a heaviness, a soothed extinction of light from which a yellowish-red spot of light, the silhouette of a house, occasionally peeks out, like a sign, a faint voice. It's five-thirty. I reside inside the train, fenced in. Jaroslaw; Prezmysl is coming soon. And I will not see it, but I will feel it. How beautifully a city announces itself in the darkness, with fine dots of light, trembling stars.

The towns drift past. Now the entire carriage, with its baggage net, cushions, valises dangles out the window, wide and high, toward the distance, and is carried through the black land. The wall, this mirroring wall, is airy and transparent; sheaves and clusters of sparks are spraying through its fine texture. How the train zooms through the darkness.

And in the morning, as I walk through Lwów, along the large avenue that is now called Legionow Street, I keep breathing calmly. The muteness is gone; German newspapers are hawked. The weather is stark, sunny. Once again, I pass a Mickiewicz monument. An angel hangs grandiloquently on a column; the angel very unhappily descends the column with his halo. And leather goods stores, hat shops, stationery shops, big beautiful boutiques, broad avenues. My heart leaps. Lublin was dreadful: that poverty, that filth, those cramped conditions. And truly: there's a big bookstore, a whole window for the stray seekers, with German books. Even the silly pulp titles delight me. And music sheets come promptly: "When I see you, I have to cry," "Where d'ya get those beautiful blue eyes?" It's a homecoming. The heavy cavalry regiment of modern culture draws up: Dostoevsky, Shaw. I give them a wide berth and stick to the beautiful blue eyes. The Poles ruled this land even before the war. Galicia was the Polish Piedmont. The governors installed by Austria were Poles; the language of courts and administration was Polish. But the Austrian influence is usually strong.

This Galician city is altogether different from the cities of Congress Poland. The people are mellow and friendly: the inhabitants of Warsaw were rigid, drilled, in the Russian manner. Who could that red sandstone man be, sitting on a chair up there? "Aleksander Fredro," says the monument.[28] I hear the tiding, but I lack the knowledge. He must have died long ago, for he has no steel pen; instead, he clutches a quill, a goose feather, to write with. Sitting there, he looks meaningless, like a writer. I think: the goose quill would have been enough. He certainly didn't write with the chair he's sitting on. But I let the chair pass. The chair belongs to a writer, it's his organ like the monkey's tail. If all traits were hereditary, then the children of writers would certainly be born with tails or chairs attached to their tailbones. Music rings out across Mickiewicz Square. The blasting is amazingly un-Polish, bad. The stout kapellmeister parades in front of the military with his baton and silver ball; behind him, the brassy razzmatazz band. And the enfilade of uncharacteristic utilitarian buildings of the big city.

In the evening, along Legionow Street. Enormous profusion of light, the brightness of day. Further back, lamps stand high; you can't see their posts; lamp globes hang big and dense, clustering in a mass of light. Underneath, on this side of Legionow Street, the wide pavement teems with swarms of people in front of the radiant and fashionable shop windows. These are tall slender Poles, with young dark faces, wearing coats in modern style, pointed shoes. Over there, in the old Russian Poland, the

women were elegant, piquant; here, it's the men. And these
boutiques also display masses of menswear, very fine items.
Women walk by, soft and sweet, feminine; Austrian style. It's a
strange thing that I see: the Russians have created an active type
of woman, the Austrians this tamed, domestic pet, a prude in
furs. Other men behind them, other morals. Here, the men
flirt, ogle, and woo; adorn themselves, almost like women. They
play the cock of the walk. In Warsaw, the women stole about
like cats, acting like wild game; the erotic atmosphere was more
heavily charged; man fought against woman. Playacting right
and left, a strangely dislocated reality. Man as creator of nature.
Again, on a different level, the victorious spirit.

Confusion, shoving on Legionow Street. Two lines of people,
a drive belt, looping around at the dark end of the street. The
profusion of light gathers the people, and the wide rows float
straight ahead, looking, looking for one another, groping for
one another with their eyes, sucking the liveliness apart. The
joy of gazing, ocular pleasure: the excitement flows with looks
and pours over to the other side. These people float on a real
current of tension; every newcomer loses his personality, supports the current.

Jews in groups and troops, in black and brown velvet hats,
which are stiff-brimmed, often creased, often merely dented;
this is the Baroque *shtreyml*. Most of the Jews walking here are
Europeanized. They speak their language loudly. Elderly Jews
hold their hands behind their backs, shuffle, slightly bent,
through the torrent of people. Sometimes, one of them halts,
gesticulating; he is pushed along. The faces of nearly all the
people walking here are well nourished.

Why do I suddenly think of Warsaw? I feel melancholy. Yes,
indeed: what sort of being is this that I carry around in my
clothes, on my shoes; what a changing creature. I think of the
churches in Warsaw, the way the women and men sat there; I
think of Wilno, where an old woman sat in front of a church
from dawn to dusk; she was blind, she had been placed there;
and now she sang; her singing wasn't all that bad. Peasants came
bustling, in colorful neckerchiefs; one of them carried squealing
piglets in a bag over his shoulders; no one paid him any heed.

And then the shabby women nursing their babies as they plod along.

Are there markets here? So far, I've only been a calm observer in Poland. I was all eyes and ears and a silent backdrop. Very seldom have I felt an urge to form an opinion. Whenever someone asked me, "How do you like this or that?" I couldn't answer: I was depressed by the emptiness that this question aroused in me. Now I walk here, and I could and I would, I almost have to, reply. These Europeans, these half and whole ones, these horribly colorless ones. That's what I have to reply. I'm almost scared that there'll be cafés here, people will make literature, they'll talk about Tagore.

And one hour later, my fears come true. I stand outside a door and see: Café Warszawa. My doom leaves me no peace; I have to go in. Bedizened women stand at the revolving door; two elderly ladies sit next to them at the counter. A girl reaches for my coat collar, pins a green number on me: 494. I'm told in German: they're collecting for patients and convalescents. I pay. And think sullenly: "You'd do better to collect for yourselves."

This is a large café. In the center, among chatting people, a band is concertizing; at the right, stairs lead to a reading room. Oh, if only I didn't have to come here. I really don't want to. I already feel such deep deep despair. How I hate this silly babbling music. Maybe I would have found it lovable this morning. At the door, the girls, with red blouses and bobbed hair, fussing, excited: empty foliage. Now, an elderly gentleman and a lady sit down at my table. He puts on a pince-nez, reads a newspaper. She makes the large brilliants sway in her ears. He informs her over the newspaper that one hundred twenty zlotys is a cheap price to pay for the thing; incidentally, the deadline's been extended, and it would cost two hundred somewhere else. The glaring light bulbs on the ceiling with their glass shades were made to give these people light in order to illuminate their togetherness. For them, coal, compressed stacks of ancient wood, are thrown under huge boilers, burned. What becomes of the water over the fire? It bubbles, evaporates as fleeting steam; the steam expands. Whirling dynamos stand in factory halls, they discharge mysterious electric power, it is conducted by wires, the energy shoots along within spit seconds, here, into this café, it becomes light—for what, for whom? For this here. Ah, it delights them, I don't wish to be unfair. They move, these human animals, they breathe, they die in light. I don't want to make a mountain out of a molehill, out of trivia. Are these trivia?

At my table, the man with the pince-nez puts down his newspaper, counts through the sheaf of money that his lady with the brilliants gave him. The band has launched into a sweet, very old Viennese waltz. If I could see them trembling, enjoying themselves. They sit side by side, matter-of-factly. The money doesn't delight him. He clutches it, has it, stows it away. He is coldness, hardness, resolution, rigidity. How proud were the things I saw among the poor scorned Hasidim, with the man who sat in his tabernacle in the dark Warsaw courtyard, speaking about the food that was something spiritual: "You think you eat and that is all?"

My goodness, I don't like these people here. There's nothing to them. I'm with the poor on the outskirts of Lublin. With the peasant who lay stretched out like a cross, squeezing his face into the floor of the cathedral of Warsaw. With the Catholics who have set up their university in Lublin, and the Orthodox Jews who are building their college, their bulwark nearby, on Lubartowska Street. Now the two girls by the revolving door are leaving; so is the blond in the long white scarf. And as she passes me—a fur trimming on the swaying hem of her skirt, a snippy young face—I see that God's infinitely vast life is flowing through her limbs, moving her eyes. But neither she nor the others know anything about it. They vend white and red slips of paper from table to table. I don't want any. I've had it. I'm resolute. The Viennese waltz, over and over. I don't want any. The customers sing along: do they have souls, hearts? Oh dread, oh horror in the world.

You, you in me, forever eluding me, forever reemerging in me, what are you seeking here? How unworthy of you this place is. Why do you stray so much, you mute subjugated self—you already sensed everything, knew everything early on, and yet you always do the wrong thing. You know about greatness, mystery, and you always seek it in life and death. Where are you, how you shut yourself off! What are you but a tiny flicker that I inherited and have to protect with both my hands to keep it from going out. You keep seeping through my thoughts like grease through paper. You punish me, but not enough—even though I now suffer, not enough. How much, how much, how much humble pie I must eat.

I have no tears. If I had any, they would run away from me now.

The restaurants are Austrian. The roast beef that I'm served at lunch is tough in a Western European way. In the Russian district, a meal was a festivity with music. Here, people fill their faces matter-of-factly in order to fill their bellies. They read newspapers, spoon in hand, eat feuilletons.

The Jews of Legionow Street have a devastating effect on me. Here I find the tense lively faces, the searching looks, the listening—the style of higglers, hagglers, hucksters, hustlers. They stand there, whole throngs, whole troops—an entire regiment. This street is a horror. It challenges you like a single black market. Anyone who goes through it knows what trading air is, what unproductive labor is. And what the nasty words "leech" and "parasite" signify. No one who cares about this nation will try to mince matters here. The sheer existence of this street shows how twisted, unfortunate, and dangerous the Jewish economic situation is for the Jews and their milieu. These are the effects of centuries of politics. A cul-de-sac. A physical and economic degeneration caused by others. It is the duty of the rulers to get the Jews out of this predicament. The sight of this horrible Jewish street must be carved into their brains. And the people who drove them here should beat their breasts.

I see men in the entrance halls. Two men glare at each other, upset, gesticulating, scolding. A group forms at the gutter, these men have modern spats, fine canes; one of them, amid approval from the others, is scornfully dressing down a stooped elderly man in a caftan covered with mortar fragments; he's unable to answer. Several men, a few with red beards, cluster outside the Hotel Bristol.

143

Polish priests on the street: blurred faces, coarse and rustic, good-natured. Aristocrats and patricians: genteel types, noble features, straight noses, high broad foreheads, smoothly parted hair, small mustaches, dark eloquent eyes full of mournful passivity. Other men are sanguine, cunning, base, gawky, with large coarse builds. Some are decidedly sullen; gloomy; eye motions that unwittingly lament, accuse. I repeatedly see a priest in a dragging black coat and a stiff black hat; he is oldish, skinny, skeptical, distrustful, glancing right and left, a misanthrope.

Green soldiers keep marching by. Steel helmets, their rifles slanting across one shoulder. Autumn strides in with gigantic steps. Lots of rain; the trees are bare.

This city is named Lwów, Löwenberg, Lemberg, "lion's mountain," the mountain of Leo, the son of Danillo, a Ruthenian duke. He lived in the thirteenth century. The Tartars were plundering the land. After one hundred years, Kazimierz, the great Polish king, captured the fortress, destroyed it, and built today's Lwów nearby. The city became completely Polish. It grew into a center of nations. This is obvious to anybody walking these streets. At the great Ring Square, there is a Russian street, an Armenian street. At the beautiful square itself, with a splendid town hall in the middle, I come upon the house of a Venetian envoy among the elegant ancient mansions. This city was an emporium, a distribution point between east and west. Sephardic Jews came here from the south and settled here. Then came German colonists and other nations, pursuing wares and profits. A Walachian church stands at the end of the Russian street. The city still has three archbishops. One is the Armenian; he's so poor that he's supported by rich descendants of Armenians, Polonized landowners. Then, besides the Roman Catholic archbishop, there is also the Greek Catholic one, for the Ruthenians or Ukrainians. And that's a whole other story. Several years ago, the sick archbishop, not very political himself, was in America, where he supposedly agitated against the Poles. When he returned some two years ago, heading toward Lwów, his railroad car was rerouted to Warsaw. After negotiations with the Vatican, he had to sign a declaration of loyalty.

Kazimierz the Great destroyed Danillo's fortress and built this new Lwów. But the Ukrainians refuse to recognize the Polish reality of Lwów. The Ukrainian nation lives torn apart between Russians and Poles, and peace is nowhere in sight. I speak with men in the city. I get the impression of a covert, but highly intense, struggle between nations. There are Ukrainian newspapers in the city; one is published at Ring Square. When I happen to pick up an issue in its Russian letters (they derive from Ancient Greek; I can read most of them; behind them is ancient Byzantium; every letter must remind them of Constantinople), when I look at the newspaper, a whole column is—blank. The space for the editorial is white: censorship, as in wartime. An empty column, which is enormously revealing. I speak with several Ukrainians. They are very fond of German culture and Germany. But many Ukrainians disgorge a terrible, blind, numb hatred, an entirely animal hatred of the Poles. The simple ones strike me as having more of a calm sense of alienation toward the Poles. The educated ones have the feeling of an oppressed nation; they try to arouse a national sense by way of culture. I can't check anything that they tell me. Some time ago, a Polish head of state was assassinated on Legionow Street. A Jew was arrested. The Ukrainians claim that the killer was a Ukrainian. I believe that they are treated severely, and that they oppose the Polish state secretly or openly. Many of them are in prison, I'm told, the ones with the best minds are in exile. Some of the Ukrainians I meet are calm slow men with sharp smooth faces, black eyes, smooth black hair. Others have full brown beards. They make an upright, rustic impression, are restrained. Lwów is a lively modern Western town, its streets are bustling and peaceful. And yet all at once, I am confronted with something bizarre. This city lies in the arms of two adversaries, who are struggling for it. Hostility and violence lurk underground and in the background. The surrounding province, Eastern Galicia, supposedly has few Poles; the officialdom and the military are Polish, the people Ukrainian, villages and towns also Jewish. The government is settling Polish colonizers in the countryside, soldiers, invalids. Their job is to Polonize. But they are small in number and feel unhappy in a foreign place. And that, I am told, is why the Poles do not want a Ukrainian university in Lwów: they fear a Ukrainian inundation of the city. An inundation that the Ukrainians believe will come anyway. This is secret and open warfare, worse than Ireland's earlier war against England. For here, demarcation lines cannot be drawn between countries and nations; they overlap. Furthermore, the Ukrainians are only just starting to awaken their national consciousness in the struggle, and the Polish are trying to weaken or even negate it, thus provoking the rage and pain of the Ukrainians.

The Ukrainians were already fighting against the Poles during the Austrian period. Count Potocki, the Austrian governor, was assassinated here in 1911. I am shown the old gubernatorial mansion on a rampartlike rise behind trees. Potocki was wearing the Golden Fleece at his death. The assassin, a Ukrainian student, was caught. But Potocki's successor was shrewd, he indicated that they should let the prisoner go. The man's still alive, in America. Like the Irish, the Ukrainians, I'm told, depend on American money.

At the end of the war, they fought against Poland for nine months, but to no avail. Then Poland was mandated by the peace conference to administer the autonomous country provisionally. The population was to decide for itself later on. But the plebiscite has never been held. In 1923, the conference of ambassadors simply awarded Eastern Galicia to Poland. There is a Polish law that grants self-administration within certain limits to a few East Galician voivodeships, including Lwów. But even this law, they complain, exists only on paper. I remember the warning expressed by the sick editor huddling in his armchair in Warsaw: "Don't listen to the minorities. They find fault with everything."

I remember what I heard in Warsaw from the very sober, very intelligent Polish politician. His hands were on the table, and he shook his head: "There are demands of daily life and there are speeches in Parliament. Here, they carry on about autonomy and lofty issues. But at home, things look different. Roads have to be built, swamps drained." Now I'm "at home." And I hear the same things that are said in Parliament. And, I would

think, the Russians spoke no differently when they sat in Warsaw and the Poles were under their fist: "We have to build railroads, we have to prevent the Poles from ruining themselves."
Occupation, and this looks the same: being oppressed, a
stranger in your own country (I feel it sharply as I wander about
here)—those are the worst things possible. Freedom is the most
necessary "daily life"! Freedom is not a political catchword, it's
as real and necessary as the air in which people have to live, and
it's more important than highways and dried swamps. Enslaved
people and those who feel enslaved are moribund people, suf-
focating people; they have no use for highways.

The Poles know all this from their own history. They know it
and—are prevented, as I must believe, from knowing it fully.

A Ukrainian national museum stands on Mochnatzki Street,
a simple building, behind a front yard. The Greek Catholic
archbishop endowed it before the war. It contains lots of religious art. Pictures of saints, liturgical vestments, church chandeliers. A Last Judgment painted on a wooden panel, with
masses of naive figures. An Old Slavonic Bible. Icons with gold
grounds and marvelously lovely and severe-looking women. The
faces of the saints are stereotyped, they have big dead eyes.
Variegated Huzulian chandeliers made of wood hang from the
ceiling. There are ancient kilims. Is the art of weaving these
rugs Polish? No: it came from the Orient with the Tartars. Dif-
ferences between ancient Russian and Ukrainian painting are
pointed out to me; I don't see them, or else they don't strike me
as major. I understand that the Ukrainians want to set themselves off against the Russians, too; supposedly, Russian paintings are more detailed, Ukrainian paintings simpler. Most of this
old religious art is tempera on wood. There is also a small exhibit
of modern Ukrainian painting: graphics, silhouettes with ar-
chaic features, delicate Tatra landscapes.

The city has a Ukrainian public high school dating from the
Austrian period. But all minds keep focusing on the Ukrainian
university in Lwów. The Ukrainians won't let their sons study
in Lwów so as not to create a precedent. There used to be a
secret Ukrainian university here: it collapsed under the perse-

cutions. There was one in Prague, where émigrés reside; but now it's gone. A plan was developed to attach a Ukrainian annex to the Polish university in Cracow. But the Ukrainians didn't care for that; they would feel torn away from their nation, which supports them; the Ukrainian professors in exile rejected the idea. In Geneva, the Polish foreign minister promised there'd be a Ukrainian university here, but then he had to cross out those lines in the protocol; Polish protest demonstrations were threatened in Lwów. That's how irreconcilable the two nations are with each other.

I travel out to the countryside, see these Ukrainian men, women, their children. An extraordinarily robust breed, rich in anthropological types. The families have many children. Masses of dwarf farms and the tendency to proletarianize. They occupy the land; they also form the majority over Poles and Jews in a number of cities, such as Stanislav, Kolomya, Drohobycz. Poles own the latifundia. They usually don't work the soil themselves, they farm it out: these leases, I am told, are now being done away with. The percentage of Ukrainian intellectuals is tiny, but the sons of farmers have a powerful drive for education. Their priests are socially radical and politically nationalistic. The clergy is the vanguard of the political movement, just as the Polish clergy was. "What is your religion?" Greek Uniate. Its rites are Greek, just like in the Russian Church: the mass, the chanting are in Church Slavonic, the sermon is in Ukrainian. They recognize the pope, follow the Catholic dogma. Striving to put their nation on its feet, they are battling for their school system. A West European has a hard time fully understanding such a young national era, in which schools are set up as an organ of the people.

I visit a private Ukrainian middle school in a small town. It has seven grades, two hundred thirty pupils, a small percentage of them girls. "Who are the men with whom you are educating your children as Ukrainians?" The teachers (unlike the Poles, they speak a surprisingly good German and are well informed about German conditions)—the teachers list: Kotlyarevski, an epic poet who lived during the late eighteenth century; a poet named Taras Shevchenko; a polymath named Ivan Franko.

Along with Polish and Polish history (a portrait of the current Polish president hangs on the wall), they teach national history in order to arouse a national awareness. A National Pedagogical Association stretches its net across the whole of Eastern Galicia.

A bizarre Little Russian/Ukrainian group, a mountain people, lives in the southeastern corner of Galicia: the Huzuls. The weather is bad, I can't make up my mind to go there. Here, in the central part of Eastern Galicia and in Lwów, people tell me and show me a lot about them. Whatever the Huzuls produce is eagerly sought. Later on, I see a colossal collection at Lwów's Royal Dzieduszycki Museum, and a few things at the Ukrainian Museum. Also, in Lwów, a private collector, a perfect simpleton, shows me his many fine pieces. There are Huzulian ceramics, weapons, musical instruments, wood carvings, embroideries, weaves, furnishings, toys. This mountain tribe possesses unbelievable manual skill and an original sense of form. Their customs supposedly have a lot of "pagan" elements. Astonishing their inventiveness in silhouettes, in painted Easter eggs. The war brought a lot of changes to them too; they came into contact with modern civilization, their specific character has blurred.

I take a slow walk with one of these clumsy earnest fateful Ukrainians. He tells me: "My nation's in a bad way. It's chiefly the fault of the good soil. It yields too much. . . . A poor soil, a Nordic soil, where life's a hard struggle, produces harder people, faster, more decisive, more determined people." Some people want to get to the soil, others want to get away from it.

The Ukrainians have beautiful and extremely odd churches. I come upon two churches in Drohobycz, a small church and one that I'm told is hundreds of years old. Legend has it that this church originally stood in the southern Ukraine, but it was taken down and transported here piecemeal on wagons, probably in return for petroleum. The brownish-black wooden building is extraordinarily beautiful; it stands in the southern part of the town, completely out in the open. I believe these people when they tell me that some Americans offered to buy the entire building.

Three towers jut out with onion domes, made entirely of bent wood. These towers and flat roofs look just like pagodas. At the base, a wooden gallery runs all around the structure. Everything is covered with greenish wooden bricks. A detached bell tower with an onion tip stands next to the church. Inside the smaller church, the back of the altar, the *ikonostas*, is covered with a painting of the apostles and the sufferings of Christ. The barn-like room has no pews; there are many crosses and candles on the shabby walls.

Eastern Galicia is in Polish hands. The Ukrainian nation feels wrenched apart. The irredenta is within easy reach. Pilsudski was intent on untying the knot, absorbing the entire Ukraine into Poland; but his plan failed. Now, across the border, Russia has a Ukrainian Soviet Republic, a fragment, calling for national completion. The Ukrainians I talk to want their motherland, but: "Our land across the border is in the grip of Soviet Russia. The Ukrainians are oppressed on both sides. The Bolsheviks likewise refuse to allow the country to rule itself." In Russia, the "proletarian nation" has emerged. The economic era has placed this type—a new type of nation—straight across the national boundaries.

Assimilate the Ukrainians, White Russians, Lithuanians, Jews, Germans—Poland can't do it. It's bitten off more than it can chew. America manages to assimilate, it's an open basin. The masses easily pour in, American civilization is large and enviable. Here, the rural population is uneducated to the point of illiteracy; the urban education is narrow with sharp national accents, and a powerful and rigid Catholicism.

Upon viewing the schools and hearing everything, I feel dejected. The boys and girls learn Ukrainian history. I have seen them learning Jewish history in the Jewish schools, Polish history in the Polish schools, German history in the German schools. There's something gruesome about today's nationalism. I lose all desire to advocate the freedom of nations. I lose all desire to comfort and threaten with "borders," which have a "tyrant's power," where I see the tyranny of nationalism. They sit here in the schools, Ukrainians, Jews, White Russians, and whoever else. Their nations are torn apart. They are not permitted to develop as they wish. And now everything is twisted and wrong. They close themselves off, are spiritually overheated. And obsessed, obsessed. What a horrible misfortune from one source, a thousand misfortunes from one. Instead of freedom, we see struggle and passion. Oh, all the hundred little languages! And history. I know how "history" is taught: megalomania is coupled with ignorance. I know how "freedom" is taught: with hatred toward the neighbor. National consciousness, national unconsciousness. However, religions still exist that do not ask about "nation," about "state," and they have a different kind of community. How blind they become, how terribly they exaggerate and cut themselves off, these nations, all of them chasing after the same Western goods. National communities are not the only kind. I will not, I shall not forget them. This is insolence and arrogance—what people call a national community, to be blindly placed above anything else. The freedom that is preached is changed by the manner in which it is preached, becoming hostile toward other equally important freedoms. I don't like the nation for its own sake. What can a body do with bad blood?

One shouldn't hide the facts: nations are torn apart by a lot of things, and these things are other important communities. I've seen masses of workers marching in the streets of Berlin. And the banner they carried was the hammer and sickle, the insignia of Soviet Russia. Their entire enthusiasm, their entire love of homeland, their entire patriotism was—Soviet Russia. For several decades, Greece glowed for intellectuals as the land of the soul, as a true and genuine homeland. And what is the homeland of true Christians?

Who will gush over a nation—one is forced to say it—and not prefer turning his back on it today rather than tomorrow, if it practices slavery, if it does not do justice, if the people there know each other only in order to climb over each other. One loves a nation and a country for the sake of their values. State patriotism, which Western and Eastern European governments demand from their masses, their subjects, is barbarity. Today's states are random entities, hardly expedient ones. Who can enthuse over them? If a machine is useless, we smash it and make a new one. Today's states are the graves of nations.

Did the Poles intend to establish this state? No. Their limbs were found scattered. They were a nation. They loved one another. They were drawn to one another. They were proud of themselves and their parents and grandparents. They wished to reveal their pride, to reveal themselves, the way people do. Their hearts and souls yearned for the state. Now they have a state, and it poisons their nationhood. The border strikes back at them. They have reached out beyond themselves. Like a revolutionary who, upon attaining power, instantly becomes a tyrant. They fail to realize that during their oppression, life went on, and that on the other side, and on all sides, and among them, nations have been living and existing, the limbs of scattered masses that are drawn to one another because they love one another, because they are one people, because they are proud and wish to reveal themselves, the way human beings do. Woeful inventions—today's big states with their greed for expansion.

A primeval phantasmagoria survives here and everywhere. The period of uninterrupted struggle against beasts went on for a tremendously long time and ended not that long ago. The insincts of that period still exist. But the beasts do not. Now, instinct spends its fury in a different way, it creates beasts. Collective feeling and fear of beasts are permanently at loggerheads. Yesterday's necessities are now phantasmagoria and delirium. We live in a period of collective fear of beasts. States are collective beasts.

But what a hard time Poland of all countries has; I want to think about today. Poland was subjugated for a century. It survived because of its sense of togetherness. Now—understandable, despite everything—it shows a national hypersensitivity. It is entirely like a man who has had an accident and now suffers from a neurosis brought on by fear. And yet Poland of all countries, afflicted with minorities, economic misery, strong neighbors, must find intelligent and modern solutions in order to achieve stability. Otherwise Poland will never become stable.

Historical memories easily turn into delusions. What a tremendous mass of dangerous memories lurks in every European state. A dreadful number in Poland. But Poland's neighbors also have memories. Alliances are good, geography is better. Russia is a neighbor. A natural symbiosis of nations must commence here, in better and looser forms than today.

I return to the streets of Lwów. Here I find stone witnesses to the struggle of the Poles and the Ukrainians. These are—Jewish ruins. In 1918, with the vast collapse of the Central Powers, the Ukrainians marched in, proclaimed the autonomy of the Ukraine. The blue-and-white flag waved on the town hall of Lwów. The Ukrainians wanted a union from Eastern Galicia all the way to Odessa. The dictator was Petrushevich. The Ukrainians ran through Lwów, drove in cars; but Poles lodged themselves at the railroad station and the high school, first a few Poles, then many. Eventually, the Poles occupied one half of the city, all the way to the main post office; the Ukrainians the other half. Now the Ukrainians opened the prisons; the Polish convicts joined the Poles, got weapons from them. The Ukrainians were defeated, the Poles marched in.

I see the post office as I walk along Copernicus Street, a narrow street; the building is new, a huge modern structure, which they are only just moving into; it is built on the ruins of the old destroyed edifice. After the retreat of the Ukrainians came the event that made this fighting renowned: the Polish attack on the Jewish section of Lwów during the second half of November. The Lwów Pogrom charged ahead, murdering some seventy Jews, looting, burning countless Jewish homes to ashes. The Jews did not form a war party, they did not interfere with the Ukrainian-Polish debate. Presumably, they argued, the Jews would be badly off no matter who won. I am told that they stayed out of it completely. That was precisely why both sides, Poles and Ukrainians, spread anxious, hateful, alarming rumors about them. And when the Poles had carried the day, they were told about anti-Polish hatred in the urban population. The city was at war, and the Poles did what troops did dozens of times to partisan civilians. They struck. Revenge for their sufferings, a desire to loot—these things are always in the blood of troops that have no solid leadership, that are promiscuously thrown together, the way these Poles were. The mass of corpses rests at the Jewish cemetery. You can see the graves. But a further monument is visible in the city, and no more horrifying and disturbing monument could be put up anywhere: the torched houses. They still stand as they did back then, after the burning and looting. Lwów has a fire department. I ask an inhabitant where the fire department was when this district was in flames—

"I could see a fire behind the theater, on Legionow Street, and I headed toward the theater. Processions of firemen were standing there. At the market and further behind it, a house was blazing away. The flames were inside the house, leaping through the window. It looked like a stage play when a backdrop is lit from behind with smoke. You could already see the looting. At the northern end of St. Mary's Square, I ran into a railroad worker, he was carrying three fur coats. He met a man and a woman and gave them two of the coats. When a second man came over, he gave him the third coat and said he'd go get himself another. When I saw the fire behind the theater, I was amazed, I couldn't understand what was going on: the firemen were standing here, and a fire was burning over there. Finally, I started talking to a couple of firemen. They said: 'Yeah, sure we'd go over and put the fire out, but how can we? There's no way. Those guys over there have guns and they shoot at anyone who approaches. What should we do? The firemen'll be risking their own lives if they get any closer.' "

It was war, a bestial state of nature.

Legionow Street, a teeming thoroughfare, runs here. During this late afternoon, I glance at the lovely broad center promenade. A fantastic equestrian monument looms between the rows of trees.

The monument and the domed structure of the theater make the promenade look like a boulevard in a royal residence. For several minutes I remain under a tree on the promenade. The tree is full of yellow leaves; they're dry, shriveled, and curled up, fluttering on stems. The wind isn't strong, it can't blow them off as yet. And now the leaves turn in the air, whirring, waving, whirling, writhing, wrenching on the small stems. Now and then, a leaf finds peace, landing gently on the ground. Huge swarms of crows come from aloft. Thousands of shrieking creatures zoom down, break up into groups, circle over one another, spiral upward. Sometimes, they vanish from sight, then they swirl again over the promenade. The air becomes pitch-black, they emit violent shrieks. As they swarm up in a colossal flock, they look like vermin—they approach me so densely, so frighteningly. And if one creature leaves the others and comes even closer, I don't see the crow. This creature with splayed wings, black, blending instantly into the flock, zooming down from the dusky sky, is an eerie apparition, sheer animal, something living, moving, approaching, attacking, dangerous. Who has sent it out against me? Now, hundreds of them float next to one another, their black bodies like a transparent gelatin. They rise and fall in masses. Few people on the promenade look up.

I pass the theater; there's a marketplace to its right. And I approach the dreadful memorial to the fighting and frenzy of 1918. Behind the city theater, behind Legionow Street, that well-paved, well-groomed avenue with its elegant boutiques, monuments, cars, electric arc lights, hotels—a swamp begins. My boots are caked with mud. This, with its teeming mass of shopkeepers, small shopkeepers, smallest shopkeepers, loafers, *shnorrers* [moochers], is the Jewish quarter. Krakowski Square stretches out; it's full of wooden shacks. The right side is occupied by an imposing white mansion with huge bow windows. Stairs lead up to the entrance. And across from it, the first ruins. A ravaged house next to a one-story brick house has caved in. Fire or other violence has razed it down to its red foundation walls; mortar and rubble lie between them. The upper part of the neighboring house is wrecked; the shops on the ground floor are still inhabited. Two surviving houses and another woeful house with a shattered upper floor. Huge crossbeams are implanted in the flanks of several houses, preventing them from collapsing. I stumble upon a narrow two-story house; its whole interior burned up six years ago. Its façade is cracked, it bares its shattered panes like dying eyes. All this is being left to decay in the open air. The owners weren't compensated for damages; so they won't pay to have their properties torn down; and why

155

tear down if you can't build. Miry, littered alleys run into the marketplace. Their ancient gloomy wretched houses are inhabited by people, chockablock. But now another house has fallen to wrack and ruin, shattered, burst, gaping with tatters of particolored wallpaper, wooden floors, ceiling remnants. One ruin slopes down: it slides as elemental as a glacier with its black moraine; that was an entire group of houses. Cheap stores have been planted in front amid the refuse. There's a Smocia Street, just as in Warsaw. Burned ruins sink into the ground on either side. A gigantic rubble heap—it used to be a mansion—was crudely surrounded with a fence; the room caverns gape toward the street. But at one point, the fence is broken, I see beggars and their children entering with sacks on their shoulders, climbing up the rubble hill, poking about with sticks, still hunting after six years. Paper, stone debris roll down the hill. A lone house has survived; then, two street corners face one another, former corners. These are wild horrifying masses of ruins, with the exposed innards of houses. These house corners have crumbled down to their very feet. And horrible, across the street, separated by the roadway, a cave-in, as if a bombardment had raged. Without a fence, all its junk, dust, morass, rubble empty into the street as if the bomb had only just struck. This house, an open house grave, serves as a garbage dump for the neighboring streets; they come, women and children, and pour out refuse. I stand in the marketplace. Bosnika Street—rubble heaps, rubble heaps. Jews go about everywhere, in European clothing or—an exotic breed—in black smocks with colossally curled earlocks, their bearded faces jutting self-assuredly, their chins thrust out, belts around their waists.

Thus the three nations live together, side by side, in Lwów: Poles, dominating the city, attentive, lively, the owners; Jews, disunited, preoccupied, and aloof, or distrustful, defensive, bustling, lively, alert; Ukrainians, invisible, soundless here and there, restrained, irascible, dangerous, grieving, surrounded by the tension of conspirators and insurgents.

Of the two hundred fifty thousand inhabitants in this city, eighty thousand are Jews.

"Why do they speak Polish and not Yiddish? Why is the Jewish newspaper published in Polish?"

"Jews are very Polish here. They start learning Polish as infants. They don't believe in the cultural significance of Yiddish. Hebrew is not spoken. That's why Polish is the language of the Jewish intelligentsia and upper classes."

There is a modern Jewish school association. The characteristic type of school in this area is the Utraquistic school: Polish language in the general subjects, Hebrew in Jewish history and literature. There are two such high schools for boys and one for girls, licensed years ago. An all-Hebrew high school exists, not officially recognized.

The pogrom of 1918 held up a strong assimilation. The Zionists took over the leadership here. I am informed that Jewish nationalism is not Zionism. The Zionists exist and have their organization; they're elected to defend Jews in the Sejm. The Orthodox Jews have not yet organized themselves as in Congress Poland; and they're also economically weak. There's a very large proletariat here; it goes "into the streets" without a specific goal.

I peer into a small Jewish hotel. The waiter, or the man who passes himself off as one, carries a tray with a cup of coffee and a glass of water on it. He heads toward a gentleman—the owner, no doubt—asks him something, points to the tray. The man reaches into his pocket, fishes out two keys, plus a handkerchief. Then he climbs deeper, rummages up the sugar from the bottom of his pocket and hands the waiter two lumps.

Someone tells me: there are people living in the Jewish district who have never come into the "new city." I'm held up by a bizarre vehicle: it's driven by a red-bearded Jew; he's arguing with a gigantic Jew sitting behind him at the other end of the wagon. Between them, a peasant woman with a brown cap and a simple face sits mutely. I find that some of the faces I encounter here have a nobler and more intelligent cast than elsewhere. Peasants toting sacks wander amid the Jews: buying and selling; the women sit off to the side in the wagons.

I look for the nation in their prayer houses. I want to visit the great "Temple"; behind the market, I stumble upon a simple whitewashed house, with a man in a prayer shawl standing at the door. I descend a few steps: a large rectangular room full of benches, full of men in hats, with or without prayer shawls. A very shrill quavering voice sings in Hebrew. At the center of the room, the *bimah*. Hats and *shtreymls* hanging on the iron bars of the fence; an agitating bustle in the room. Boys run up and down the steps of the *bimah*. The wall bears a series of evenly spaced paintings: landscapes. An old man with a book wanders along the corridor, praying, all the way to the door; then he runs into someone; they exchange greetings; he returns, murmuring, with his tattered book. Meanwhile, the chanting on the *bimah* continues; soon it stops; and then it resumes quite suddenly. Behind the small barred windows, there seems to be an area for women, but I see no women. There are many other prayer rooms on the same street. A marvelous sight at one corner: three boys coming up through the morass, ten to twelve years old, in long, black, not very clean coats, black skullcaps; full pale faces, beautiful boyish faces, long twisted black and brown earlocks, an image from Gura. The earlocks dangle on either side of their faces, from the ears to the throat, proudly swaying as they walk.

Then I reach the temple, a large fenced-in building with a round dome. Well-dressed gentlemen and ladies step into various doors. It's like Tlomacki Street in Warsaw. The man with the prayer shawl in the vestibule is wearing a real concierge cap, and it also says *"portier"* (concierge). Two glass doors: the room is chock-full all the way to the doors. Total silence. The bright clear singing of the choir. These prayer rooms reveal a difference of worlds. Only occasional whispers in the throng behind the benches; the center aisle is also filled. The room is a large wide circle, and lo, it has three genuine tiers with a balcony, it's built like a real theater. The tiers are empty; a tiny number of women in very fine modern clothes are sitting in the first one. The men crowd downstairs, soldiers among them. In front, the clergymen stand in black coats, each wearing a round skullcap with a button. The man in the middle is the cantor. Splendid, splendid singing. I've come here only to see and then leave, for

I despise what the liberals of all persuasions call "divine service."
But then he sings. I don't understand what he sings, but it's the
finest artistry. What trills, what coloraturas he produces, how
he shapes the tone. Everyone stands and listens. And it's not
mere art, the art of concert halls; there is such a thing as religious art, even if it's not as sublime as religious non-art. The
praying begging praising emotions express themselves here with
a thin veneer of civilization. He sings in the lofty foreign tongue.
Now the concierge goes wild, he makes room in the center aisle.
The singing cantor comes down with the rabbis. They carry the
Torah, wrapped in red velvet, around the seats, and the singer
rejoices and laments as he walks. From all sides, the men stretch
out their hands to touch the red velvet, to kiss the Torah.

And I continue investigating what the life of this city produces. The wooden fences show posters: circus, movies, and
death notices. I am haunted by the name "Salomea Hausknech-
towa."

A black flag hangs from a window. A corporation has lost a
chairman, shortly after the death of his predecessor. I'm told
that when the young chairman heard of the old one's death, he
hurried after him, so that his predecessor wouldn't run him
down in heaven.

We are walking along the ring for quaint farm wagons with
small brown horses. Some have white manes. And many stand
there with drooping heads, stand with their shaggy hair and
protruding ribs. A huge fence: there used to be a house behind
it. It collapsed in broad daylight, in the middle of the city, killing
thirty-five people working there. Another house was evacuated
just before it caved in.

Today,[29] my colleague Henryk Sienkiewicz is being laid to rest
in Warsaw, at the cathedral. The former parliament building
stands there, pompous, straddle-legged. Allegories sit fat and
sassy along the façade; there are also useless columns. How I
despise these buildings. I turn away. And here is a big park with
a thousand children playing in it. I cherish any diaper of theirs
more than the allegories. Dozens of babies lie in their carriages,
basking in the sun, sleeping like birds.

159

I climb a hill on the border of the city, early Sunday morning:
Unia Lubelska Hill, piled up in memory of the Union of Lublin.
A Polish president of the Austrian imperial council broke the
ground for this monument after the collapse of the Uprising of
1863; it was one of the many proud Polish "nevertheless"s. I
encounter Ruthenian peasant women; they're going to church;
flat gentle lovely faces, calm patient eyes, the creatures of a
fertile plain. Past a huge barracks (horses are being walked in
the yard) on the cone of the hill, which is green, covered with
trees. Stone steps, bushes. A stone lion squats at a bend, with a
gaping maw. But he squats comfortably on his hind legs, he's
merely a heraldic lion. Leo's animal: first he bit for the Ukrainians. Now he's a heraldic animal, historic mortar. The sun is
white and low, the trolley clangs. I look down at treetops, everything drops steeply. In the end, I spiral up higher and sit under
a tall flagpole in a full storm.

The city radiates all around; to the right, it dissolves into
streets; to the left, it vanishes behind hills. That area too is
inhabited. Someone built it, someone else destroyed it and rebuilt it. Then Turks, Walachians. Then Cossacks with Tartars,
Bogdan Chmielnicki, Tuchai Bey, Vasil Buturlin. Once, they
all became aristocrats down there, because they refused to surrender to the Tartars. Then Austrians; and so much for that.
And when the Poles rebelled, the Austrians decapitated the best
of them. Goddamn tug-of-war. This is known as "growth":
punch a hole here, a hole there, rip off an ear, pull out a
tongue, smash a brick into the brain, attach a wooden leg, and
the organism is complete. Now the Poles and the Ukrainians
are digging their teeth into one another. An awful wind is banging against the flagpole. There are the houses, the Cathedral of
St. George, the Cistercian church, the former parliamentary
palace. The soil peacefully bears grain. The city has beautiful
stairways, small decrepit houses, drab courtyards. Milk women
clatter their cans.

The days of All Saints, All Souls.[30] Obsequies: dreary rainy
afternoon. In the twilight, people come from the center of
town, small troops, whole processions, down Kochanowski

160

Street, a long road leading to the cemetery. The entrance to the street is blocked by policemen with rifles; people have to mount at the right. From the side lanes, more people merge into the cortege. They hold flowers in their hands, big wreaths, fir twigs, candles, small flags. In front of several houses, peddlers stand with the small flags: small white-linen banners each with a red cross sewn upon it, two crossbeams; small white-and-red flags with a Polish inscription. Police guards at every corner. The road is soggy; people keep switching sides. Now beggars, blind men hugging the walls; eight blind and horribly crippled men lined up at a bend in the road, lamenting, shouting. Then, in an open field to the right, twenty in a row sit, lie, squat: raggedy women and cripples, mere torsos with heads, exposed arm stumps, leg stumps, artificial limbs thrusting out; some people lie in small handcarts, wheelbarrows, one person sings, one plays a harmonica.

Yellow trees on the boulevard; the wind shakes the remaining leaves. A crowd of people. Scores of trolleys, automobiles, and droshkies. This is the iron gate, the entrance to the cemetery. People are shoved in. Mute, unseeing nuns behind tables, on which pious pictures are set up. Small flags are hawked. The cemetery: a dense splendid deciduous forest. Wonderfully thick treetops, many still full of colorful leaves. And at the entrance, the grave chapels, to which steps ascend. Several people go up, to the candles burning inside; the interiors are very bright, they're peaceful, warm, solemn. And everywhere, on the grave mounds, in the chapels, amid the tree trunks, the small, delicate candles flicker, the tiny red flames, while the dreary twilight presses toward them without reaching its goal. Foliage, yellow, brown, red, has fallen upon the graves in thick heaps. Rain drips down. The people under the long tent of black umbrellas pour through the main roads, dissolve in lateral aisles.

They speak Polish, perhaps also Russian. These are large people, slender young men and women; many females in the coquettish mourning garb of the countryside: white crepe over the forehead, a long, trainlike black veil. Now they cluster at the graves, planting flowers, candles, very small fir trees into the beds. They press the candles like flowers into the lawn, two, three, ten, twenty, a gentle burnt offering: at times, whole rings around a grave. The cemetery is full of lovely simple tombstones, statues, small sarcophagi; lanterns with homey variegated glass burn in front of some. The small flags flutter down from crosses and broken columns. People work by their dead, speak, obtain more adornments. Three young, slender cadets with fixed bayonets come marching in; a soldier behind them lugs a huge bundle of fir branches; they march through side lanes to a guard of honor. The cemetery undulates; its green surface, filled with trees, is beautiful. The hilly terrain slopes up and down; from above and below, the candles flicker through the rain. The rain douses many of the flames; but boys standing in front of the large graves relight the candles. And as I crisscross through leaves, through rain, a singing resounds. And men holding hats are standing about a grave; a male choir sings a Latin song: I hear "*Requiescat.*" It rings out so soothingly under the treetops in the rain. Everything is so soothing. They decorate their graves, light candles as if decorating their homes, peer into the tiny flames, murmur a prayer, speak to one another, straighten the flowers. And slowly go their way, back to the masses of people, past policemen, dripping beggars, into the illuminated streets.

On the street, an intelligent man speaks to me softly. "A state is an equilibrium of oppressors and oppressed. But in Poland, the stratum of sufferers is growing. Poland is democratic, basically and intrinsically more democratic than Germany, precisely because of the Poles. However, our country is poorly organized. Our trade and industry are too large for Poland. They were right for Russian or a Russian dominion. Now, we are in the process of reducing something that was too big. We need East European support. Poland has a weak domestic market, and our exports are too expensive." Even more softly, he says: "There are Polish patriots who already see that the current solution to the Polish question cannot be a definitive one. No politics can buck economic necessities. Some peer anxiously, others look hopefully at Russia."

In the afternoon, a different man guides me along the

crowded streets, through a rather elegant stroll down Akade-
mika Street: this man is an inhabitant of Lwów, fat, obstinate.
He likes talking about politics, and even more about something
else. He shows me a large literary café, Roma, then takes me to
the center of town, the Zalewski Coffee House. Here, art, theater, and politics sit next to and amid one another. And there's
a total-recall prodigy at the coat check: the man who hands out
no wardrobe markers, relying purely on memory to return
everything to the right person.

At the round marble table, the fat man whispers to me: "It's
insolent of women to get indignant when a man breaks off with
them. They claim they gave the man so much pleasure; they
say: first he enjoys, then he sends them packing. That's so insolent of those women, so ignorant. They enjoy a friendship and
its opportunities as much as a man does. It's no small matter for
a woman to get a man; for a time, he gives up his independence
for her. A woman should be ashamed to say something like
that."

"Like what?"

"That she's being abused, that a man enjoys her and then
sends her away. It's the other way around. She robs and enjoys
the man if the two of them are at all compatible. She consumes
the man and not vice versa. And afterward, she insults him."

I probe sympathetically: "Is this an acute case?"

He growls: "No, no. But something like this is always acute.
It hasn't been new for me for a long time."

After a while, his face brightens; there's more room at the
table; he points out men and women at the neighboring tables.
Then he happily whispers:

"Do you know, without a creature like a woman, the world
would be unbearable. In the morning, when I lie in bed, weak
and listless, facing a dismal day at the office, the thought of a
woman galvanizes me like a shot of camphor or a glass of wine.
There's something to the idea that we're an incomplete half
without them. It's worse than anyone thinks. It occurs to me
that each of us, male or female, is castrated. It's also nonsense
to assume that two different creatures of a single animal species
are running around. There's only one running about, a her-

maphrodite. When it was separated, a mutilation took place, a castration. The sexes and love are symptoms of deficiency, like in eunuchs. As castrates, we are sick and pathological with our love. And every so often, we are not eunuchs: namely when I'm with her, and she's with me."

I drink my coffee, listen. I notice I don't have to speak. He's got ulterior motives. Maybe he likes me and wants to bare his soul. Or else he's terribly overwrought. He smokes agitatedly, probes the tables, then, smiling arrogantly, he turns his broad back on them:

"Women are right about one thing. They have good reason to make fun of men. Those men over there—they understand so much about women. Every woman wants to be taken in a special way. That's something that such a bull doesn't understand. The erotic zones. What do you think a man thinks? You must have made your own observations. A guy like that pounces on a woman—slam, bam, thank you ma'am—and the woman, yes, the woman. She feels half nauseous, and no wonder. Guys like that don't deserve the existence of women. They're freebooters, predators; all they care about is their stomachs. I don't give a damn about myself. Who am I anyway. I'm no egotist. What I care about is the other person. If she's enjoying herself, then I'm in heaven. I can thank God that He's given me things to help her enjoy herself. You think I'm a troubadour? I'm just not a bull, I don't rage about in a china shop."

Once again, he puffs away, but only for a short time; then he gets too close for comfort:

"A woman's erotic zones. One woman has them in one place, another woman has them in another place. You have to get away from the so-called genitalia. That's nothing but anatomy. That's gross. If you're attentive and love the creature you're with, then you discover her beyond the 'genitalia.' Amid nothing but genitalia. The complete other person lacks the other person, the complete one. I have a girlfriend now, I can't let go of her. I've got to come right out and say it. You'll probably laugh. I can scarcely find what's female about her, in the anatomical sense. In the anatomical nonsense. Yet she's sensuality personified. The fusion of spiritual and physical in the sensual, the *unio mystica*, has succeeded perfectly in her. I'm here for her, from head to foot. The philosophers philosophize past that; they know nothing about that state of affairs. Sensuality, I give you my word—and I've got a lot of experience—is more mysterious, more enigmatic than the apodictic a priori judgments that the philosophers investigate. I experience the enigma with her every day. For me, our love is an experiment with nature. I can't get away from her, because she haunts my mind and body, I can say both physically and metaphysically. Haunts me incessantly. It stops only when I go to work. If you saw her, you'd say: a female, a beautiful woman. Someone else would say: It must be nice to have her. To 'have' her. You hear that vulgar expression. I mean: to discover her, to discover oneself in her. What this woman experiences in her throat, her breasts, is something that another woman's entire special organ couldn't accomplish. I'm amazed, amazed. Maybe you could express it in a special language. I find that it beggars all description. It's like an act of primal procreation. Yes, when we get together, that act takes place. Just stroke her back, and she gets so excited that she nearly drowns in the flood. She starts trembling (why won't you believe me?), she turns her back away, moaning, and then has to get closer. Magnetism, no, how ridiculous—it's the elemental birth of new senses. She can sit in front of me, with other people present, and then our eyes meet. I hold her. I hold her tight at a distance of several yards while I'm talking to other people, and I can see that she's getting excited, she's turning pale and red, she's clutching her chair, reaching climax, while other people sit next to her, and the conversation keeps going. I can pull it off with my eyes, gazing right into her eyes. By talking, I can arouse her sensations and get her to come off. It lurks in her and breaks out everywhere. It's more than magnetism between us, between male and female in general; it doesn't need organs, it turns the entire body, entire body into its organ. Ah. But. . . . You understand."

I can see how excited he is. He's all pale and trembling. He's suffering, he's consuming himself. It's more than he can stand. Is he enslaved? His caustic face has become strangely rigid.

At tea, a refined old count, a former governor in Austrian Poland, chats with me, shows me his Italian paintings, complains about all the things he lost because of the Bolsheviks. Then he, a professor of public law, hands me his card, so that I can easily view the collections at the Ossolineum. This is a library and museum established about a century ago by Count Ossolinski and Prince Lubomirski. It contains some seven hundred thousand books, a sign of the incredible collective thinking of man. Walking through the rooms, which used to be a Carmelite convent, then a military magazine, I think to myself: They are fighting for ten leagues of border—half the earth is empty—they are confronting one another with weapons, the idea of a United States of Europe sounds utopian: yet a common brain has existed for a long, long time. Its utterances are here, in seven hundred thousand books. But the brain has no motoric zone, it has no effect as yet on its muscles. The organism is not adjusted to the brain. The human body is frazzled, one part does this, another part does that. We have absolutely no inkling of how collective we are. This building, which originally served Polish nationalism and liberation, has all the books about Poland. Glass tables contain very old chronicles and prints, postils, large collections of drawings and engravings. I am taken to the Lubomirski Gallery by a young Pole, whose fine features and noble, piquant nature absorbs me more than these paintings. And now I stand in front of the picture of the Union of Lublin, which I have heard about everywhere. The painting hangs in a glass-covered hall. But the room isn't completely airtight: every few seconds, a heavy drop of rain plops down from the ceiling to the floor in front of the painting. It interests me greatly. It's been nicely arranged for me. I walk through the room, look at the fine Pole, I glance at the drip and salute it.

In Lwów, a Count Dzieduszycki built an entire museum on Theater Street, near the big ring. At times, it's good to take the guns from people; they then see things differently. Counts too then discover nature, which is normally in the hands of scientists and day-trippers. I think it's charming when counts, barons, and the entire old nobility begin studying nature. It's

suitable for them to do so, if only for reasons of piety and gene-
alogy: after all, most of nature is even older than they are. But
they would also bring in new concepts; morality breaks through
in the concepts; our science, ruled by the middle class, could
acquire different tones.

I visit this house, and I present arms to the count. He didn't
donate his money like a Rockefeller (for whom signing a check
was the summation of the intellectual act). The Polish count
accomplished something. After mounting the stairs to the second floor and entering a room, I stumble upon dozens of young
girls. I would never have imagined how appealing an institution
the Dzieduszycki Museum is. The girls sit on chairs, kneel,
squat. There are many positions found by these thirty young
girls of fifteen, sixteen, seventeen.[31] This was arranged by the
intelligent count. For he set up a lot of cases and cabinets with
stuffed animals for the girls: and the girls draw them. Can they?
As soon as I approach them and look at their drawings, the girls
turn them over, speaking Polish, as if to say: "Keep your mouth
shut." I keep it shut, but not my eyes, not my ears. They whisper, smile, murmur on and on. A teacher walks about. The
supervising owl. Yes, look at the birds, children dear. You won't
be stuffed. When we're dead, we're thrown away; there's no
higher species as yet to shoot us down and display us in museums. The age of the superman hasn't come as yet. Here they
are, the conquered nations and animal breeds. Tall long-legged
stilt birds; then taller ones, storklike, with distended bills. Whole
flocks of gray ducks squat in cabinets and, all the way at the top,
bevies of sea gulls. What gigantic eagles now show their hacking
beaks. Some don't resemble birds, they look worse, like ground
animals; their legs are planted far apart with tensed muscular
thighs; their feathers are unbelievable. The flocks of cormo-
rants: they're like miniature kangaroos, comically helpless, their
wings degenerated into fins. They hug the ground with bodies
on colossal legs, on which they jump when they're not waddling.
The mass of climbers—the whole school is now standing in
front of them, laughing, drawing, erasing—the eagle owls. The
way birds build nests. I had to travel to Lwów to see this. The
birds wrap dry grass and reeds around rigid blades, they take

stable blades into their lairs. You can barely see their grass; they sit inside it. The Good Lord has imbued the animals with mutual distrust; it's a kind of correction, a very belated one, which the Good Lord, distressed, attempted to apply to his own work. Other birds actually pitch small tents between dry oat blades. But how does the *Aegitalus pendulinus* behave? Its life-style is utterly Baroque; this little bird ties a thick closed woolen sack to a supple branch, which bends under its weight. It leaves a comfortable wide opening in front. But it doesn't glide right into the nest; first, it inserts a tube. The bird can slip through, but intruders can't. Then the bird coats the entire bizarre apparatus with grass; this *pendulinus* is a skeptic, a shrewd security commissar. I walk past the terrible super-ox, the bison, past moose, past cabinets full of hares. Some hares are as small as cats and act like cats; but some cower, black and fat, and look awfully dangerous, preying on someone or other. In one glass case, small thin bushy animals scurry about: the sign says, "Martes"; they bare their incisors and white whiskers, and behind them, their young, a tiny ratlike brood, twist and climb up the tree trunk. Foxes, scads of foxes. And fish. Vipers curling in high glass cylinders. Here, an egg has opened; a tiny snake is developing on the inside, a thick black head lifting the shell and poking through. To think that snakes lay eggs just like fish and birds. Snakes are in between. Laying eggs is a cagey old method used by animals; they can bury them, leave them while they save themselves. Holding eggs and hatching them inside the body is really a foolhardy idea of land animals. It makes them move so heavily; they can be killed and eaten up together with their brood! But perhaps the dangers besetting the brood were so great that the land female had no choice but to make the nest inside her belly. Now: it's high time we returned to laying eggs. The air is pure, other predators are no longer dangerous. Now that would be something: a woman goes to the incubation institute and lays her egg. Mine and yours are no longer an issue. Or else she keeps it, inserts it into the brood tube or cans it for better times. One could, of course, preserve eggs and put them by for future centuries, perhaps immure them in a cornerstone along with coins. How does the woman emancipate herself from the uterus?

I see a magically fine snake skeleton: the semiarches of the countless ribs swing off, left and right, from the spinal column. They're as thin as fishbones. This makes for a fine elastic tube, which swells down toward the threadlike tail. And the pattern of the snakeskin: regular rectangles. An excavated rhinoceros has been set up in one room. The black dreadful entity lowers its head, ominously thrusting out its sickle-shaped horn. And then, the primordial form of the elephant towers from behind a wire: the skeleton of a mammoth, its black skin. This creature is one story high. Its hipbones are so thick, its shoulder girdle is as wide as a woman. The heavy arch of its spinal column bends at the top; the bone eminences stab high. The totality is a crude load-bearing structure, stronger than bricks and ashlars. Masses of rhinoceros fat and innards have been bedded in formalin. Both primal creatures were excavated from mineral wax. They may be some twenty thousand years old. There they stand. This was how they opened the royal tombs of Egypt, this is how they open the earth, hauling up coal, the wood of primeval forests, using it as fuel. Or learning from them. We're such cunning human animals, walking around here, laughing, sketching. Our bones are much weaker then theirs, but our brains are gigantic. Yet a bit of global upheaval, of mineral wax may take us down a peg or two.

How refreshing, I find, how anything but melancholy to stroll about here. It would make no difference to me if I were to stand here like this one day, perhaps be blasted into the air by fire. I —am and remain invisibly visible. After all, I am the self that shines on everything here. That shines from everything: nothing knows it. The self is here. The driving, urging, feeling self. I am the truth of all the rats, foxes, mammoths. This is my gallery of ancestral portraits, my hall of fame. These are my accomplishments, so far. Dear rats, dear foxes. Too bad you can't run around with me, so that you could see yourselves and me. It would boost your self-confidence. You come from the finest backgrounds. Look! What battles have been fought—all the way

169

to us. And what still lies ahead. How great, how strong—am—
I! How indomitable, inexhaustible, unapproachable—am—I! I
am very legitimate. I will never be unworthy of you, you rats
and foxes.

Behind the trees at Theater Square, another museum wants
to catch me, the City Gallery. Good morning, Arthur Grottger.
What simply lovely little watercolors you have. You paint the
way old Blechen painted in Berlin: comical variegated life. Yes,
it's comical and variegated. Sometimes life seems like snowflakes: you practically drown in it. But the paintings in this gallery! Paintings upon paintings! God, how much has been
painted already. Not all of it has to be art, and if it is art, you
don't have to view all of it. This Matejko fellow all too often
loses his way in big subjects. He drew his own portrait in pencil:
a dismal expression, a loose goatee. You don't have to transcend
yourself. You have to be thankful for what you have. The place
has a crafts department. I see cups: what a joy to drink from
green cups in the morning. Haulms of grass sprout high, red
flowers. How deliciously this raises your joie de vivre; you touch
and see beauty, which exudes warmth like the sun, and you get
closer to yourself and indeed to God as well. I can understand
why a person dotes on such things and fights for them and fights
over them. And how well I comprehend the Greek king who
waged war for a creature of flesh, a living female, with a head,
mobile arms, legs, hair, senses, moods, for something that no
artist can create, that only a tremendously clumsy, exceedingly
sly nature, who knows all the tricks of the trade, has produced
in the course of millions of years as the fruit of immense knowledge. With how many changing things does she stimulate a
man, does she get him to feel himself, awaken and intensify his
self.

I walk past creamers and coffeepots; yes, food is important,
and vessels are its clothes. I have gotten into a happy mood
from nothing, from nothing. I bask in the sun of what I see.

And I really have to celebrate an item that's displayed here. It
stands on a low buffet, and it's made of porcelain: two young
people, a couple, dancing. Both in modern clothes, she in a
skirt with slit sides and a feathered hat, her shoes tied over her

170

ankles. His arm is around her waist. Her left arm swings aloft as they dance; her shoulders are bare, her neckline veers across her breasts. And that fine hue of the china, that discreet matte tone of the couple. His suit a soft greenish-brown; his shoes a wee bit lighter; his hair, smoothed back, a wee bit darker. Her richly pleated dress, her feathers, her shoes are a light flesh color. Both their faces whitish. Their right legs are raised in dancing, the knees bent; the tips of the feet are sinking. How enchanting the sight of such youth, fine, modern, gracile. I exult upon seeing them: she is older than he, he's just a big boy. This gives the couple a special intimacy. Flowers wind very delicately around the pedestal under their feet.

Oh, how it makes me feel. I'm absolutely enchanted. When I go outdoors, a scaffolding is set up in front of a house, its cross-beams marking the sky. And I—am delighted by the ladders, the rungs, rafters, over the open jagged brickwork! A scaffolding, a house—as if it were utterly, utterly crucial. It is more than grown, it is a resurrecting mystical sign! As if I were suddenly seeing the primal world, eye to eye. And nothing is unclear, uncertain, everything is completely present, open—transparent and exposed to its innermost core. Not only the building—the entire street, the people with packages, walking along the pavement, the rattling car, the dachshund leaping from the house vestibule. I am summoned back by the scaffolding, the high ladders, the rafters. I focus on them as if through a burning glass, a center—as if piercing rays emanated from there.

I walk slowly down the narrow street, stand in the gigantic rectangular marketplace. The tremendous city hall is surrounded by market people. In the square, fountains cast out water. My feeling is already waning. I glance back down the narrow street. The air quivers around me.

And in the evening, all churches and secular buildings have vanished, sunk away. The evening is the daytime of the shops, the people. The shiny stores. This is the hour of young men and young women, of officers with sabers and kepis.

Around this time, St. Mary's Fountain near the bad Mickiewicz monument is indescribable. Down below, the dear pious water springs into a basin and tells stories. Mary stands on top, opening her arms in a simple beautiful womanly movement. Her head is circled by a wreath of stars; she is the queen of heaven. A light burns at her feet; a large oval of light bulbs surrounds her naive figure. A sweet eloquent image.

A church is nearby; I don't know its name. I enter the illuminated room behind many women and men. The effigy of an old bearded man in armor is engraved in a central pillar; he holds an hourglass while sleeping on his side. Next to me, a young man kneels on the floor, he's got a briefcase, he's coming from his business or office. He crosses himself, stares unswervingly into the altar flames, barely moves his lips. Then he's finished. He crosses himself again, and softly hurries into the evening of the city. What was that? He has fortified himself. Perhaps more. Who can say that what he has just done is purely subjective. Who knows the real connections of the part, of humanity, with the universe? It is a connection with the universal totality, a connection that the worshiper quickly established. The sciences do not touch this issue. The dismemberment of the world is too big everywhere. What was that? Practical wisdom. How wise he now is: he dipped his hand into the water, back there, in the font. He chose to touch a cleansing being, a beloved being, a beloved hand, a beloved head. And what comes over him? Strength. Who knows all the ways things work.

After eight in the evening, the city is still; unlike Warsaw. I see and hear *Lohengrin* at the City Theater. But only one act. I am fast asleep before the swan ever shows up. During intermission, I try to keep awake with my companion, a cheerful music critic. But he can't resist either. Ortrud's nocturnal conspiring fails to reach us; when the trumpets blast in the morning, we both jump up. But then we have to get out into the fresh air. The singing and acting were excellent. But the totality is awful. That "Grail magic" exudes whole clouds of boredom. This is a brassy and whimpering Romanticism, sheer theater and bombast. Which have tripped over a fairy tale and trampled it to death. I can't watch. "Ah, never shalt thou ask me." Naive fairy-tale gestures, blasted out by trumpets and wrapped up in psychology, modern psychology! I've got to get out of here.

Stolz's *Pojaz* is more decent. Tomorrow, nobody will know about him. The old fable of the man who disguises himself and visits his married love, taken to her by the unsuspecting husband himself. This time, the husband doesn't think he's taking a doctor, but a jointed doll, which he gives her in a department store. The doll then stands there at her bed, inviting her to play. And the playing can start. I can't remember how it ends. It was merry and not pompous. I kept watching a beautiful whimsical actress, who played the beloved. Because of her, because of the way she fluttered and aroused you with all desires for life, the play was good, the music masterful.

# THE PETROLEUM DISTRICT

*The mountains are covered with tiny flames.*

I travel toward the south. There, two hundred and fifty miles of petroleum deposits run along the northern slopes of the Carpathian Mountains, between two rivers, the Raba and the Cheremosh. Boryslaw and Tustanowice are the centers of the oil industry. I ride across a rich plain filled with arable land. Meadows come, stubble fields, huge herds of black and dappled cattle, horses run free with young chestnut colts. White spots in the green, moving, craning necks and yellow beaks, shrieking: geese. More and more herds of cattle; shepherds in white linen trousers, black fur caps, Ukrainians. Here are their tiny farms, draw wells with wheels; the peasant woman, barefoot, a loose-fitting flowery calico skirt, her white babushka knotted under her chin, reaches into the spokes of the wheel, pulls up the bucket. At a railroad station, a little boy dashes after the train; at another station, a barking dog. At a small station, a water faucet wrapped in straw looks comical; the big suffering thing has a pail hung from its mouth and it has to drip into it. The land rises, hilly, with more and more trees. Always, the red and yellow flaming trees; in between, earnest deep-green conifer forests. Stry lies behind me. After two hours on the express, I am south of Lwów; the train enters Drohobycz.

174

A crowded station; pairs of peasants lug covered sacks and baskets. Jews in the background raise their long, black coats as they cross the tracks. At the other side, on the platform, a man shouts through his hands: "Oettinger, Oettinger." Tickets are not checked at the exit [as they are in German stations]. Outside the station, men shout: "Pannje, pannje, cab." Some twelve or fifteen open one-horse carriages stand there in a row, the coachmen swinging their whips, beckoning, pointing at everyone who emerges from the gates: "One zloty!" I sit in one of those old crates; the driver doesn't start for a time, he hails and beckons others. Then he grumpily lurches and lumbers off; over level ground for a while, then uphill, into deep potholes. What unbelievable houses come along! This is a village, a long boggy road; low-drooping shingled roofs, small wooden houses, some grouted, whitewashed and painted, in bluish, yellow, pink hues. Many green porches, their roofs resting on wooden poles carved round into columns, some bearing primitive ornamentation. On the road, two peasant women in colorful skirts and high black turndown boots tread briskly through the curdy slough. The highway slowly flattens out, the left-hand road is aswarm with people and wagons; we turn off, I am in the great square.

A vast rectangular marketplace. Booths and stands, horses, rigs, rows of fiacres. And everything sinking into mud and a refuse made up of straw, debris, trash. A line of tables runs through the garbage, displaying bales of particolored cloth. Kerchiefs, linen are hung up in booths. Behind them, male and female vendors, Jews, only Jews, with German names, chat and shout. Groups of peddlers in soft caps, dirty clothes, talk in the square, outside the one-story houses. Stooped old men, greasy, in dreadfully tattered caftans, raggedy trousers, burst boots, poke sticks into the garbage on the ground. One oldster has a long yellowish-white beard, a stiff hat full of holes, its brim half torn off; he keeps murmuring, playing with his thick fingers, begging. And then, emerging from the throng in the square, an elderly, very ugly, crosseyed, unkempt woman begs. And then a younger one, holding her baby wrapped in a babushka on her breast. And then a barefoot boy. And then a man in a trilby, eating a big apple, chewing and simply spitting out the peel. They all murmur in Yiddish: "Give me something. *Zait gezunt* (good-bye)."

A high rectangular tower with a clock stands dreadful in the middle of this marketplace. The tower is alone, no church, no house attached. It's a leg that's been ripped from a body. A bombardment must have taken place here; the walls at the foot of the tower still loom; up above, you can see the walls of rooms, whitewashed walls with shreds of wallpaper; but the rooms are gone. A mountain of rubble at the bottom. This was the city hall; they tore it down before the war in order to renovate it; after the war, it had to remain as is; now the ruin stands. To the right, a broad road flows past a red church. The swamp in the middle stretches quite a way; lovely trees stand on the side, tolerable houses. In front of what must be a public building, there is an empty pedestal: this was Mickiewicz, the national Polish poet. Several years ago, the advancing Ukrainians shattered the bust.

But below the market, beyond the garbage and the grisly tower, there are narrow streets. A dreadful area. Anyone who hasn't seen these alleys and "houses" doesn't know what poverty is. These aren't houses, these are remnants of houses, shacks, sheds, huts. Windows covered with boards, windows without glass. Houses without closed roofs—decrepit barracks, in serried ranks; some with basements, which are lined with bricks, but look like caves. Each dump is overcrowded. A big, freshly whitewashed house shines, horrible, in the midst of this woe. Is this their Citadel of Uri? It's the synagogue. It too was ruinous, but then it was renovated. And I can't help thinking that it shouldn't have been renovated. These houses were slated to be demolished long ago; the matter was debated, decided. But the war came. And now, real victims of the war are decaying in these holes; now, the war cannons are still booming away at them, inaudible. A wretched populace, squalid, massive, keeps house in dugouts, shielded against invisible pilots, barely scraping along from day to day.

I, skeptical, ask experts: "Are these people really as poor as all this? Are they assimilated to the filth? Do they refuse to leave it, even when they're better off?"

"Some ten or fifteen percent may have gradually reached that point. By now, they know nothing else. But the greater mass— they have no choice. They can't budge."

I put myself in the hands of a dishonest coachman: in the afternoon, I drive down to a crude-oil refinery. "Coachman" and "dishonest" are synonyms here. However, during my weeks of moving through this poverty, I think differently about dishonesty. Fraudulence is the primal and normal condition of trade, honesty is possible only under lofty circumstances. In nature, there are no fixed prices. All that the dealer wants to do is make money, and only special circumstances, the competition in Western Europe, can force him to give up a position— namely, the psychology of the buyer. The seller automatically takes the buyer, his man, into account; that is: who wants and how badly does he want? A deal involves establishing something: the seller competes with the buyer, from case to case; and it is only during the negotiations, the tug of war, that he ascertains the price, the value of his ware. That is the "dishonesty," the elementary, elemental, the actual action. Compared with this peddler, the Western European businessman is an anemic civilized creature, an official.

When you walk through the factory gates, you are encompassed by a different world. Vast modern facilities—tracks, pipes; typewriters clattering in brightly lit offices. Well-dressed white-collar workers, men and women, walk about, sit at tables. Outside (this one factory employs over a thousand people), rails run for two leagues. Crude oil, pipelined all the way from Boryslaw, is processed here. Stored in huge tanks, it is preheated; then the distillation begins. I see the huge boilers. Here, Polish, Jewish, and Ukrainian workers work side by side. In a special building, the white, light benzine, shielded by glass, spurts from the distilling pipes. In another facility, the lubricating oils, following their specific gravity, run down angular gutters: the heavy lubes, the light ones, blue oil. Then, paraffin: in one building, candles are poured around the retracted wicks. Resi-

177

dues are boiled down. How bizarre—this light porous coal that I pick up. It's coal and yet not coal. Supposedly, it is highly inflammable.

I want to go to Boryslaw and see how the petroleum comes out of the ground. I spend the night in Drohobycz. The slow train carries me for almost one hour. Down below, a white-haired beggar, holding out his cap, bows deeply to the lumbering train. The landscape grows more and more hilly. Now, blue and blackish masses emerge more densely on the horizon. Mountains, mountains! Carpathians, the foothills of the Carpathians. Outside the railroad station in Boryslaw (masses of vivacious people get out): once again, the coachmen. An entire procession of vehicles starts moving along a precipitous highway. A tollgate, a bend in the road and now—a narrow, boggy, dead-straight road, with wagons careening insanely in both directions. The wagons zoom; left and right, people climb up to wooden boards mounted on high wooden planks. Refuse, mud flows under the planks. The morass oozes down from the higher sides of the street. Oil used to float on this water; it was gathered by the poor. Throngs of people in the center of the village, a dense crush of wagons. The men wear caps, stride briskly. Russian, Polish, Yiddish posters. Meat is hawked in horrible wooden shacks; whole beef carcasses dangle from nails. Scaffolding around pitiful ancient houses; boards and rubble block the road. At every ten paces, telephone poles loom on either side, each pole sheathed in a mass of white porcelain insulation. This is an entire forest of poles; I roll and walk among them, down the long straight street. White spots lie on the rising greenish mountains; the spots look like snow or barked wood. Now I see: those are plumes of white smoke. The smoke puffs densely from the ground, by the derricks. Slender, wooden, house-high pyramids—they already stand here, next to the highway, singly, in groups; but on the mountains, they stand in bevies, in the middle of the green, amid tree stumps. All the trees around them are polled. A heavy gutter slants down from the top of each heavy pyramid; the storage for its long ropes. I travel up the mountain, to a tower. They started drilling twenty-five years ago; first wildcatters, then whole companies. The land speculation began at the same time. One man bought an entire mountain, and now everything belongs to him. He leases it out, receiving a percentage of the yield, the grosses that encumber the enterprise.

A tarry black pool is to be found near the derricks: thick heavy petroleum with soil, spooned out of the drill hole. They are boring over five thousand feet down. Polish oil, I hear, is heavier than American oil, yielding five to nineteen percent benzine, thirty-eight to sixty percent petroleum, five to thirteen percent paraffin, fifteen to twenty-five percent lubricating oil, and three to six percent tar. In 1909, an enormous amount was hauled out: two million tons; then came a decline; now, they extract about seven hundred fifty tons a year. And how many places are they drilling in? Some seventeen hundred. But this number is changing; productivity is going down; every year, they tap the earth in three hundred new places. A strong stench of petroleum everywhere. No coal is used in the boiler house; the drilling itself yields natural gas, which is used as fuel. And the flame beats with colossal violence against the wall of the boiler. Now and then, fires break out. They have to be smothered with sand; this task requires courageous men. There are Jews, specialists, who are experts in this field. Under wet burlap, they creep over to the fire; then they bury the fire in sand. Here, this derrick, the timberwork, creaks dully, in fits and starts; the ground is being drilled. The facilities are simple: pipelines from the drill hole for the gas; enormous tanks for the crude oil; underground lines in which the preheated crude is driven by steam to Drohobycz. Some twelve thousand workers depend on these works; in the village, another fifteen to twenty thousand people are attached to them.

As I travel downhill through the mutilated forests, the first stars twinkle in the black sky, a host of lights twinkle on the mountain slopes, and I hear roaring and blasting everywhere. A policeman with a fixed bayonet patrols the high wooden paths. A locomobile with a broken wheel lies halfway across the road. What a mob of people. It's like the Wild West, haste, speculation. An American creation that got stuck in the swamp. No settlement for people, but an object of exploitation. The owners don't live here, they consume their money in Vienna and Paris, the money of this country.

In the train that evening, the passengers talk. One man complains: he has to commute between Boryslaw and Drohobycz; no homes are being constructed in Boryslaw. This is how his life goes: in the morning, when he leaves, his kids are still asleep, and in the evening, they're already asleep. One man gloats about a man who owned grosses, shares; he speculated, and went bust. Who benefits from the oil wells? The managers themselves are employees, capable men, they have to slave away. Whatever's here is their doing. But not even the managers know who owns the derrick, the ground, who reaps the harvest. It changes kaleidoscopically: companies form, dissolve. There were owners who couldn't read or write, they didn't have a clue. Some lucky speculating, and they were rolling in money. One man, the instant he got money, had nothing better in mind than to order furniture for his villa, like Emperor Franz Josef.

In the darkness behind me—the forest of masts lies way, way back—the electric lights flash. The mountains, the plain where derricks stand, are covered with the tiny flames.

# CRACOW

*I have devoted my heart to the mighty reality, the slain man, the executed man on the cross above the worshipers. The trolley is no more real than what I feel.*

Candles are burning in the dark vaultlike entrance. Sharp sunlight, bundled into beams, drops from high up, falling to the right, into the nave, across the pews, along the pillars, down to the stone floor. Tremendous, utterly tremendous, the nave rises, then concludes in a point. Small golden stars are strewn into the blue up there. And at the entrance to the altar, over the entrance, a Christ on a cross: enormous. He hangs under the ceiling, he hangs down from the ceiling, his arms spread out; the cross intensifies his body, the vertical and horizontal lines of the dead body. A dead man, an executed man above the worshipers, the living, in front of the deep variegated hues of the window.

I have already encountered this person, this dead man, Christ, in the other cities. But I overlooked him because of the Marys. I am a bit startled to see him here. The pious walk forward between the wooden pews, kneel down at the pillars. Behind me, the women with market baskets, whole rows of them. Suddenly, they've all become incomprehensibly alien to me, wondrous. At the high altar and the side altars, sacristans scurry about, genuflecting as they move. They light dozens of candles. The living flickering innocent red stands out powerfully against the violent white blaze of the sun.

Sorrow is in the world, suffering, a struggling human/animal emotion is in the world. That is the dead man up there, Christ. His wounds, his execution, his perforated bones. He emanates horror. They pray to him. To him, not to the columns, the pillars, the colorful hues. These people have gathered only for him. An everyday occurrence, and how astonishing for me. What faces these people get. Do they experience it as I do? Hearts of stone taken from their chests, replaced with hearts of flesh, and now they can see. One does not see with one's eyes. Pain, woe in the world: a tremendous, illuminating emotion. Dreadful: and this is written everywhere in the churches, the secret is so open, anyone can read it. You have to spread color, beauty around to make it bearable.

I tiptoe on. Past a huge crown; inside it, one man of the cross baptizes another. People lie, kneel in the penumbra. A side chapel with a grating, tomb figures. Standards in the side aisle. The milky sunlight keeps flowing in. Ancient effigies hang at the foot of the pillars. Sometimes the sun is blocked; the church lives and sinks into it.

Outdoors. White edgestones all around the church. They look like genuflecting priests in canonicals, a long row with bowed heads. The beggars mob the doors: a young blind man with empty eye sockets, a pockmarked blind man. Two elderly women in thick ragged skirts have shiny-red creased faces, their lower right arms are bent, their hands open. And thus they stand, they stand. With towering windows, the ancient church walls rest on the marketplace. They send two spires upward; a small structure, like a church model, surmounts the left-hand spire, a gold crown hangs near the tip. The crown shines far. A plane buzzes overhead. Mary, the crowned queen of Poland; this is her church. The clock strikes twelve, the bell tolls deep; a trumpet blasts, drowned out by the bell.

I'm back again in the morning. Darkness throughout the vast space of the church. A few candles flicker on the pillars. At the front, left and right, the side altars are illuminated. The church floor, as I gradually see, is covered with black kneeling bodies, human beings. An organ resonates; its sound is small, like a pillar in the building, like a single picture. A priest whom I can't see sings weakly. Then hush. A ringing, very loud, at brief intervals. A young priest walks forward, in very wide white robes. The ringing continues. The young priest is carrying something, he walks up the steps, then puts down what he's been carrying. Amid constant ringing, he walks back down the steps very slowly and solemnly, then halts in the middle of the side altar and kneels quickly and lightly; other priests next to him. Then he turns around. Meanwhile, some people are leaving. Others cluster in front; he makes the sign of the cross over them. And again, the beggars mob the door, trembling in the awful cold.

Another morning. I've doffed my hat and spent a few minutes standing and gazing at the countenance of the executed man; now, I'm strolling in the pungent air. It's a blissful morning. I experience nice coincidences. I wake up early as if sleep had led me down a road; then, it grows lighter out; sleep opens the small door, motions, bows, speaks gently (an old friendly gentleman) in the doorway, "*Auf wiedersehen*," and closes the door behind him. As I stand up, my comb drops from my hand, lands on the rug, indicating a small piece of newsprint on which I wrote an address. Afterward, I sit in the breakfast room; the waiter isn't here; I get up and think I ought to call him; the other guests are also waiting for him. Then he comes in, zooms straight toward me, with an agitated face, apologizes: without realizing it, I had leaned against the wall, right on the button of the bell wiring, unintentionally buzzing him. I had been led to the bell. Now I amble along behind others, entering an old church located on my route. For a long time, I see nothing inside; I hear a deep lone voice singing. Then individual organ harmonies. I venture into the darkness with a few schoolchildren and I see that I was standing in the wrong place: I had entered the church from the side.

And to my left . . .

To my left, a gigantic fire blazes with wild incomprehensible

183

lines. Just where is the music coming from? It's not in this church; it has to be in another church nearby. It sounds just like violins. My eyes gradually adjust, the church stretches out. The rushing and roaring of the house-high glass windows never abate. And lo and behold, a whimpering sound begins—how weird I feel. Is it here, is it overhead? A very high lamenting. It must be coming from the other church, the lamenting stops of an organ. I turn around: I can see two white-clad priests; they emerge from under the flaming window, they vanish in the wall. Slowly the distant organist pulls other registers, roars once, twice, and then hums again, plays violins, the sixths meet up, the lamenting thirds. I head toward the glass windows. I don't know the meaning of these surging gushes of color, these gushes of black, surrounded by billowing gushes and rushes of blue, laced with green, flooded with yellow and gold. Are those human beings? Sometimes I believe I can make out fairy-tale eyes, long hair. I don't wish to recognize anything; just as I don't need to understand the distant male singing. The lines in the glass flicker. A dark-green floral window. And to the right, the most burning of all colors that I have seen, a bright yellow, a satanic red-yellow-brown, one color more burning than fiery red, only just born from the marriage of the living light, of the sunshine pouring in, with the slumbering gushes of color.

Now the room is bright. I can survey its entire depth. Its vaults are not as high as those of the Church of St. Mary. But it has the same azure up above, the same gold stars. And now the walls have emerged from the darkness and they're articulating themselves. They are painted discreetly, brown-yellow, greenish-blue, a dawning and brightening; the room grows and blurs into them. Fantastically animated pillars, gigantic surfaces turbulently ornamented. Sheer color, quivering lines. These side windows—what can I say about them? Huge white lilies stand between green plants, or something resembling them, flowers; and higher up, an intimate, tremendously intimate blue flows over everything, and slowly a crown emerges, a head. It must be the queen of heaven.

The church is plain, grayish-red. Gray buildings adjoin it, a cloister. Wyspianski painted the church and made the windows. The flashing sun strikes the outdoor effigy of St. Francis.

And churches at every turn, well cared for, some splendid. In front of one church, on Grodska Street, the commercial artery, two ecstatic holy figures made of stone stand in the sunshine. Wawel, the old royal castle, which is dilapidated (the Austrians had barracks up there), has a powerful church with two tremendous steeples. One steeple has huge gold clockfaces on all four of its walls. At its foot, a wild horse stands on a pedestal, menacing, bearing a rider on its back. He's the untamable Kosciuszko. He wants to ride down the road, straight down the castle. Inside this church, the kings of Poland lie in beautiful sarcophagi in cellars, chapels. This is half church, half triumphal avenue. I roam past mute houses, ancient homes, which make me feel good; monks and nuns live inside them. I encounter several in the street: with processions of young children and older girls, whom they teach. Many centuries have left their stone thoughts of God and mystical things. The eleventh century built a house on Grodska Street in honor of St. Andrew. A colossal church was constructed for St. Catherine; a stone arch crosses the street, connecting the church with its convent. And another earlier century moves here, raising its ancient eyelids like a tortoise: the rock church on the Vistula. It used to stand right next to the water; but in the course of centuries, the river retreated. A thousand years ago, a murder was committed in this church. Stanislaus, a politicizing bishop of Cracow, betrayed the king, Boleslav the Bold. The bishop fled from the furious king, seeking refuge in this very church. No use. The bishop was gruesomely mutilated and executed. But within a short time, the pope succeeded in forcing the overly bold Boleslav to leave the country, and the exile died a wretched death. Today, people come here on the eighth of May to obtain dispensations. The well in the garden has healing powers. Now it's frozen. A stone man, perhaps the saint, is freezing in the midst of the ice.

Noon.

A man with long curly hair, wearing top boots and a billowing coat, stands on a rectangular marble pedestal, holding a globe in his hand. The inscriptions identify Copernicus, who studied here in 1491. A title is given: *De revolutionibus orbium caelestium* (On the Revolutions of Heavenly Bodies); he was born in 1473, he died in 1543.

He is surrounded by a very noble rectangular courtyard covered with asphalt. It is lined with arcades, balconies, decorated windows, small stairways, a jutting roof. Grinding iron gates open arduously. I'm in Cracow, the old city of spirits. I come here in the evening, from Wawel, the royal fortress. Wawel is shrouded in haze. Above it, the dazzling moon hovers in the milky whiteness. The towers and the mass of Wawel are like shadows. The cutting moonlight is very sharp, deathly white on the arcades. Slowly, something emerges from the blackness, something lofty, silent: the column of Copernicus.

A Polish Faust, a man named Twardowski, lived in Cracow during the Middle Ages; Twardowski was a magician, he had commerce with demons. I grope my way through the Jagiellonic Library: it was founded by pious Hadwiga. Here's the huge manuscript that was supposedly owned by Dr. Twardowski; you can still see the inky imprint of the devil's hand. Astrological calculations, planetary tables drawn in red and blue. I stroll through tremendous library rooms; *Collegium maius* and *Collegium minus*. The blue vault used to be an auditorium. The old Jagiellonic Library from the fourteenth century, colossal tomes, Nuremberg and Lübeck editions, treatises, speeches. Manuscripts from the fourteenth and fifteenth centuries, penned by professors and students. A theological lecture course commences: "God is the subject of theology. Theology is a single science. Theology is a practical science." A splendid, splendid statement! We are gradually beginning to understand it again. Back then, it bored the students in the classrooms. Lecture halls, corridors, refectories; everything crammed with books. Old globes, marvelous French books of hours, the wonderfully elegant codes of the municipal scribe Balthasar Behem.

A beautiful ancient city. Straight and winding narrow streets with houses, their walls reinforced at the base—I don't know why, perhaps against earthquakes. At the town hall, I open a glass door; a peaceful courtyard lies before me. I walk up; the stairwell is very plain, almost cubic. This is the secret of all these old buildings: they inspire peace and security. Their effect is natural, they are flesh, they have matured. I felt it in Wilno, at the university, and in an old Lublin tower. This entire inner city —its structures are poignant and profound. Modern-day people are going about. On the vast ring square, the fruit vendors with their colorful baskets stretch out in charming rows. Women spread ladles and wooden whisks on the clean ground in front of them. Tar steam wafts from a black kettle. The trolley clangs. How gracefully the Cloth Gazebo capers in the center of the market; the people with their wares rest all around. The Gazebo has been decked out with an attic. Its flanks are adorned with archways. In front, a pointed arch spans the dark entrance. In the basement of the long long vault, electric bulbs are burning, like lanterns, a double series, showing the darkness, not dispersing it. The darkness is the light, the lamps are red shadows. The vendors sit along the walls in these red shadows, and their stands are chock-full of valises, baskets, toys.

In the evening, I often steal into this slender decorated building, as airy as lace, the home of a dense darkness. The tremendous wealth of the arc lamps is spread out across the large square. The ancient fragile structure appears clearly in the whiteness, like a ship on the vast ocean. Confusing, poignant— this proximity of two worlds: electric light, modern promenades, automobiles—and that, the Cloth Gazebo, and also that, the slender church of St. Mary. How they crowd each other, encounter each other, kiss each other over their shoulders.

Is it a dead world and a new world? I don't know which is dead. The old one isn't dead. I feel intimately and violently attracted to it. And I know that my compass is reliable. It never points to anything aesthetic, it always points to living, urgent things.

I know that I've spent a few days being handed from one art lover to another. I've already done the big art collection on the second floor of the Cloth Gazebo, the Czartoryski Museum. Right by the Florian Gate, I saw Rembrandt, Raphael, Matejko, and porcelains, ancient Polish rugs, weapons. Tremendous paintings hung upstairs in the Cloth Gazebo. Once again, ceiling-high Matejkos, the excellent painter Malczewski. Roaring strength in a picture of a drive across ice: four racing farm horses yanking a wagon across ice,[32] four fat draft horses kicking colossally, four animals smashing right into the middle of the room. Also charming Grottgers, like the ones I saw in Lwów. But then comes the moment when I realize I'm not listening to what my companions are telling me. They are incredibly knowledgeable about art. They can't show me enough stylistic transitions. But I couldn't care less. When my final companion asks me whether I've already visited the art chamber at Wawel, I, dismayed, lie, "Yes," and I'm glad that she feels reassured. During the entire hour that she's been showing me old frescoes, I've only had eyes for her, a person of flesh and blood. I heave a sigh of relief when she starts talking about her family, her brothers.

For days on end now, I've been feeling such mysterious rheumatic twinges of yearning in my heart. I wake up with it, visit the Church of St. Mary three times a day, for five minutes, ten minutes at a time, with the vaults hanging over my head and collapsing. I'd like to have more of this, of this. I feel the lack. Or: I've got it and I need more of it. If only I could hear more about Dr. Twardowski. I'm thoroughly haunted.

One day, I again amble around the Church of St. Mary, which has captured my heart for a thousand and one reasons; and then I spot a balcony on the structure, on the side façade; its style is palpably Renaissance. I realize what I want—and I don't want what this balcony is and is meant to be. These are the awful theaters, the antique buildings in the cities. Looking at this balcony and thinking of these Greek columns and triangles, I feel that my reaction is more than a distaste for imitation, for empty art cliches. I unconditionally reject and repudiate classicism, Hellenism, and humanism. They are bourgeois easy chairs, deep, lazy lounge chairs. When I approach the Middle Ages, which waft toward me here, cooling forth from the dark vaults, hushing around the churches, the monks and nuns, around the houses with fortified walls, I know where I belong. I'm a born enemy and adversary of serene classicism and overly beautiful Grecism, an adversary of their emulation and their very doctrine, because they are perishable. They may have been something once, but they've been corrupted by the people who've used them. This is not the time to do right by them. If you want to do the right thing for yourself, you've got to avoid them. I'm an enemy of normal, lukewarm, shabby humanism. Just as I despise today's democracy, that name for a nonentity. Where can I feel it more sharply if not in the city of the cathedral, the bleeding Man of Sorrows, the executed rebel.

Like a horse that gets mud on its hooves and bangs it off on rocks, I've pushed away art and art lovers and now I'm moving without a plan through the town. The center of town is St. Mary's Church and the criminal under the ceiling. A human being, Veit Stoss [a German sculptor], hauled him out of his agonized soul. I walk without a plan and feeling my plan. I avoid the neat modern houses I was shown on the other side of the ancient city wall. I feel drawn to noisy, bustling Grodska Street. I sense disquiet, filth, poverty, suffering, formlessness. Once I'm past the ecstatic saints, the street opens up without becoming a square. A laughable building stands there: it's high, palatial, but old and dirty; its name is Hotel Royal; it's visited by Jews. A tall man in a brown cape and a black trilby walks past me—there's a hill to my right. Crows circle and caw over the red, bricklike round tower. And the hill sports a structure, surrounded by a red merloned wall, which descends abruptly all the way down the hill, depositing its mass on the road. This wall encloses mediocre, freshly whitewashed houses. They're like barracks. I walk along the foot of the hill, through a neglected area, with bare trees; trucks unload in front of grubby sheds. The crows keep cawing; a broad road leads upward; I don't want to take it. Yes, it's Wawel. The much-lauded castle. But I'm completely hindered from going up. It's my feeling, and it demands that I walk about below. I'm like a man to whom a woman is reciting a lyrical poem, but he keeps looking at her heels and thinking: What do her shoes cost? How is she getting along? What does she live on? Why does she want to recite? At the corner, at the sharp bend in the wall, rocks crop out. Now I'm entirely out in the open. Girls are walking dogs. Brown and white cows are grazing on the slope of the hill. A chaotic field: dump heaps of rubbish. How rhythmically the cows pull grass and occasionally stick out their long white tongues. The field slopes down. But now it's no longer a field; I didn't see what's below: water. Yes, there it flows, a broad expanse of smooth black water. And no ship moving across it. A locomobile steams and charges on the other side. Again the Vistula, again it's been excluded from the city. I wade through morass, leave the wall, mollycoddle the river. I'm delighted to hear its voice rise up to me at a bend and roar. This is how the river is treated: mortar and garbage are dumped down its banks. When the morass becomes insurmountable, I have to get away from it. I turn around at a small dirty house, with ripped towels, red and white aprons hanging from its rusty barbed wire; I am following the wall again. It retreated on the green hill; now it's returning with windows and a circular structure. The imposing castle church stands up there, Kosciuszko on his horse rides in front of it. The main entrance to the castle: the wall along the ascent has been lined with a mass of patterned tiles. On them are the names of cities and persons who have contributed to the restoration. And here is the pièce de résistance (I can already see the miserable Hotel Royal): up there, on the energetically aspiring wall, stands a building, renovated, with columns and a loggia. In the street, a farm wagon with small tinware: the woman inside, on the straw, is munching on a roll; she's covered the horse with a shapeless cloth, as if for a funeral; the horse is nibbling on its shaft, peering through sleepy eyes.

The Hotel Royal! I'm supposed to return to it. Yes, that's where I have to go. Am I not looking for Faust, Dr. Twardowski? The Jews! Jews are going there! I want to see the dead, the perishing things that live. I don't want renovations. Those people in black coats and fantastic fur caps on the sidewalk! Don't I recognize them? The Jews! The darkness in the marketplace, illuminated by electric light. The magic ship rising on the ocean. I have to see these things without further ado.

I know what the enlightened gentlemen, the Jewish Enlighteners will say. They laugh at the "stupid backward" members of their own nation, they're ashamed of them. They'll poke their shallow fun at me. The world was born with them and has reached utter perfection with them. The mere notion of telling the old fairy tales that the stupid backward people concern themselves with: what nonsense, what ignorance! None of that stuff is real, after all. I, neither an Enlightener nor a member of these national masses, a Western European passerby—I view those "Enlightened" ones like Africans who flaunt the glass beads they've gotten from sailors, the dirty cuffs on their dangling arms, the brand-new dented top hats on their heads. How poor, how shabby, how unworthy and soullessly devastated the Western World is, giving them those cuffs; how are they supposed to know.

In the evening, I see the groups of men emerging from small brightly lit prayer rooms on the narrow streets of Kazimierz, the Jewish district of Cracow; they wear half-shoes, white stockings, colossal fur caps over their ears—the *shtreymls*. My companion is telling me—I lap up his stories—about a bizarre old man, Berishel, whom you encounter in the streets; he's covered with hair, like a mountain man. He used to be more liberal; now he eats no meat, wears prayer thongs and a prayer shawl outdoors, puts stones in his shoes. People are scared of him.

When prayers are over, I enter the old synagogue. It used to be the library of "Emperor Kazimierz"; I saw a plaque outside; Kazimierz sitting as an angel, old Jews with Torahs thanking him for allowing them into Cracow. In the *pollish*, the anteroom of the synagogue, the chain still hangs on the wall—the chain for those condemned by the judge, the rebbe, and the pillory where they were spit at: theology as in the book at the Jagiellonic Library—a practical science. There is a group of "custodians of the sunrise"; they gather at the crack of dawn, old men. If one of them enters the synagogue before morning, I hear, he knocks on the door three times: the ghosts pray in the *shul* at night. You shouldn't walk past the *shul* at night. One night, someone did walk past it; he was called up to read the Torah inside; nothing happened to him; but he wasn't allowed to look back when he left. Someone tells me about the books they read in the prayer room, and about the Cabbala. You study it when you're older. One Jew was too young, he was only sixteen when he began reading the Cabbala. Secluding himself, he read and read. He no longer spoke, all he ate was bread and salt. He stopped speaking to his mother. Soon, he passed on; his father was a rabbi who composed Talmudic utterances: "Secrets of the world" are in the Cabbala. It tells about the angels who guard every human being. The Cabbalists parse every word of the Torah, explain the meaning of every letter, they tell when the Messiah will come, and they talk about bad angels, about Samiel and his wife Malka-Shvu. That's what I hear from these people.

Jews know about the thirty-six tsadiks. These are not rebbes, but anonymous righteous men in the populace. They are not allowed to reveal themselves, and no one guesses who they are; they can be cobblers and tailors. The world rests on these silent hidden thirty-six righteous men. If they didn't exist, the world would go under. Whenever one of them dies, another is born. Once, the great Polish queen Hadwiga wanted to wipe out all the Jews. The Jews were at their wit's end. Then their greatest rebbe consulted heaven, and heaven sent down a tsadik. But he refused to reveal himself. The poor coaxed him, lamented, and he finally gave in. He went to the royal court and said: "Anyone who puts his hand in his pocket will take out whatever he wishes." And that was what happened. But Hadwiga pulled out a snake, which wrapped itself around her entire body. The queen pleaded with the tsadik and asked him why. He said: "It happened because of your verdict." So she rescinded her orders, and the serpent disappeared.

In a book for women: the fable about the knight at the well. A knight found a well in the desert, he drank and accidentally forgot his money pouch. A pauper came, he also drank, found the pouch, took it, and went away. After a while, the knight returned at a hard gallop, looking for his pouch. At the well, he found a different pauper, who had just drunk from the well. The knight asked him about the money pouch. The pauper knew nothing about it. But the knight wouldn't believe him and he struck him down. Moses was sitting in heaven. God saw the murder and showed Moses what had happened here. Moses was horrified, he said: "A terrible injustice has been committed." But God said: "I will explain it to you. The knight killed the beggar who hadn't taken his pouch. But many years ago, this same beggar killed the knight's father. That is why the knight has killed the beggar now. And not he but the first beggar has the money pouch, and he's delighted. And who is the first beggar? He's the man whom the knight violently robbed of all his worldly goods and turned into a beggar. That's why the pauper is now taking back his property."

As we walk through the narrow streets, my companion laments. A young girl whom he knows has been missing for a week. She was intelligent, a hard worker. A week ago, she attended a lecture, he was there too. She was in high spirits, she visited someone after the lecture. She casually asked whether a person is buried if he has committed suicide and how he's buried. Then she didn't come home. Her parents believe she's been kidnapped by a white slaver. She was pretty, petite, her body wasn't very developed. But she had a lively mind, and she was always so merry. I can't really comfort him.

I walk across the broad marketplace in front of the Kazimierz Synagogue. It's surrounded by small decaying houses. Part of the area is walled in and closed. That's the old cemetery. I'm told about a house that used to stand here. One Friday, they were celebrating a wedding. It went on into the holy Sabbath. Whereupon everything and everyone sank into the ground: the entire house with the bride and groom and all the guests. A great rebbe used to live by this marketplace, the Remos—an acronym for REb MOses Isserle. His cottage is still here, he resided in it two centuries ago, he's buried in the old cemetery. He lived for thirty-three years, he wrote thirty-three books, he died on Lag b'Omer, thirty-three days after the festival of Shevues [the Feast of Weeks].[33]

I spot an odd-looking slip of paper. It looks like a leaflet, and it comes from the house of a woman in childbed. During her

labor, such "leaflets" were pasted on all four walls of her room.
The slip of paper bears Hebrew words, which are oddly arranged
in a column. This is what they say:

"Protect me, God, because I trust in you, protect me like the
white of your eye.

"Conceal me in the shadow of your wings. You are my protection. You save me from the enemies that surround me. Just
as sixty heroes of the heroes of Israel stood with swords around
Solomon's bed, each hero with his sword in his belt because of
the king's terror at night.

"Felicitations for the protection of the child, made by the
Baal-Shem. In the name of the God of Israel, the great, the
sublime; his angels will protect you on all roads. God, tear Satan
apart.

"Sinat, Wassinsanaff, Wassmangalif. Abraham, Sarah,
Moses, Aaron, Isaac, Rebecca, David, Jacob, Leah, Solomon.

> *"Do not let a sorceress live.*
> *Let a sorceress live: not.*
> *Not—let live a sorceress.*
> *Let live—not sorceress.*
> *Let live—sorceress not.*
> *Not—sorceress—let—live.*
> *Adam—Eve—inside.*
> *Lilith and her followers should remain outside.*

"I raise my eyes to the mountain. Elijah was walking, and on
the way he encountered Lilith and her followers. He said to her:
'You, your uncleanliness and your followers go with you. What
does that mean?'

"She said: 'I go into a birth house, in and in, to give the baby
a deathly sleep and stamp out its life and squeeze out the mar-
row of its bones and leave only the flesh on its body.'

"Elijah said: 'You should be banished from the sight of God
and remain as mute as a rock.'

"Lilith said: 'My Lord. Let me go and I will flee, and I swear
to you in the name of the God of Israel that I will give up my
designs on the mother and the child, and whenever I hear my

name or several of my names, I will flee. And I will tell you my names. And whenever anyone pronounces any of my names, I will be unable to harm the mother. And I am willing to tell you our names, and you should have them written out and hung on the wall of the mother's home. And I will then flee immediately. And these are my names: Lilith, Shattrinoh, Absta, Amiso, Amitrefo, Kashash, Odam, Ick, Poddu, Eilu, Pattrittu, Assihu, Kata, Kali, Bidna, Taltu, Pakusha.' "

A conjuration, and this is an amulet. These amulets are known as cameos. I hear other formulas and conjurations from an ancient tome, The Book of the Angel Raziel.[34] All this can easily be shrugged off as superstition, but it survives illegitimately. Survives like the cult of the dead. It's concentrated cabbalism. It stems from the old faith in a connection, nay, identity between words and reality; it emanates from an ancient mystical feeling. A great ancient way of thinking. The Hegelian notion beckons from far away or intimately near: "Whatever exists is rational." Modern-day people are content to study the state of history: words and signs issue forth in visible animal life. Here, in the beginning, the word begets. The Faust of the German Goethe begins by rejecting that proposition; he's not an ancient, not a genuine Faust. What a blend of naiveté and profundity.

The Book of Raziel advises that during a difficult birth, you should whisper the name of the Evil One into the woman's right ear and say: "You and all your followers, flee!" If you want to conquer a woman, you should take sweat from your face, put in into an unused glass, take a copper mug, and write *Citron* on a slip of paper. "Throw the slip into the glass and say: 'I beseech you, angels, make the woman's heart turn toward me.' Take the glass and hide it somewhere on the last Thursday of the month at four A.M." This is redolent of the German Middle Ages. It circulates around the world. We moderns control and utilize natural forces from the exterior; we've given up directing them from within ourselves.

I hear a few things from the ancient *Sefer Yesirah* [The Book of Yesirah];[35] I understand little, I remain with obscure inklings.

*Sefer Yesirah* (who knows how old the book is), followed by a whole library of commentators; there's nothing more mysterious. As if a different human species were talking. How foolish not to listen, to rely solely on the wisdom of a brief era like ours. What did Neanderthal man think, what sources did he investigate? What do locusts think, or birches in the forest? *Sefer Yesirah:*

> Yahwe Sebaot sketched thirty-two hidden roads to wisdom. He created a world with three numerical principles: number, enumerator, and that which is numbered. . . .
>
> Ten naked numbers, their appearance like that of lightning, their goal endless. His word within them is a dashing to and fro, and, at his orders, they race like a storm wind. And they cast themselves down in front of his throne. . . .
>
> Twenty-two letters: he drew them, he raised them, he purged them, he weighed them, and he interchanged each and every one of them with all the others; with them, he formed all creation. . . .
>
> Twenty-two basic letters are written in the voice, hewn into the spirit, and attached to the mouth, in five places. . . .
>
> He created Something from Emptiness and made nonbeing into being, and he raised huge columns from ungraspable air. . . .
>
> He bade the letter *het* rule language, he placed a crown upon it and fused them together. With them, he brought the ram into the world, the month of Nissan in the year, and the right hand in the body. He bade the letter *vav* rule thinking, he placed a crown upon it, and fused them together. With them, he brought the bull into the world, the month of Iyar in the year, and the left hand in the body. He bade the letter *zayin* rule walking, he crowned it, and fused them together. With them, he created the Twins of the world, the month of Zivan, and the right foot in the body.

The scorn of the Cabbalists: the historical tales in the Bible are supposed to be divine revelation; it is supposedly important to know how many oxen Jacob had, how the king fought. Since this is divine revelation, we can understand only if we know that everything signifies something else.[36]

And now for the Book of Raziel. I see the fantastic drawings in it. Someone reads me a passage:

God took a name and turned it into three drops of water, and the entire world became full of water, and the splendor of God was over the waters and divided into three parts: one part is dependent on his word, one third is in the sources, one third is on the water. Next, he took the second name and squeezed three drops of light through it and divided it too into three parts: one part on this world, the second part for the future world, the third for the Messianic world. Then [he took] the third name and squeezed out three drops of fire and divided into three: from one, the angels; from the second, the sacred animals; from the third, fire. That was how water, light, and fire came into being. To the right of God, fire; to his left, light; below, water. He took all forms of matter, blended them, took water and fire: from that, he created heaven; from water and light: his throne; from fire and light: the sacred animals. . . .

One angel is named Arzizo: that is why we call land *erets*. God thereupon created dust from the earth, and the angel over the earth is named Admiel: hence, Adam. . . .

God took counsel with the Torah: How should he create the world? And the Torah was written by God's arm with white fire and black fire. And God's name was written on the Torah with his right hand. And he was all alone in his world. And then he promptly held out his hands and took a name, and he made three drops of water from it. . . .

The size of the entire earth is five hundred by five hundred. And the entire sea turns around the world by the foundation of the world. And the horizon, the world, and the great sea all stand on a column. Its name is Tsadik. Because it is written: The Tsadik is the foundation of the world. And the column and the world are on a scale of Leviathan. Leviathan dwells in the lowest part of the water, like a small fish in the sea. The lowest part, compared with the highest part, is like a small wellspring on the shore of the sea. The lowest waters are called the weeping ones, because God parted the waters and took the highest water; whereupon the lowest wept and wanted to be higher: but God pushed the lowest down. And the weeping waters remain suspended over the lowest [part of] the earth.

In the cutting wind, I walk along the dark silent winding streets. On Friday evening, the streets of the ghetto have suddenly died. Almost no one is out. No commercial vehicle runs. The trolley silent, empty. Window after window is bright; they sit around the father, at the festive candlelit table. He sits royally, he sings.

Could I, could anyone else go back to this level? How long I had to stand in the Franciscan church until I made out the walls and niches, thus—my eyes penetrate the darkness and indeed penetrated it long ago. Not the darkness of these teachings, but the darkness of the era that calls itself modern.

An educated Jew, an Enlightener, joins me. The little Orthodox Jews, he says, are firm in maintaining the tradition absolutely. They picture Moses as wearing the fur cap, the *shtreyml.* The educated Jew says it's characteristic of the Hasidim to believe in their rebbe. He disapproves of the things I describe about the obsequies in Warsaw: people have only unclear notions of the existence of the soul; he doesn't like hearing about these things; instead, he emphasizes that these Orthodox Jews reject the modern secular school.

He seems to believe that there is only one solution to the Jewish question, and that the Jewish question is merely a Jewish question.

Someone else joins me during my random zigzagging. He regards the rabbis, the miracle-working rabbis, as intelligent men and as the real pillars of Orthodoxy. As usual, those Brahmans are against the elimination of castes, because it would hurt their money pouches.

Yesterday, during the festival of Joy in the Torah, they danced with the Torah out in the streets of the ghetto. At full moon, the pious pray outside their doors.

And when I cross fish markets, walk down a Dark Street, and come to Esthera Street, I find a large Orthodox school for boys, a Talmud-Torah. Groups of boys dash out of a gateway; the building is large and old. Two barking dogs leap into the gateway; a boy fearfully cries, "Mamme, Mamme." A very tall lanky young man with a red beard is guiding me; we are joined by several otl.ers in long coats. A huge white-haired man seems to be part of the school administration.

The old man has a kind fatherly bearish face, intensely crimson; he is very broad. I no longer notice the white flecks of mortar that come from the walls, and that they all carry on their shoulders or sleeves. The old man eyes everything with good-natured crabbiness; sometimes he smiles indifferently, sometimes he growls fiercely. For decades now, he's known it all; his hands are thrust deep down into his coat pockets. Very slowly, he ambles ahead of us through the old stone gate. And I instantly realize: this school doesn't have a trace of what Western schools have: rigid discipline, harsh authority; things are serious here—but in a different way, of course—patriarchal and intimate. Ancient doors hang in the wall. The old man opens: "Some pupils are probably still sitting in here." This is a class.

Yes, a class. A young man with a long brown beard and a round skullcap thrones on a raised platform; a book lies on the small desk in front of him. A strange dialogue that I don't understand ensues between him and a boy at his desk. The pupils sit at small desks around him. This is no dialogue, this is a duet. Sometimes the boy's neighbor joins in. The boy purrs, then goes on singing. At the last desks, two elderly men with books are listening. Suddenly, without saying a word, they reach back and shake my hand. The old man has trudged on ahead; I'd like to stick around, but he wants to visit another class. This one is filled with singing, purring, speaking. The teacher is on a platform again, a boy with a book next to him: an eager repartee between them. Meanwhile, the forty other boys, between eight and twelve years old, sit around at their desks, behind books, swaying their upper bodies lightly or intensely, some quite wildly, whispering, speaking, singing, prattling. "They are learning," says the red-faced old man from above. [The Yiddish verb *lernen* means "to study a holy book."] They all wear lovely black round skullcaps; they're all squeaky clean; their earlocks are long. They stand up, class is over, they run past us to the door. Some walk gently and earnestly. What a black, melancholy glow in their eyes. And a new class, older boys studying a passage

199

from the Talmud. The rooms are separated only by wood; the purring, the confused talking, the chanted learning resound from right and left. Over nine hundred pupils in this huge old house. I've never seen a school like this.

I visit another school run by these pious Jews, a modern school, for girls. They study religion as well as decorating, dress-making, housekeeping. Otherwise, the pious Jews would ignore the girls.

Along Grodska Street to the ring: Cloth Gazebo, St. Mary's Church, the executed man. Everything's symbolic; the executed man and *Sefer Yesirah* on one and the same level. But I reel at the sight of St. Mary's, the women with bowed heads emerging with rosaries. Icons, incense—I don't care for any of this. I've turned my heart toward powerful reality, toward the executed man. And how can I carry Leviathan in, the weeping waters under the lowest earth. I may have to carry them past. I am haunted by the executed man. I am drawn to him. The righteous man, the tsadik, the pillar that holds up the world: that's the executed man, the hanged man. In stronger colors, more intense, hues, like those in the stained glass windows. He, again he. He—stronger, stronger or different, struggling harder. Like a man who stands and walks calmly, and a man who has been thrown into the water and is about to drown: thus, the righteous man and the executed man.

As I walk past the down-to-earth shops along Grodska Street, through the well-organized confusion, I see the businessmen, the hurrying lawyers, art lovers, students. Just let them hustle and bustle, businessmen and intellectuals. The unsafe insidious rabble of intellectuals, whom I hate. The prostitutes of the mind.

The trolley, I know, is no more real than what I feel. The trolley is nothing compared with the powerful reality of the righteous man, the executed man. Compared with the unkilla-ble dreadfulness of the soul.

My companion was right: the young girl who's been missing for a week has been found. Floating down the Vistula. Why did she kill herself? Supposedly, the corpse can only have been in

200

the water for a day. What was she doing all week? Her mother continues to insist that the girl was kidnapped and killed. The corpse is going to be dissected.

This city of Cracow, to which I return, do not return, from the churches and Cabbalistic darknesses, is clean, beautiful, the cleanest, most beautiful city that I've found in Poland. But what can I do with the streets: I'm suddenly corrupted. What a world. On the ring, I see the powdered feminine beauty of Poland, in light-colored stockings, the sharp, piquant, sexy faces, the full figures. They're not isolated although they're walking ten or fifteen feet away from me: they head toward me through the air, the light carries all of them to me. I recall a painting at the Museum of the Cloth Gazebo, a female nude. The head was unpleasant; but the carnality was seen and captured beyond the familiar norm. The left leg moved forward, utterly animal; I saw a horse with a special skin, a higher equine breed. This intrusiveness everywhere in the streets.

Blissful laughter, strolling in the evening. The cafés are filled, people emerge from the pastry shops, holding small bags of candy. How solidified everything has become. How they sway and barely move in coziness and delight. Solidified. They're sated, they sate themselves, the pleasures steer them to themselves. The executed man hangs in their midst, but in a church. They've heaped up pictures and gaudy things around him.

Life must always be roused; this is easily forgotten. Life wants to be heavy and sated.

I walk, am hindered at every moment; things cross my mind at every moment. I can't understand it. At a construction fence, a movie-theater poster announces the films *Nathan the Wise* and *Count Cohn*. Henri Marteau is scheduled to play the violin in two days. An old gentleman with glasses, a bald head, and a thick mustache has had his photograph taken; underneath, it says: "The famous interpreter of Chopin."

An idea pokes into my brain, something that afflicted me in Wiesbaden years ago when I saw the people, the sick and the healthy, sitting in front of the spa orchestra. They lie in masses in the earth, corpses, horizontal, six feet, sixteen feet, thirty feet below, huge hosts of them, entire armies. They lie below, stretched out, the people who waged wars in Napoleon's day and earlier, who marched to India with Alexander, all of them. Romans, Caesar, Tiberius, and the Germans across the Alps— all of them horizontal in the earth. For them, Rome and Germania are nothing now. What is there for them? Just as Rome and Germania, Cracow and Berlin will be nothing for us. Colors will be nothing; music, the development of art, all the hubbub will be nothing. What do the millions of dead men care about the cathedral here. It doesn't exist. It has been—exhaled from them. The market, the paving—exhaled. A few, who passed here every day, died yesterday; something of their gaze is left in the windowpanes. And what are the ring, the great church for them now? Evaporated. For me, the square, the street are still something. But as if I were already retreating from them. As if I were gaining detachment. As if they were veering away. They are growing colorless; they are far away; congealing. As if I lay dying. Dying in this instant.

I have to lock myself up in my room. Then go to the city, only to the city.

A photographer's showcase. A very well groomed lady sits in an easy chair, her chin on the back of her hand. In her late twenties, with her opera cloak dropping away. A white satin gown, elegantly exposing her bosom. A small coquettish hat low on her forehead. She smiles opulently, very knowingly. Her eyes shrink when she smiles.

Next to her, the bourgeois woman, smiling a smile of deep understanding. She's very young, her hands are folded in her lap, she sits casually on her chair. Peacefully, trustingly, she gives herself up to your gaze. Her young smooth face is nice and maternal. It's good, it's friendly walking here. I have to find my bearings, see what's what.

I like the name Florian Street at a corner. This street is narrow. Students and modern women stroll about. In a shop window, a blissful mother stretches in a picture, her baby rides on her bosom. What I mistook for a small church at the end of the pretty street is an ancient gate that lets the trolley pass through. The old brick structure stands rectangular, surmounted by a

green dome. A wall adjoins it on either side; that's the remnant
of the old city wall. Droshkies run below, priests get their coats
dirty, toddlers clutch women's hands. Then I'm out in the open,
in a square. Parks line the wall, the Planty [public gardens]. A
sort of crenelated castle stands in front of the gate. An old Jew
with a colossal swollen nose walks about, peeking through the
apertures. Modern houses and streets are developing. The Polish Bank has a dreadfully modern sandstone building; up on a
scaffold, three red sandstone females are being attached; if they
were to topple down. . . . I stumble as I wander straight into a
broad street; the curbs are made for giants. In the middle of this
street, I find Kaiser Wilhelm, the First or the Second, or Franz
Josef, or Sobieski. He sits on a horse, with a pedestal underneath; he's got laurel wreaths too, no doubt. Coming up close,
I see "Grunwald"[37] on the socle; a dying knight is falling from
the pedestal; on the other side, somebody appears to be pushing
a plow: but the sun is blinding me. At the moment, I'm interested in a different horse: a butter wagon is trying to enter a
house near the monument. But the house is too high above the
roadway. The nag falls, pulls itself up, falls.

Soldiers, officials, students—the city has lots of them. The
students used to be badly off. In the early postwar years, I hear,
their clothes were terrible; many were the sons of poor peasants,
living cheek by jowl with the locals; often, they slept two to a
bed. Things changed later on; now, many students are well-to-
do; often elegant, they dominate the scene. I see them strolling
through Ring Square in the evening, a gathering of the young
intellectuals of this country. This is a masked ball. First music,
droll animals, futuristically painted emblems; a speaking chorus:
I hear that they are demanding financial aid. The masquerade
is the curtain-raiser for an Academics' Week throughout Poland. A class demands financial aid; that's how things are today.
They could be mailmen or washerwomen; but these people
would be more earnest. The young intellectuals as a class; why
do they make such a fuss over themselves? Other people are
worse off.

I'm told about the university and the intellectual life of this city; half lost in thought, I enjoy listening. Warsaw has become the big waterhead of Poland; Warsaw pumps out the provinces, Cracow has been drained. Someone curses: "It can't go on like this with the Warsaw economy." This was a Polish haven in times of misfortune. Poles migrated here from the Russian territory. When Pilsudski fled from St. Petersburg, he settled in Austrian Galicia, where he formed riflemen's associations, a cadre army, supported by the Austrian general staff. The workers and the Socialist youth stood behind him. When the war broke out, they marched across the border as Polish legions, poorly equipped. In Cracow, they founded the Supreme Polish National Committee, headed by an Austrian Excellency, a professor of law, Ladislaus von Jaworski, an adherent of Vaihinger's "As If" philosophy.

This city has an impressive story. Its university, with four faculties, was launched way back in 1400; the aims were pious: to fight the Russian schism and consolidate Christianity. Queen Hadwiga sold her jewels to foot the bill. Later on, Hussitism forged its way here too. Hordes of Reform refugees appeared in free Poland. There was a Polish Arianism; Anabaptists, Italian freethinkers like Sozin and Garibaldi found refuge here. Later on, the backlash came, as it did everywhere else; the Polish kings continued to be humane. Bishop Hosius of Ermland [in East Prussia] fearfully taught: "One heresy draws the next, and the ultimate end is sheer atheism"; the Jesuits consolidated the terrain; the Old Believer peasants and the lower clergy, the calm, obtuse populace kept the upper hand over the innovators.

After ancient bourgeois Cracow, after Jewish Kazimierz, I want to see Podgorze, the suburb, the proletariat, iron industry, chemical industry. Grodska Street, the fortress, the Hotel Royal lie behind me; I am walking through Kazimierz. Shop after shop; in the upper stories, businesses after businesses. I read the names on the shingles: Affenkraut, Stieglitz, Vogelfang, Goldstoff. Bales of cloth are being unloaded; many redheaded Jewish women walk about. How badly groomed these young men; they're not allowed to shave; the black down grows thick on their throats and cheeks. Slender boys march in black top boots; their heads shorn smooth, their long earlocks wafting behind them.

204

The stores become more wretched, the houses are thoroughly squalid; this is Krakowski Street. I've walked past the old building that bears the plaque for King Kazimierz; it's an elementary school now. In the marketplace to the left, the farm wagons are scattering straw; shabby booths display produce. Through the tiny side lanes: urban and rustic proletarians roam about, hauling loads next to woeful Jewish figures. Horrible tattered coats, sloppy women, and, in the wretchedness, beggars hugging walls; pale children. Jozef Street is narrow and thronged; peasants and workers pant under heavy sacks. Oh, what a little Polish ragamuffin in front of me: she's five or six years old. She shuffles gingerly in ripped oversized shoes, her legs are bare from the knees up, her dress is a ragged sack, she has a torn greasy kerchief over her blonde head and her shoulders. The streets are filthy; piles of refuse and garbage are stewing on the paving. I passed through a meat and fish market, then a goose market. Among peasants climbing down from their wagons, an old Jew wanders bizarrely in felt slippers and a loose, black-belted coat, holding his prayer shawl in a green velvet pouch under his arm.

This is the Vistula, the great full Vistula torrent. Its banks are powerfully fortified with ramparts; people fear the river. Ice floes drift by. Look, we've had a freeze. We've had a freeze. So that's how long I've been away from home. In Warsaw, I could leave my coat in my room. I've gone through Wilno, Lwów; now I'm going through Podgorze. Cities after cities. What are my roads.

As I leave the bridge, I see a small fat dog in a shop window, eating from a plate. The houses are all one- or two-story, and so run-down. Tattered posters stick to the walls: appeals from political parties, no doubt. They appeal, excite; human beings love being excited. The posters probably contain promises and goals to be achieved. Then, once elections are past—the windows remain shattered, work remains the same from dawn to dusk, people groan the way they did yesterday, and they will keep groaning tomorrow.

The vast rectangular square ahead of me is a jumble of booths and stands for baked goods, knickknacks, vegetables. Work vehicles charge left and right. I want to mount the steps to the huge red church that terminates the square; with its steeples and its crown, it resembles St. Mary's Church. The beggars on this stair are extraordinarily ragged. Women sit in the cold; they're shapelessly wrapped up in tatters and parts of old trousers; old skirts dangle over their shoulders. And there they sit, immobile and trembling. I—don't—want to enter the church.

I wade through people down a long suburban street. Two nuns lead a bevy of girls in black caps. Warehouses for provincials, cottages, a butchers' hall. Behind the houses, green hills loom over walls. Factory fronts. And through miry side streets back to the Vistula, past awful houses. Masses of dogs playing around, sniffing the garbage. I hear bickering from basements. Again I stand on the stone enclosure at the river. Gigantic chimneys to the left spew out heavy smoke.

Down below, the flickering iron-gray water.

The political physiognomy of the city:

There is a respectable old conservative newspaper, *Time*, which used to be loyally pro-Austrian; now it represents the viewpoint of the constitutional state; there are the Social Democratic *Forwards*, the Christian national *Voice of the People*, the Jewish national *New Daily*. At the Sejm elections, the city gave two mandates to the Christian national coalition of the so-called Eight Parties, one mandate to the Socialists, and one to the Jews.

I enter the treatment room of the health insurance association, the lovely new rooms of the provincial health plan. Students then go into the surgical unit, and I join them. A steep amphitheater, huge round windows. Down below, the professor, with salt-and-pepper hair and a white smock, is lecturing behind the white table; his beard is nicely trimmed. A man with a terrible hernia is lying on the table; now and then, the professor touches the hernia and demonstrates. Throughout the lecture, a young man in a military uniform with a yellow belt around his waist and a strap running down from his right shoulder stands in front of the professor, stands and listens. On the wall below, pictures of hernias, the course of the cutting in the operation. Sutures. Younger and older students have draped their coats over the backrests. The room is full; they are stand-

206

ing at the top, in the round, under the harsh cold sun. The red and lilac blouses of the female students glow pleasantly in between the browns and blacks of the men's clothing. Fresh young men with long hair combed back and with bored faces lean back. Two chat, their hands over their mouths. Pert bobbed hair, girls with black hair and piquant faces, prop their chins on their hands, half leaning over their desks, dreaming downward. The professor talks uninterruptedly. Several students prop both arms up broadly, some doze comfortably, leaning back, some peer at the circle overhead, some scribble on the desk tops.

As I descend, a crippled boy stops at the entrance and passes his water. They yell at him, ordering him to go to the eye clinic, where he belongs.

I visit students cramming for exams. They are pessimistic about a later medical practice; they complain: what a time this is! Others tell me that they are wandering through the Polish cloisters, monasteries, and churches, traveling to Italy, writing about their experiences in books and periodicals. Just like us— and in Paris—and in London—and wherever.

The face of the modern movement, the pragmatic one; the issues are institutions, progress, better jobs. And they, the younger people, are doing the donkeywork. Sometimes they feel it, sense something. I've known it for a long time: the younger generation is not revolutionary. It's simply wild. Following the law of nature, it repeats the childhood of the human species. Dear Fatherland, thou need'st not fear.

Outside the main post office, I ask a policeman for directions. In fractured German, he amiably guides me across the street: "Well, first here, to the right—then" (he peers about) "another right and another right, and then" (his left arm lunges out), "take a left, and then" (his face twists in a smile, he thrusts it against mine), "then another left." He bursts into jovial laughter; I join in.

At one pillar of a gateway, I encounter an old, ragged beggar. With his hat wedged between his knees, he spoons squashed potatoes from a tin plate. A small pale tattered girl, his daughter, stands at the other pillar; she brought him the plate; now she stares rigidly at him with big brown eyes, with big eyes that lie in their sockets. They rigidly follow his every movement as he eats.

The autopsy has been performed on the eighteen-year-old girl whom I heard about from my guide through the Jewish district; and these are the findings: heavy injuries, rape, death only a day ago. She was kidnapped, abused, murdered, her body thrown into the water.

The sixteen-year-old daughter of a physician has vanished. She's been missing for four days. She was found on the road, raped, moronic, insane.

The woman with the unpleasant head in the gallery: the flesh, the animal movement of the leg, the horse, covered with human skin! The intrusive faces! The biting animal, the raging animal, the flailing animal, the animal shrieking in pain!

Sunday morning; it's ten o'clock; people are strolling in the brightest sunshine. Now a blood-red banner comes across Ring Square from the church side. The flagpole pokes high above the square. The men carry red inscriptions on bands; women, girls, children are also demonstrating. The procession, four hundred, five hundred people, moved very peacefully, very middle-class, across the square, towards the Planty. Then it was swallowed up. The sun shines white; the ladies and gentlemen are promenading. After a quiet while, I free myself from the sun, look for the side street that they took. Through the gardens, along Du-najewski Street. They stand in massive groups at the Labor Union House, along Dunajewski Street. It's cold out. Factory crews with red flags. Gigantic wreaths, the posters say: "For the Victims," "For the Fallen." Bands march up. Railroad workers in blue caps. Female workers with red carnations. Associations with banners. A year ago, a general strike took place in this city. There was an inflation, the lower-ranking rail workers demanded higher pay. When their demands were turned down, they went on strike. The government sent troops into the factory, declared martial law. The other workers then began a sympathy strike. The government tried to crush it with violence. A battle was fought. The workers entrenched themselves in the Labor Union House. The army and the police blocked the entrance. The workers got hold of weapons and fired at the cavalry, which was sent out first. There were many casualties on both sides. The afternoon brought an armistice, and the episode was settled peacefully. The government's drastic methods found no sympathy even among the middle classes; the workers were known as peaceful; the government had acted Russian. Sixty workers were put on trial because of those events—and acquitted. The funeral of the dead workers was attended by ten thousand people and no priest. Government and clergy participated only in the obsequies for the soldiers who'd been killed. It was the sixth of November. On that day, I saw a coffin in St. Mary's, at the high altar; the coffin was covered with flowers and surrounded by a very high ornamental frame, which sported wide yellow ribbons. Late in the afternoon, at the onset of twilight, a company of lancers rode over from the ring: uhlans, four abreast, on huge high horses, rifles slanting across the men's backs, lances decorated with pennants on their right arms: a booming tableau. But now the others are marching, the thousands, here, along Dunajewski Street, toward the cemetery. Their fluttering red flags!

The red flags! Of all the flags that exist, these are the most resolute. I can understand them. I haven't gone astray in the city of the Church of St. Mary and the Righteous One. The blood-red flag. The oppressed fettered people of the machines. And the safe and secure, who rigidify the world in a sense of well-being, in a stringent order for the eyes.

The safe and secure world; bloody flags above it.

A teeming swarm in the evening, at the railroad station. I have no business being here: I've been here twice already, and now I prick up my ears: my hour has come. The people mob the corridors, shove into the third-class waiting room. Policemen patrol the corridor. One, carrying a fixed bayonet, escorts a prisoner in a brown uniform. The prisoner laughs when he enters the waiting room, his fresh young face beaming broadly. As if freezing, he holds his manacled hands together on his chest. Inside, in the throng at the buffet, he instantly addresses a young woman; they laugh together. She puts a roll on the table

209

for him; the prisoner settles on the bench by the wall, jolly, looking at everyone; he squeezes into a corner; the policeman at his side. People cluster around the table, chatting with the prisoner. A man hands him cigarettes; the fettered man reaches very gingerly with his manacled hands, trying to conceal his chain. The man gives him a light. The policeman buys sausage.

A dismal young man comes through the door with a young woman and two clean little girls, all muffled up; for an instant, they glance along the benches. The careworn man ensconces himself on a bundle, the woman next to him; she lifts one child to her lap; the other child, with a finger in her mouth, gazes into the smoky room.

Throughout the middle room, the men, the workers, stand around the pillars, full healthy faces, women and girls with shawls and kerchiefs. Many of them so young and beautiful. Two factory girls whisper together; then they pounce on a new-comer, a young girl, grab her hands, shriek, laugh their heads off: they've experienced something; the newcomer shrieks with them. Working girls, adolescents of sixteen to eighteen, form a circle. Behind them, boys, as tall as trees, wearing caps, smirk, play pranks on the girls, who respond. They push one another, girls and boys, with their backs. Eventually, two girls hurry around the group of men and through the exit to the platform. As they leave, one boy unabashedly tries to grope their breasts. The first girl pulls away, the other takes it in good stride, grinning, without moving. As they leave in a row, another boy gropes their hair through their kerchiefs, holds them fast for an instant. And every girl pauses for an instant, not batting an eyelash, not shaking her head, then hurries on.

# ZAKOPANE

*The fog opens in utter silence, divides.*
*And round mountain massifs emerge, are there, carry*
*snow.*

I've been in Cracow too long already. You finally reach the point where you know everything that's available to you, and you have to decide: either move on or settle in, surrender. So I climb into the wagon. The martyrdom of leaving a city commences: not the wrench of separation, but the struggle with the hotel staff, with the insolence of compulsory gratuities, of tributes to inferior people. I, a free man, am suddenly dismissed and handed over to arbitrary creatures. My fury at having to encounter these people disrupts my every night before my departure. In Warsaw, the chambermaid informed me through a Pole who was visiting me (she had already motioned toward me mysteriously) that people pay her weekly tips. People pay her. In the same hotel, a bellboy who had to shine my shoes every morning because I'd been forgotten by the colleague taking care of this series of rooms shook his head as he gazed at his hand after I gave him fifty groszy. He stood there, saying nothing, and left only after receiving fifty more. In Lwów, the bellhop in charge of my room carried my suitcase down, but, ominously thrusting his hand into my droshky, he refused to let go: "It's

211

too little, it's too little." He got a bigger tip for carrying my suitcase downstairs than someone else would have gotten for lugging it to the railroad station twice.

Now, in Cracow, early in the morning, I glumly descend the stairs of my hotel. It was nice living here. But from now on, I'm no longer a guest. I'm an outcast, I have to run a gauntlet. Strange the way the rumor of your departure spreads through the personnel. I told the night clerk yesterday evening, and today the entire house knows—a tribe of robber barons. Agamemnon's system of signal fires after the fall of Troy can't hold a candle to this network. Normally, when I take the stairs (they're covered with nice clean carpeting), I don't run into anybody. If someone was mopping the floor, he never stood up, never got out of my way. Now, all roads are beleaguered. "He must go through this empty corridor." They're all here—people whose existence I inferred only from the notice in my room. The text warned: There are bellboys, chambermaids, waiters; each has his bell signal. My departure is their call for a general inspection. As a rule, they innocuously moved about somewhere or other, wearing white aprons (which meant they were chambermaids) or green aprons (which meant they were bellhops), or carrying dishes from some room (not mine) while soft-soaping one of the chambermaids: the waiters in black tuxedos, tip-top, scurrying down the stairs. But now I have to struggle to pass through, pay tolls, road fees. I drink one last glass of this hotel's water, cursing the place; then I open my door and sneak inaudibly across the hallway carpet.

Holy Shiva, what can go wrong! I'll manage to get out. In half an hour—it's most inconceivable—I'll be sitting inside the roaring train, heading toward Zakopane. In half an hour, what's about to happen will be far behind me. Now, the first greeting flashes, the first shot: "Good morning." Then the second. How friendly these insidious women are, how they manage to stop cleaning the carpet just when I have to walk by. They're already standing up, smiling. Smiling expectantly—these women. I know that smile. That's the guises they use for their baseness. They mount assaults, sound the attack. If I fail to nourish their smiles, then I'll experience the lunge, the mocking mouth movements. Insults that I tremblingly anticipate. I ask: "Which of you belongs to the room I was staying in?" One of them is at hand; she dons that smile and approaches me, in accordance with the rite. She's put down the broom in order to keep her hand free. Too bad she doesn't use the broom to cover her face so she can give up that damn smile. She receives a banknote, scrutinizes it—and I've passed the test! She nods, the highway-woman nods, her eyes flash. She speaks Polish in her emotional exuberance. The other one nods too. They have my purse, my life is saved. I live two flights up. Now just two more corridors: they're open. I know that the main barrier is downstairs. There, barricades are set up by the robber barons who had bell wirings up to my room and whom the hotel took on under the discreet name of "domestic staff." Downstairs, they'll form a guard of honor: making my every step difficult, laying booby traps for me all the way to the door, all the way out to the cab.

I ask the desk clerk for my bill. He sniffs portentously: "It will be ready in a moment." I wait. Now and then, he scrutinizes me, searching me, assessing me, the condemned man. He smokes, whistles, summons an apprentice waiter, acts un-abashed. I notice that in the lobby, more people than usual are sauntering about, almost assiduous, or rather, lurking. The lobby is crowded all the way to the door. The latter is a four-part revolving door. Two boys stand there. I look ahead: a boy will make a motion, then I'll be inside the structure. Then the other will make the second motion. But first, each will doff his cap and stretch out his hand. If they don't like what I give them, they'll let me get stuck in the revolving door while they have a coffee in the lobby, saying they'll get a locksmith at some point during the day, but now he's asleep. The hotel is really quite accommodating, it could even station four boys at the door. The other two are probably at a different door, pouncing on a fellow sufferer. All at once, the clerk exclaims: "Your bill is over there, with the hotel chambermaid." The hotel chambermaid? How can that be? I just ran into her. That was my first escape attempt. Is she going to show up again, that abominable freak, and is she going to smile again? Flabbergasted, distrustful, hesi-tant, I approach the opposite room. Here, at a table, I find an

213

elderly woman with papers. I wonder: Where's the chambermaid? The woman addresses me in a language that Poles apparently call German and Germans insist on calling Polish. She says (and I grow confused, a feeling of helplessness lovingly comes over me) that she's the chambermaid. Hers truly. The hereditary chambermaid of my second-floor room. No one but her.

I gather my thoughts: "How did you get down the stairs? And on the other hand . . ."

"On the other hand what?"

"On the other hand, you looked different a couple of minutes ago. Upstairs. You looked younger. You were holding a broom, in front of your face."

"I was holding a broom?"

"Yes, you've been transformed. You've gotten so much older. What's going on here anyway? What's happening here? How did you get down the stairs? What happened to you on the way down? And besides, what do you want? When I was upstairs I already—"

Suddenly the door opens, the young girl from upstairs glances inside and instantly scoots away. I gain poise, composure: "So that's the story. Sneak attack!"

I spray anger: "*That* was the chambermaid. She's the chambermaid. Not you. You didn't grow older at all. You were standing here, waiting to ambush me. You were old already. Ancient. You know the trade."

The woman retorts pityingly, then calls the desk clerk, who comes to the doorway and, scrutinizing me with inquisitorial severity, crows: This woman is the hereditary chambermaid. Thereupon, he folds his arms, remaining at the threshold in a Napoleonic posture. He and the woman exchange glances. What are they planning? "I'm all alone in this vast plain." Should I jump out the window? Berlin has a fire department and a riot squad. I inquired yesterday: you can't call Berlin from here. You can't call Berlin until you get to Kattowice. Should I gallop to Kattowice, alert the riot squad? My rage at my helplessness grows. Grows beyond me. Grows so intensely that I *can* do something after all. I ask for my bill. I begin speaking out loud. Too loud. Positively screaming. These are screams of distress, clad in anger. All I am asking for is my bill; I am not concerned with the metamorphosis of chambermaids, the sudden aging of chambermaids, or the duplicity of chambermaids in this hotel. I am not a theosophist. And I pay. And holler. My wallet emerges, thick, from my coat; swollen with prosperity. I bare my money shamelessly before the eyes of the desk clerk and that woman. I have a fabulous amount of cash. Including U.S. dollars. They dare to smile for a moment. But I slam my money down so hard that the foundation walls quake, the guests tumble out of their beds, the doors fly open, and a ubiquitous lament resounds on all stories. I slam down some more money. The panes shatter in the street. The elevator shoots up. The woman is terror-stricken by the detonations. I too am terror-stricken. It's so nice feeling rage. Her false teeth have slid out to her lips, the better to peer at me. I leave the room, I swing the bill like a trophy. At the exit, the bellhop tremblingly receives me with my valise. The boys have scattered. The revolving door moves on its own. I sit in the droshky. The coachman's back is in front of me. I'm sure I'll wrestle you down too.

I'm told this isn't the right season, the right time for Zakopane. But there's always a time for Zakopane. There's always a time for everything. Nature is present in rain, fog, snow, hail, as in light and warmth. A chicken's a chicken, when it's healthy and when it's sick. Normal beauty gives me encephalitis, sleeping sickness. Nature ripened last night; the meadows with their stubble look piebald. I travel with a small valise and my yellow briefcase. I've cast off my worthy wardrobe trunk, I've bought a ticket for that green abomination, which has brought me joy, but also burning heartache. I've dispatched it to Danzig, to the chagrin of all bellhops, who've pounced upon it greedily, in order to grab hold of not it but me. It'll wait for me in Danzig, I'll greet it across the barrier, then the two of us will peacefully head home.

How empty all the trees and bushes are. The branches poke black into the air. The trees are skeletonized; cringing, they let the frost pass over them. They stand in packs on the rows of

215

bluish hills; they ought to be freezing, but they're smart: they conceal their energy ahead of time, play dead. All that's left above is their empty summer home. Azure-painted cottages whiz past on long stretched-out mountain pleasures; the cottages are all wood, with old low roofs. I feel as if the hills and mountains are growing higher; they stand blackish-blue, with broad yellow spots. Now, a fir forest on a rise descends in a straight line. Red tile roofs flash bizarrely; the house walls are blue. I ride in amid bare woodlands; they look like a shriek with their hundred erect branches. A wild black agitated pleading. The ravens perch nicely upon it; staggering up the trunks and sagging to the ground. A black fir-covered mountain draws closer and closer, and now it's so close that I can make out its trees. The firs are blended reddishly with hardwood. In the very white air, I see the various depths of the forest; it looks astonishingly spatial, three-dimensional. I'm amazed at the perspective; the way the tree trunks grow smaller and smaller, round and standing behind one another into the depth. A stereoscopic spectacle. And that's just the curtain-raiser.

Am I awakening or is the landscape awakening? It moves more richly. There are stubble fields slowly rising over hills and mountain chains. Colors appear, strangely delicate; green grass or moss in the reddish-brown of the stubble; the entire tableau whitened over with frost. Such a fragrance of white. At times the scene is dominated by the red of the stubble and the soil crust, at times by the heavy green. The breath of the whiteness lends them charm as they grow weaker and stronger, vanishing or emerging. The frost fuses soil, moss, grass, and stubble into a unity, subtly modulating it.

Black mountain blocks keep towering toward me with red roofs, churches. Valleys open. A lake lies there; its edges white as if it had formed salt crystals. But that's ice; black and dead the hole in the middle. The countryside changes so abruptly. It's extraordinary. I have to stick to looking. Suddenly, a slope is covered with big, garishly red leaves. The sky is gray as if snowy. Far away, everything is brightened with grayish-white. And to the right and left of the blackish-blue mountain blocks, long rectangular tongues of fields dart toward me. Then come reddish flames of trees and low shrubbery. I don't know why I keep gazing, so anxious, so absorbed, at those slopes, which keep approaching me every few minutes and then twisting away into the background. The solid, physical, three-dimensional quality of the trunks, blades, shrubs is so distinct. As it was in the fir trees. They stand side by side, so vividly in the ditches, trenches. Everywhere, space. Everywhere, something occupies the space and separates into it. Separates into the space. And then dons colors and moves in the wind. There is something very mysterious about the way things stand on the slopes and show branches and haulms. A remarkable, delicate intimacy. Afterward, I feel as if the very essence of spatiality has touched me at those moments.

The trip lasts two hours. It seems a lot longer. Just three hours ago, I was still sitting in the hotel lobby. We zoom past small smoking white-powdered villages, shoot up elevations, rattle through a flanking of fir trees. A wide black body of water lurks below—a group of small frozen brooks; beneath a vault of shrubbery. Now men step out of a lonesome house. Wearing thick brown coats and high black caps, they turn toward the field in back, swinging their sticks while talking. Under the frost, the field wears a wonderful light grassy green. Black horsies run along the highway, pulling timber carts. Everything melts before the profound green carried to me by bluishly shadowed mountains and before the reddish radiant yellow of the treetops.

For a long time, the polymorphous landscape rocks past me. It looks wan and chilled; I viewed it through closed eyes. The hoar is molded with cautious and poignant finesse on even the smallest things. This station is named Jordanow. Now, a touch of sunlight peeps from the clouds straight to the right; a dazzlingly white cold shine. I already noticed the sun's presence a short while ago: the frost flowers on the window were growing hazy. Their fibers ran together, they buckled: wherever a feather landed with bold swings, the flowers dripped. What a magnificent, terrifying power—the sun far off behind the clouds, barely visible. It emerges further, the flowers die, and I'm delighted. What a chaos life is. I'd like to meet the man who can discern an order here. The day grows lighter and lighter. Now the sky turns blue. The higher I travel, the more thickly powdered the trees. A strange black brotherhood assembles on the mountains; colossal black firs. They wear white cloaks. They stand up there and preach into the valley.

I check my suitcase, my overnight bag. With my hands in my coat pockets, I stroll out of the station. People are taking cabs; but I've got lots of time. I stand, wondering which way I should go; where is Zakopane? People have been watching me. Boys eight to twelve years old. Snotty ragged little boys; first there are four, then six, seven. They congregate on the street outside the station and follow me. Suddenly, one of them accosts me and talks to me. The others surround him, watching my mouth. I laugh. I know what they want. They've been sent out by small landlords. But I want to sightsee in peace and quiet. I laugh, shake my head, say my *"Niemiec, nie rosumiem* [German, I don't understand]." I march on. They argue among themselves, are suddenly behind me again. I halt. So do they. A physical interdependence exists between us. We are opposite electricities. But I don't care for the gang; I want to walk alone. I snap at them in German, I make an international annoyed face and cross the street. They stand there. To hell with them. Is there something about me that makes them run after me? I compromise myself with this society. They cross the street. Trees stand in the way, a long highway. I'm going to stroll along it until the village comes. Now the boys are on my heels. I put up with them for a few paces. Then I turn around, holler. Tone too has an international resonance. They say something, again offer me their hospitable homes, their lousy hovels. Where's a policeman! Are people here fair game for the riffraff? Now a gentleman comes along the avenue, sees me, hears me yelling, and addresses me in German. What's wrong? The boys won't leave me in peace, they're actually following me. Could he kindly tell them to get lost, I don't desire their help. He parleys with them, then reports that they've got a good cheap room nearby, I'm obviously looking for one—would I like to see it? I'm absolutely not looking for a room. I'm not looking for anything. And certainly not with them. *I'm walking alone through the woods today*

*and looking for nothing along the way.* The man doesn't understand. But I stick to my guns; I'm an enraged Goethe lover. And
in Poland I can get away with it. Now I'm strolling to the village.

"The village? This isn't the way to the village."

"What? Where's the village?"

A young woman, out of a clear blue sky, is standing next to
the man. I already saw her back at the station: she was staring
at passersby. The man tells me that this young woman is here
and intends to guide me, she too. She's willing to take me if I
want to go to the village; she can show me a hotel or rooming
house. They won't leave me in peace. Why oh why oh why does
she want to guide me? I'm not to stroll under the cool mute
trees. I'm not allowed to enact government-approved German
poetry. The man asks me, while the boys lurk, whether I wish
to go to the village with the young woman: she knows several
good places to stay. My role is ludicrous; I'm making a fool of
myself with Goethe. In the Tatra Mountains, people don't understand Goethe. In any case, I've got to get rid of those kids. I
ask the man to ask the Polish miss whether it's a decent place in
God's name and whether he or she happens to be personally
acquainted with it. After a bit of Polish, he replies that he *is*
personally acquainted with the place; it's a reputable rooming
house; the people here are all having problems because it's off-
season, that's why they're sending out errand boys.

"Fine," I decide, "I'll go with her. Thank you very much. And
above all, miss, please drive those kids away."

She understands a smattering of German. The man says
good-bye. The boys, under a hail of invectives, dash across the
roadway, cursing, yelling back. I walk with the young woman,
but only briefly toward the village. Then she has a brainstorm:
she's got an aunt who speaks a good German. She lives with
her. It would be better if she took me there. I'm flabbergasted;
if you've got an aunt, give her my best. In Germany, aunts are
dubious creatures, they belong to the realm of mythology; ad-
vanced Biblical exegesis has utterly shattered all faith in them.
Should I really accompany her to her aunt's place? She says it's
not far. The kids are gone; now comes the aunt. I find the
weather beautiful, the boulevard very pleasant; I'm delighted by

219

the bare swarthy branches. Why shouldn't I go with her to her aunt's if it's along this route? I feel bright-eyed and bushy-tailed. We turn around. We leave the village behind us.

My young guide is named Niusia, pronounced Nyusha. The Zakopane chapter begins.

Her hat is pressed deep down on her face. The visible part of her hair is straw yellow. She's of medium height. She's wearing a very simple black jacket. Her shoes are anything but elegant. And she conceals her hands, in her pockets, on her bosom. Her hands inspire lots of confidence; they're in ordinary brown cotton gloves, torn. Usually, she walks ahead of me along the muddy road, consoling me now and then, assuring me we're almost there. She may be twenty. Her figure is solid, more rustic than urban, her hips are solidly developed. The conversation often bogs down, she can't find the German words. Finally, we come to a simple wooden house with a veranda; we walk across the yard; she exchanges a few words with a man. I stand in a large dark hallway filled with smells of food. The young woman gets a key. Then she opens a door on my right. We enter a large bright room. This is supposed to be my room; do I like it? And she apologizes; she's getting her aunt.

Upon seeing this room, I am slightly moved, and I know I'm staying. A real piano, a big black instrument, stands by the window; plush furnishings of the old caliber: these people have come down in the world. They take in boarders. These are the remnants of their good furniture. It's cold here; I don't really want a room like this; where have I landed? But I won't disappoint them. I'll be freezing here, and I'd have more comforts at the hotel in the village. But I see a different sort of comfort here: they address me respectfully, I am somebody in their eyes; and I—cannot say no, nor do I want to. Nyusha comes back with another woman: mid-thirties, slimmer, skinnier, faded, yet fresh, charmingly lively and friendly. After exchanging a few words with me, the two women whisper together (I'm still in my coat); and when I ask what they're smiling and talking about, the second woman stops talking to Nyusha: "We both find the gentleman so nice. He's so attractive." The room's too big for me, it gives me the willies; I ask about the bed. The two of them whoosh out to look for another room in the house. And I sit alone and tinkle on the piano. The room's ice-cold. What was the hotel like? I had my room number and the bell; here, two women go back and forth; it'll be too much for me, but it'll work for two days.

When they return, they've changed, they've done themselves up. Bobbed hair, light blonde. Red stub noses, their hands show signs of rough work. They lead me to my real room. And for an instant, I'm truly startled. This is really too much. It's nothing but a naked alcove. Board walls; two cots along the walls. The room's on the ground floor, no curtains on the windows. The door can't be locked. An iron stand for toiletries, a table, a chair, a closet: that's my room.

"We'll turn on the heat," she says.

I'm dreaming; yes, I say, it's cold.

"And we'll bring the gentleman hot tea and lunch."

"Please do." I'm dreaming.

The older woman keeps moving diffidently at the table; she manages to get it out: she'd like me to pay something in advance.

"Fine, fine"; suddenly, I'm lost in thought. They obviously can't even afford lunch. I pay. They leave. I stand at the window. Those awful kids across the road. I might have gone with them. What am I up to again? Why am I standing here? I've got cash in my wallet, and I'm in this wretched alcove. It's so icy cold I can't even take my coat off. I sit at the table in my hat and coat. My hands are dirty; no water and no towel. I'll sit here awhile, then travel on. I'm utterly lost in thought.

Lunch is over. Nyusha wants to go to the village with me. I was intently focused on the street; Nyusha is walking next to me, speaking or not speaking. And now I learn something new: how to both pay attention to her, watch her, and view the countryside. View the countryside through her. My estrangement, my aloofness disappear. All at once, I've been here for six weeks. She says: there's nothing to see there and there, and I'm willing right off the bat, I amiably see nothing. It's funny and friendly. A long road, a bridge. New buildings, mountain chains to the right, and then the village, the church, a quiet main street with resort shops, picture postcards, dry goods. It draws past me very far away, gaudily painted, oddly tinted.

She takes me between lovely villas, leads me out into the open fields, along a broad promenade. The terrain rises. The village with the church spire gradually sinks behind an undulation. And in front of me: a red evening sky above a jagged massif. Upon seeing the cloud bank, I'd like to capture every last detail of the tableau: the way the colors blend in the sky, their edges, their intermingling. It's so interesting, so thrilling: the colors change from minute to minute. But Nyusha chats: about her aunt and how badly off they are. She's lost both parents; her mother, who died young, was the sister of the woman she lives with. Mother and aunt compete with the hues of the clouds. Now, says Nyusha, she's in a cheery mood. And German is a very fine language and very beautiful; but also very difficult. She had a friend, a tourist. He taught her French. But all she knows now is: *Je suis très malheureuse*. She asks if I know what it means. Yes: very unhappy. At that time, she was very unhappy, but not now; it wasn't a natural thing anyway. Overhead, everything has unexpectedly turned black. As if photographic paper had been placed in light, forgotten, and overexposed. Dismayed, I think: I hope it's all repeated tomorrow; after all, I came here to see things like this. Or why have I come here? I remember my wooden alcove, I start daydreaming again, squinting; I think to myself: I want to think about nothing. Let me take a walk, I'll be leaving for Lodz soon enough. Nyusha meets a peasant woman, converses with her. Time to head back. Her hands are frozen in her torn gloves, which she hides from me. I'm frozen through and through. Where is there a coffeehouse around here? We sit, almost alone, in a plain long room. I drink coffee. Nyusha eats cake. She sure can eat cake. She licks the landscape clean—everything the waitress brings her.

In the evening, I hung my bed cover over one window, a towel over the other. In the morning, I'll take the towel down for I do have to wash myself. Outside, everything is white. Snow glitters in the gray air, whirling like flights of swallows skidding to the earth. There must be air currents on the ground; the snow doesn't merely sink down, it veers off horizontally and wafts for a short stretch. The whitish-gray heavens are tremendously high. They don't stop. Where are trees, mountains, where is Zakopane? Everything is absorbed in that sky. Standing at the other window, I peer through the fringes of the bed cover. Yesterday afternoon, a mountain loomed over there. It's still there. But a wall of fog is now dropping upon it. The fog is like a stage decor, like a gigantic curtain hundreds of miles long. The wall sinks into the fir forest of the mountain, the fog thickly pushes forward and downward, shrouding the blackness of the mountain. Yesterday, the nearby trees at the foot of the mountain were a single cohesive black; now they are being shredded, dissected by the gently drifting fog and its snow. It molds every single tree very finely, setting it down, contour by contour.

I receive the aunt's friendly greeting and I stand in the alcove, still in my hat and coat, gazing at the outdoor spectacle. I don't know what to do. The snow cloud sinks lower and lower upon the mountain. The foot of the mountain is bluishly darkened, but the whitish-gray cloud of haze is already above it, inexorably drifting down minute by minute. I am a man in a small wooden house, somewhere in the world, in a blizzard. I don't know whether I can escape the squall. I've been overtaken by a natural occurrence. We are in God's hands. I want to probe deeper, more densely into the weather. It lures me. I have to get into it. The house is silent; I sneak out. Nyusha is asleep; I'm going to have my own eyes again.

Walking along the avenue toward the village, I feel that I'm still in their field of energy, between magnetic lines of force radiating from the house behind me. I wade through loose deep snow; I think and feel backwards. I am not a free blowfly flitting here and there, I am resting. Part of me is still resting in the feeling of the house, of its inhabitants, in their life together, their poverty. There they are, the two of them: the one with the torn gloves, who brought me from the railroad station; the other one, who has given her children away to relatives and brought me the coffee. I am accompanied by a friendly mood, which nods on all sides. I do not go naked. I wear a garment, from the house back there.

The snow drops by the cartload. I can't make out the house

223

over there. Small black flecks emerge from the air: chimneys snowed in on one side. The roofs are invisible, they're part of the vast snowy sky. Walking softly across the snow, I feel cheerful, sprightly, I'm at a masquerade. The snowfall has something carnivalesque about it. I see that the passersby have also been touched by it. You don't have to buy a ticket, and it's fun. I, little animal that I am, snuggle into the natural occurrence. I clump across a small wooden bridge, past sanatoriums, military convalescent homes. And on the small frozen pond under the bridge, two boys, shouting for joy, are skimming across the ice, each on one skate. The village lies up to its ears in Sunday peace and snowy weather. I pass through it in the gentle flurry of the heavenly feathers. The full hush of the landscape, any landscape, has embraced me, is trying to embrace me tighter. I don't know whether fields or mountains are coming: the wall of fog, the cloud I'm walking in is too thick; but who cares: the subject is nothing, the brushstroke is everything. Lone cottages still lie along the way, villas, small farms. Now a flock of white ducks cringes on the edge of the road, around a runnel. They lie flat on their bellies, quacking, slurping, dunking their yellow horny beaks into the trickle. They produce a noise like someone quickly clicking his tongue. And as I shift my eyes from them to the fog, the fog starts thinning out as if opening before me. It opens in utter silence, it has opened, it divides. And round mountain massifs emerge, are there, carrying masses of snow. The massifs rock the snow on high treetops. The backgrounds and depths of the mountains are molded by the fog. Its long patches slide into valleys that I haven't seen. It all brews soundlessly back there, moving in huge dimensions, and it's charming and involved in a soft game. The firs near me have green feet. They stand like brood hens, broadly expanding their lower plumage, squatting, covering and warming the ground. At the top, the white head moves, trembling in the wind and peering about.

I venture deeper into the blizzard. It's gradually dying down. This is a mild maternal landscape. The village has sunk into a basin, the church steeple was the last to submerge. And now, what a spectacle: all all all clouds and fogs in front of me rise as if obeying a signal. The mountains hoist their clouds like a shirt. The haze gathers above, they let it drop downward.

The mountains have risen to the right and the left. A creek roils and roars along, it's full of detritus. I've wandered into a ravine, a long drawn-out gorge. The hush of the landscape is no more. Zakopane, the mountains are here. The creek gushes right and left over the path. It pesters you like a child. The entire tableau, having opened, is agitated, nor do the settled masses of snow provide relief. Four rock columns stride all the way up to the path, slender high-shouldered rocks, like statues of men. These are strange wild figures, and I have to get closer to them. And when I stand among them, I see that they are weathered rock, which has crumbled down from the great rock mass; dark, clay-colored defiant creatures, refusing to die. They add a streak of violence to the landscape. What lies on my hand when I stroke the rock? Two large six-cornered stars, wonderful symmetrical snow crystals. My skin is cold, they don't melt. What beauty in their plumage. They dangle from tiny hairs on the back of my hand, displaying themselves to me from all sides. Perfect, they've become perfect, with three rays from the center. Not a single flaw in them. The cold welcomed them freely; they formed in its lap, evolving out of pure water. Now they've glided down from my tiny hairs to my skin. Ah, my hand, what's it doing? It's a lions' den. They snuggle in, lie intimate, flat. And they sinter, sinter. Their corners rise, the center sinks. They shrink, become transparent. They are drops, drops. The snow has come to me, to my home, it has put on my clothes, taken my warmth—and has died. The way Buddho took the poison in the goldsmith's home and died without a peep. Our lives pass in such narrow margins. Then we melt, are snuffed out, crushed between two plates. "We," I say: I and the snowflake, the myriad snowflakes with me, the ones that I stamp on, have to stamp on, that I vigorously keep melting with my breath.

In the evening the aunt and Nyusha come to my room, my alcove. The kerosene lamp is burning. The aunt's an author; she tells me about the stories she's written, and she's going to translate them for me. Nyusha has a cat; she has long conversations with it, laughing, screeching, and roughhousing with it.

The dark evening has set in rapidly. The morning refuses to come. The snow keeps squalling incessantly. It roars out of the air in whole salvos and broadsides. The air is piercingly cold. There's no softness left in it. The white masses are as deep as my feet. An element has thrown itself across the mountains. The wagons on the highway slowly struggle forward. The sky is a washed-out gray-white, almost blackish-gray; the mountains hide within it. The Gurals, the local drivers, jingle by in cab sleighs, sitting up front, their bodies sideways, their faces toward the sidewalk. I trudge through the enormous masses. I'm on a sea, I'm rowing a small boat on a shoreless sea. The human faces have grown smaller, gray, wrinkled, hard.

The village streets are empty. I can't advance along the storm-swept highway. I spot a house with an inscription: Tatra Museum. I enter, find admission, I meet a young assistant curator. While the night is settling in again outside, he shows me his treasures, gives me hot tea to drink. He tells me about the art academy. And Gurals live here; I've seen them on the street: the inhabitants of the High Tatra. I saw whole bevies of them emerging from the church. Men as tall as fir trees, extraordinarily powerful creatures, some with the wild beauty of highwaymen. These are Gievonts, the aunt told me: Gievont is the name of the high mountain near Zakopane. These men wear strange snug white trousers, decorated with ornaments in front, under the groin. Flat lid hats on their heads, beautiful embroidered leather jackets hanging over their shoulders. A skillful breed with a natural sense of art. They speak a Polish dialect, they have their special customs; some of them look like American Indians.

In this warm room, the friendly Polish curator tells me about them and their mountains: about their economy, their superstitions. Some of them were highwaymen; one, who was very famous, was hanged in the late eighteenth century. Supposedly, bears still live in the forests of the Tatra mountains. There's a horrible wind here, a *foehn*, which drives cottony clouds along. The winds rip out whole forests. In winter, it brings thaws.

In the evening, as I grope my way home through the darkness of the snowy waste, I can't hold out any longer. I'm paralyzed by the horror of the awful weather. I spend a few hours with Nyusha and her aunt in their upstairs room. They're a bit sad and very cordial, because they know what I'm planning. The aunt lays cards to read my fortune: I will have great joy at home, very great joy; everything, everything will be good. She says she's never read such good cards. And Nyusha beams: Yes, I ought to have faith in the cards. When she picked me up at the station, her aunt had read the cards: a gentleman will come to their home; and that was me. She tussles tenderly with the cat: "There! She kisses both your hands. She can dance nicely. She's very smart." Nyusha kisses the cat, shrieks, shows me letters in Polish from her sweetheart. At eleven o'clock, they take the lamp and see me down the stairs.

I stand on the dark street, I walk. I want to, I'd like to, I have to go to the station.

# LODZ

*The hell with materialism: it's empty, but it heralds the future. That's why I don't like all the hollering against it.*

Past Wieliczka, the salt mine south of Cracow. I had expected nothing, it didn't even live up to my expectations: a tourist attraction with guides, enormous rooms, a ballroom, a Kunigunde Room, a Pilsudski Room, chapels. Everything is made of salt, which is supposed to amaze me. Had it been concrete or candy sugar, I would have been just as indifferent. I got to see the salt in adjacent corridors: the guides hurried past it with lanterns, trying to surprise me with electrical light effects. My mouth felt like gaping in a four-story yawn. At the very bottom, there was a smithy, engines humming, fire glowing, an anvil, a live horse; there were shafts far away, factory facilities. I would have liked to see them and the workers. But I, a "tourist," was driven like cattle; they had another monster of a room and one more *in petto*.

I walk across the pavement of Lodz; I am filled with friendly warmth upon viewing the houses, stores, markets; I've been to Zakopane. I've seen these mountains and the winter passing across it. The house in Zakopane is still in back of me. I had joy and warmth with them. It's as if I had taken part in a family festivity and am now encountering the members of the family

228

in everyday life. I sat in their home, even though now, a stranger as always, I wander outside, along the house façades.

And lo and behold: the painted female faces, the eyes, the legs in light-colored stockings—the black-haired Jewish men, bearded, in caftans and skullcaps, the wretched crumbling houses. I'm in Russian Poland, Warsaw is here. I celebrate our reunion. I like them all. I love the Russian blend, I love it more than the Galician street; the latter was too smooth, too West European.

A strip is drawn all the way through the city, from top to bottom; I've never seen a strip like this in any city. It's Petrikow Street. And, on this street, amid millinery shops, restaurants, sales of men's furnishings, I read a sign in German: a German-language newspaper in Lodz. So in this city I'll be guided better than anywhere else; I'll be reading a newspaper myself, local items, ads.

And I sit in a restaurant and read. "Don't drink unboiled milk." That's the thick warning in the middle of the text. Oh, why not? This triggers deep probing. Is dysentery going around? I cast a shuddering glance at the town's sewer system. So far as it exists. *Ecce:* Russian dirt also has its dark sides. An article instructs me about Gedurol, a cancer remedy: "The recent report on the invention of a new cure for cancer is further evidence that the public is following every advance in cancer research with alert eyes." I stop in my tracks. I'm at sea. Does a different causality exist in Poland? The recent report cannot possibly have issued from the alert eyes of the public. Or if it did issue from there, how did it get there in the first place? Is the report itself perhaps a cancerous tumor in the eyes: if so, then it could be treated with Gedurol. Alarmed, I hop over to a different passage. According to the wire service, the Sejm has approved the sum of two hundred thousand zlotys for unemployed intellectual workers. Now you're talking! If there are just twenty thousand unemployed intellectual workers in this country, then that comes to ten zlotys per man, and he's got his work cut out for him: he can try and figure out what he could do with ten zlotys. The Sejm could have gotten just as far with five zlotys —or only one; but the Sejm is generous. On we go: "On Saturday, the Evangelical Lutheran Women are putting on a huge fair, with surprises for old and young." The Butchers' Club is having a dedication of the colors in the hall of the Volunteer Fire Department of Lodz; the Kraft [Strength] Gymnastics Club, following the example of King David, is arranging a "victory celebration with dancing." Oh, this Lodz. Evidently, the factories develop faster than the people. For a long time now, I've been of the opinion that the inorganic world is more dynamic than the organic world. The organic propagates its vices under the pretext of heredity; top priority is given to stability, preservation of the species and of things not worth preserving. But if the inorganic is struck by lightning, then that's that. Things are at sixes and sevens; you don't wait for ruins in order to let a new life blossom.

I skim the Szeptycki-Stpiczynski duel; it's an unspeakable affair. The health statistics grab my eye:

In the 1923 Lodz Yearbook, we find remarkable figures on the activities of the Municipal Scabies Institute during the past few years. The number of people who had to make use of this institute came to 12,805 in 1918, 11,337 in 1919, 8,283 in 1920, 5,203 in 1921, 4,337 in 1922, 1,409 in 1923. We may infer from the compilation of these data that scabies, which was widespread in Lodz during the war, has been declining since 1918. On the whole, it has been established that scabies is more widespread in the Jewish population than in the Christian population. This leads us to conclude that the hygienic conditions of the Jewish populace leave a great deal to be desired. After all, in the year 1918, fifty-seven percent of all scabies sufferers were Jews, while the Jewish percentage of patients treated at the Municipal Scabies Institute was fifty-one in 1919, sixty-two in 1920, sixty-seven in 1921, forty-six in 1922, and eighty-two in 1923.

From scabies, I casually shift to "Art and Culture." The German Theater is doing two plays, *The Post Office* and *Eternally Amen.* "Wildgans's adaptation of Tagore—the difference was great, but it provided, I might almost say, a textbook case of realistic literature in contrast to a series of witty ideas, poetry transplanted to the stage." Inimitable, I might almost say. The difference between Lodz German and normal German is great, supplying a textbook case of the textbooks and the German that's taught here. Wouldn't it be better simply to speak Polish, in contrast to the double Dutch, or should I say double *Deutsch*, that's smeared into the gazette. Incidentally, "the content of Wildgans's play is very short, it is limited to fascinating dialogue," which is gratifying for all concerned. In regard to a French play done at the Polish Theater, the writer reports "that the production was successful on all scores; one can safely say that it couldn't have been better." I think: One can safely say it; why, my son, should you not safely say something like this? It will do you good, it's no disgrace. Granted, the fact that the performance couldn't have been better is slightly unpleasant. But what can you do. And who's lying on the ground in the advertising section? A "victim of uric acid"! Didn't I say so? Didn't I guess it right off the bat? Only uric acid can wreak such havoc. For years now, I've been a staunch opponent of uric acid. I intend to speak to the "inventor in Warsaw" first chance I get. I've already read about this cancer medicine, Gedurol; also about the two hundred zlotys for intellectual workers. Just what's going on? I can't read newspapers anymore.

Two men converse across from me at the table. "In Lodz, only the big numbers catch on, anything else is completely worthless in Lodz." What do they mean? Coats, actions, people? They whisper very mysteriously; now they turn their backs on me. I don't understand: How come only big numbers catch on in Lodz? How come? Dark things are afoot in Lodz.

The women on the long strip, Petrikow Street, have their stockings splashed on all the way up. Cocky boys in high school caps stroll in threes and fours, hands in their pockets. A girl of twelve or thirteen is wearing a blue coat, her freezing hands are thrust into her pockets, her eyes are on the wet ground. A tuft of brown hair dangles over her forehead, her blue cap is pushed down on her face: thus she walks in the crush, her head drooping sadly, her face blossoming; she ambles, not knowing whether she's a girl or a boy. Elderly gentlemen glance at women coming toward them. How incredibly painted they are.

Beauty spots on their chins or in the corners of their mouths. Their black coats are pulled tight around their waists and rears, and their buttonholes sport glaring red roses, broad, wild, luxuriant floral creatures that die, croak on this black cloth, spreading arms and legs in their final agony. Something about the terrible wet roadway forces me to think of Warsaw, of the hotel and the funeral procession that trudged by. And while I'm thinking, I hear music. And it blares. Blares, comes closer. Someone in a white surplice is carrying a black cross. Behind him comes a black flag. Behind the flag come three male mourners, giant wreaths with violet ribbons. And the trumpeters. They're the ones who are blasting with all their hearts and might. The procession advances step by step. Note by note, they drag on, drag the mourning retinue to the grave. Behind them, a company of policemen with shouldered rifles. Now a small voice sings in the street din, all alone, a human being, a priest, book in hand. The trolleys stand still. He wanders, sings. The hearse containing the dead man rolls on; a woman buried in black is led along. Sorrowful civilians, a group of officers chatting.

And when I enter the lobby of a hotel, a man in a desk clerk's cap is standing behind the desk, his face crimson, liquored up, an exquisitely stupid fellow. Speaking German, I ask for a room. He grins. French: he grins. The liquor's got him. He emits something Polish. I have to flee from the liquor and the stupid fellow. And half an hour later, I'm smiling in a real room. Lo and behold, it's got a deep sink with a wide mirror and running water, hot water. It's got a wide bed. You don't ring; I noticed the light signals in the corridor. Unlike Zakopane, distant beautiful beautiful Zakopane, I do not stand at the empty window in the poor alcove, dreaming: Where am I, what's happening to me?

There's also a night-table lamp, even though it's not working. A lovely red window curtain, even though its drawstring is torn off. A broad couch on which I can flop down—if only to receive a hard counterblow from the offended object. You have to approach it gingerly. It's a Polish original: it's disarmed down to the bones, it has no springs.

I ask a German to enlighten me. Lodz, the city, has half a million inhabitants. Oh, how regrettable. That's too many. A Polish city is big because of its diversity. Once it gets bigger, it organizes itself and is already smaller. Lodz was supposedly built by Germans. And indeed, a lot of German used to be spoken here; now, Polish has gained the upper hand. Germans are industrialists, factory owners. There are German schools: high schools, some thirty official elementary schools with German as the language of instruction. However, enrollment is dropping; every year the parents are asked to provide a special declaration stating that they wish to have their children taught in German. Their religion is mostly Evangelical. A German writers' association exists in Katowice. The Germans have a theater. Yes, I know all about it. And the newspapers review the productions regularly; I know, I know. The actors are mostly Austrians; it's hard to get performers from Germany.

Now just how do Germans, one hundred thousand of them, get along with the Poles? Oh, very well—the richer they are, the better. How come? The rich are the fastest to assimilate. So, does patriotism increase with the melting away of money? Or does intelligence increase with the size of the purse? No. A poor man is simply needy; poverty makes you belligerent, it prevents compromises. But the rich man wants something for his money, and also imports his glamour from abroad: gold vs. nationality. The Germans socialize together, as is appropriate, in clubs. There are about thirty clubs. The Germans have formed two political parties: a German middle-class party, which is rather weak and barely active; and a socially engaged party with a nationalistic streak, a German Workers' Party. Upon hearing this, I ask him, insidiously, about the elections: for instance, whom do the German industrialists vote for? And I get the answer I expected: the industrialists do not vote German; they voted for —an industrialist, who, incidentally, didn't get elected. What about the workers? Yes, their party teams up with the Polish Social Democratic Party.

The Poles in Lodz number one hundred fifty to two hundred thousand. Most of them are workers. They vote Christian Social and Christian Democratic. The Catholics have a bishop here; the city has five Catholic churches, two Evangelical, two Russian.

Along with these Poles and Germans, says the gentleman, the city also contains Jews, as I have already noticed. In fact, I noticed a few at the station. And if there were no Jews in Poland, speaking German with me, helping me at railroad stations by telling me when my train stops and leaves, then I wouldn't have gotten beyond Warsaw. Of these Jews, there are all of one hundred fifty to two hundred thousand in Lodz—a nice round number. They are economically powerful, producing industrialists, merchants, and craftsmen. I bet that whole battalions of them are starving. I'd rather not ask him anything else about the Jews: he's a Prussian, and I know his colors.

Ah, my dear Germans, my dear Jews, here I find you side by side. What a bizarre situation! Now both of you are alien nations! With equal rights amid inequality of rights. Lo and behold, an odd kettle of fish. You're got little else in common; maybe you can now find something worthwhile in one another —it doesn't have to be baptism for Jews or tefilin [prayer thongs] [38] for Germans. Now I am walking along Petrikow Street. And—my demon is guiding me—I stumble upon a bookshop, a German one. My heart leaps, my ears prick up: I'm in clover. The bookshop has two windows: I ignore the Polish one with its hieroglyphs. Then, two paces to the left: *The Sin Against the Blood*. I can read this, I don't have to translate it. Ah, I'm home again, a thousand greetings. "Mother tongue, mother sounds, oh so blissful, oh so sweet." *The Sin Against the Blood*; a whole row. Nothing but German words, German to the core! Meyer's encyclopedia: a book about lacemaking and artistic knitting ("On Saturday, the women's clubs are putting on a big fair with surprises for old and young"). The Gospels, so many Gospels. Yes, the Germans here are Evangelical. It must be Luther's translation. But why so many Gospels? Is this a new translation? Why are they propagating the book about the executed man, the memory of whom makes me close my eyes. These are such strikingly thick tomes. The four ancient books can't be all that thick. Do these have commentaries? And then

I see: the swastika on the cover, and the name of a German nationalistic agitator above it. His Gospels! His! Yes, that's good, now I'm in the picture, now there's order in the shop window. No doubt he's proved that Wotan is the true God, or else Christ came from Mecklenburg. Yes, that's what makes the book so thick. He could have made it thinner; people would still believe him. Dear homeland, a thousand greetings. Just how are things with the interesting situation of the Germans and Jews? They will walk together for five paces. But I doubt whether the Germans will be putting on tefilin.

I love hearing about olden days. Pious German missionaries came here during the twelfth century, the sons of the Cologne bourgeoisie dwelt in monasteries here. During the fourteenth century a prince named Wladislaw of Lenczyca bestowed the village of Lodza on a bishop of Kujawy and the bishop summoned German settlers. There was prosperity and decline. In the mid-eighteenth century, Lodz had fewer than two hundred inhabitants, and by the end of the century 89 men, 90 women, and 11 Jews. (I can't determine how many males and females among the Jews; as far back as in ancient Rome, slaves had no sex.) There were 44 houses, plus 44 barns and 18 unbuilt lots. The people and Jews lived with 18 horses, 97 oxen, 58 cows, and 63 head of black cattle. So Lodz was first Prussian, then Russian. And the Russians, those cursed people who let everything go to rack and ruin, issued an edict around 1820: a factory community had to be built with 200 building lots. During those thirty years, 200 people grew to 800, 44 chimneys became 118. The Russian fiat of 1820, with its eight articles, was extraordinary; it enticed foreigners, and a special statute detailed the privileges that foreign manufacturers and clothmakers were to enjoy in Lodz. Weavers and textile workers were now the bearers of Western culture! Western culture had changed radically. Western Europe had deigned to put the main emphasis of life on making money. They still built churches, but for the most part they erected factories. Now, when people came from Cologne, they didn't settle in monasteries. The ancient knowledge, the ancient yearnings and sources of knowledge died out. To conquer, to possess, to increase the power of the state: these remained. O humanity, how beautifully you stood with your palm branch at the end of the century, in proud, noble vigor, minds open to the world. Those were wonderful times for foreigners in Eastern Europe. But the kick lurked in the background: the thanks offered by human gratitude for services rendered. This kick was not recorded in 1820. Incidentally, the concessions were extended to all "foreigners." "Jews, however, are not permitted to reside in the new industrial colonies. Nor shall any Jew, in the future, be permitted to maintain a tavern or to manufacture spiritous liquors." Jews are neither foreigners nor natives. What are they then? This strange nation enjoys such preferential treatment everywhere. A chosen people indeed. Their neighbors tastefully and affectionately call them "bedbugs."

A master dyer named August Sänger (a good Polish name!) regulated the old city and founded the first dyeworks. Saxons and German Bohemians were brought here by the cotton industry. A man named Louis Geyer from Zittau built the first large cotton mill. Then came the Evangelical church and the town hall; by 1829, Lodz had some 4,000 people and 400 houses; ten years later, there were 20,000 people, and it was the second-largest city in the Kingdom of Poland.

Soon this number was increased by Karl Scheibler. He brought 180,000 rubles along and built his colossal factory. The West mounted the great attack. By 1864, Lodz already had 38,000 people: 7,000 Orthodox, some 12,000 Catholics, 13,000 Lutherans, 6,000 Jews. "We by God's grace Alexander the Second, Emperor and Sovereign of all the Russias, King of Poland, Grand Duke of Finland" decided on and decreed the building of a railroad line connecting Lodz with the Warsaw-Vienna line; the contract was awarded to the bankers Johann Bloch, Eduard Frankenstein, Josef Zablkowski, August Raphan, Karl Scheibler, Matthias Rosen, Moritz Mamrott. They appeared to have been mostly Germans—and bedbugs.

When the railroad was opened, a Lodz newspaper greeted the fervently longed-for day: "Never has our city worn such a festive air. Upon descending from his railroad carriage, His Excellency

Governor Count Berg was welcomed by a deputation of citizens with bread and salt." That's a Russian custom that Germans are following in Poland; but given the teeming crowd, what's one nation more or less. That evening the entire city was illuminated; meticulously made signs bearing the name of His Majesty the Tsar were set up in many places. First the governor reviewed the dragoons stationed in Lodz; having been recruited in Siberia, they were the only natives.

During the banquet that the governor enjoyed, he condescended to announce: "The city of Lodz owes its prosperity to German industry, to the enterprising spirit of the Germans, and to German hard work. I believe I am giving these people good advice when I encourage them to emulate loyally the virtues of their fathers and to maintain the German character. It is the determination of our Very Gracious Monarch to give every nationality in the Kingdom of Poland that which belongs to it."

In Wilno and Warsaw, I read old Russian posters: IT IS UNLAWFUL TO SPEAK POLISH. Language obviously does not belong to this very graciously tolerated nationality. Especially, I assume, the Polish language. Here we have an extravagant appreciation of the unique situation of the Polish people. One can intensify this feeling of esteem to the point at which one assumes that life, too, does not belong to the Polish nation. So the Poles are killed. And the experiment was carried out, over and over, 1863 and later. Except that sometime later, something utterly unexpected happened (just as nature loves it): the tsar and his government kicked the bucket, and the Polish nation could now exhibit all the attributes of a normal living creature, very openly, in peace and quiet; it could even demonstrate the dreadful appetite of the hungry, and the heedlessness that leads to dyspepsia and diarrhea.

On the day of the celebration in Lodz, the Germans were granted permission to open German schools taught in the German language: "Gentlemen, you must realize the profound significance of this wise determination! Strengthen your industrial capacity for the benefit of the great state in which you have found your second home." The Poles must have gotten a stomachache; nor could the Germans have felt all that comfortable with that Polish stomachache; sometimes high-ranking people are insidious in their graciousness.

Gaslights were not long in coming, asphalt sidewalks were introduced; a certain Israel Poznanski made himself agreeably noticeable. Lodz was approaching the nineteen-eighties. Stone houses supplanted the old wooden ones, 150,000 people lived here; the big city became unmistakable. But when telephone lines were installed, the inhabitants of Lodz grew nervous; the mysterious abomination of telephoning settled in only very slowly. Contemporaries were already reporting on contradictions in the city: on the adjacency of shacks and luxurious buildings, on a charred ruin that remained for a long time at the center of the city, on nations and religions.

The terrible hatred between Germans and Poles! The nations telescope into one another from east and west. The country was settled by Poles; then the Poles themselves called in the Germans, the more highly cultivated group: a cultural, economic upswing came, spiritual and intellectual assimilation, national jeopardy. People didn't remain what they were—on either side: they became mutually acclimated. But the urban centers contained groups that couldn't accept this and that were interested in maintaining hatred and so-called tradition. A ridiculous proverb was already circulating during the sixteenth century: "So long as the world remains the world, the German will never be a brother to the Poles!" The Teutonic Knights, summoned by Polish princes, were defeated at Tannenberg. The Polish clergy fought for the Polish language, the German elements were Polonized; the more highly cultivated took on the vernacular of the struggling peasantry and aristocracy. But then the Poles ruined themselves, and foreign dynasties subjugated the nation; one such foreign dynasty was Prussia. There was only one intermission in the hating: 1848. Mieroslawski waved the black-red-and-gold flag in Berlin; the political inmates were released from Moabit Prison. They marched across Castle Square. Amid the din, Count Schwerin declared that the king of Prussia was confident that the Poles would henceforth work closely with Prussia and its royal house. The leader of the Poles gave an impassioned address at the university, he spoke about the Polish-Prussian alliance against Russia: "To ensure the safety of a free Germany, an independent Poland must be erected as a rampart against the Asiatics. . . . Today, the gigantic heart of a nation that has been yearning for freedom since time immemorial beats destructively only when fetters and obstacles are placed upon its mighty stirrings." On the morning of that day, March 20, 1848, Polish colors waved in the Prussian town of Posen [Poznan]; Poles and Prussians exchanged cockades when the Berlin Poles arrived. But then the interlude ended; the provinces were in chaos; armed bands wandered about. The Prussian troops concentrated on the forts. First they sang: "We embrace you, all you millions." Then it went: Bang bang! It was nothing but a Polish uprising; it was crushed in the usual way.

Now Germany is chewing on the "Corridor" and Danzig, Upper Silesia, forced treaties—it certainly won't swallow them. And Poland—has to be scared! No border will change this; one can decide either way.

Today's concept of the state has to be mellowed. Banalized. Borders themselves are a tyrannical power. People have become persons, the nations have been called upon to practice self-determination, the ancient monstrosity of the state cannot survive. Space must be made for the stronger, older, communities of human beings. As well as for new ones. In our era, the lives of nations have long since overlapped political borders. The old state still stands between them, fat, complaisant, and admired —a mammoth has-been, a lazy ichthyosaur that must be eliminated by modern-day brains.

But it is even more urgent to address the individual, the self.

I am flabbergasted by the incredible violence inflicted by the thing that calls itself the state. In the old days, dynasties conquered these territories for their own purposes; it was understandable that the state used its fists, violence; the individual was helpless against the state. Now, states are merely utilitarian

239

forms, remnants from the era of dynasties, and we have to make do with states as they are. And the delusion of the unique significance of the state and the recognition of its power live on.

The truly human groups, the truly rational sphere of the self, of the individual, must be rallied against this entity. Its usefulness is incontestable, but it is only the living self, it is only the rational human groups and ties, that give this usefulness its status. The individual suffers, lives and dies; he and his connections exist; but masses and organizations, groups hiding behind abstractions, try to make the individual inferior and ridiculous as they withdraw into a majestic anonymity that is borrowed from the old despots. The individual vegetates as a private person. He is degraded and enslaved; the dynasts are only seemingly gone. The public sits on the throne, the real human being has been reduced to a mere shadow of himself, the theoreticians of the state are willing to deny the very reality of the individual. Even man's unearthly relationship to the maternal elements of the world, what he calls his religion, is, in practice, openly or covertly reduced to something trivial—in other words, a private matter. And it *is* a private matter, but in a different way from what the abstract dynasts mean: namely, a direct expression of the momentous things of the world to the individual, confirming his reality for him and placing responsibility upon him.

The state has grown beyond all bounds—a direct or abstract matter of concern; no one can now grasp it emotionally. The fond sense of homeland, attachment to family, love for friends, love for one's tribe; all these things have been devoured by the state, a monster that turns them into goodness knows what. The state is a giant factory and that's all it should be, nothing more. What awe and groveling are cultivated before this practical or impractical entity, what grandiose names are applied to this groveling. In the war, very few nations fought for their freedom. Most of them marched off to battle without knowing why, and not even the leaders knew why. One must embrace the self in order to know what it is. The self must reduce to irrelevancy that which is irrelevant.

Sunday, Memorial Day. The tenth anniversary of the dreadful battle of Lodz. Leaving from the factory station, I take an hour-long train ride out to the country. The man I am visiting is not in the station; we meet at the barrier. Vast fields, soil thrown up, the ground muddy, loamy. We come to a village: a German colony. Clean cottages stand in a row; the Evangelical church. We stroll through the park by his home. He shows me remnants of the great battle. The cast-up embankments for setting up cannon. Here is where the Germans were stationed. The embankments are lined up in a wide semicircle; now, they are bushy, overgrown. We approach a pond; it's supposedly filled with guns and ammunition. A dreadful bombardment took place; the steeple of the Evangelical church was destroyed. At the pond, we come upon wide, ribbonlike depressions; young saplings are rising out of them. Those depressions are the trenches. They are already being covered by the forest, human beings don't have to cover them. Those German peasants over there retain their language and their ways. I don't know how much truth there is to a poem I am handed; it was written by a German in Poland:

> But I celebrate the Children's Land.
> The fathers lived, the fathers are dead,
> The fathers do not really need our work.
> Behind us broods the eternal night,
> But before us the glowing day awakens.
> Soon its light will enclose the land,
> From which new crops and men sprout forth.
> We Germans are the land's sun and rain,
> Its nourishment, its blessing, too.
> So up! Till the soil of the Children's Land!
> To found a new German world!

Today's concept of the state is nothing.

Fog in the streets. I suddenly find myself on Petrikow Street —evening is approaching. Lights shine in some stores, extraordinarily huge masses of people are trudging along on both sidewalks. All at once, I realize that I feel as if I were in Warsaw, on Marshal Street, which I recall with pleasure. It feels so good walking here, so homey, and more; it's exciting to swim through this teeming crowd. These women in furs, their heads drawn in between their shoulders, their hats in their faces, the slender girls with a touch of perversity, big dangling earrings, heavy overshoes, black gazes. They are starting to dress up their faces. The tall men, the yelling newsboys; hurried Jews wearing black coats, in twos, in threes, conversing loudly. Tanned soldiers as tall as trees, greeting the trolleys. The posters announcing the Labia concert, green, the Szymanowski concert, red.

There's fog out, it's late afternoon: I want to comb this street. It looks fabulous. After ten minutes, it turns slummy: tenements brutally alternate with teensy cottages, storage sites. At times, this road reminds me of the derrick road in Drohobycz. The spirit of Western civilization, the industrial, technological spirit has forged this far. When I walk about here, I feel exactly as if —a different era—I were stepping into St. Mary's Church, the Franciscan Church in Cracow. Tough Polish workers trot along —muddy boots, high caps, drooping mustaches. Now two Poles thrust cigarettes between their lips and puff. Laced-up brown overcoats, heavy, clattering canes—that's how they strut along the sidewalk. Truly, the faces of lords, arrogant, passionate faces of lords.

I've slid very quickly from the commercial town to the red industrial town. Fences, chimneys—I've turned off into a narrow cross street. Huge gates stand open; engines hum, whistle. An elegant open coach sails softly on rubber across the morass, chestnut horses in front, liveried footmen on the box; and in back, a gentleman has his hands in his lap. Panska Street is broad; one sign still has the street name in German: Herrengasse [Lord Street]. Tracks run down its center, wires through the air. Everything is neglected, indeed chaotic. New chimneys, new streets, squalid, crudely covered with stones. Suddenly, after lots of fences and walls, comes a solid block of houses, then a corner: shouting boys hawking the evening papers, two street-cleaners working vehemently with coarse birch brooms. But to the right, where the trolleys turn off, the street spreads out wider, workers, factories, smoke. Danzig Street, workers, smoke and smokestacks, red walls, fences, groups of apartment houses

with crumbling fronts. The high-tension wires run, colossal, from one pole at a corner straight across the street. Kosciuszko Avenue, like a boulevard: the lower portion with the red, dirty factories is swampy; the upper portion has modern apartment houses, crude tenements. It's grown fully dark now. I enter Petrikow Street with muddy boots, splattered trousers. Suddenly, the brilliant crowd no longer appeals to me.

In the morning, I push my way through toward the north. The trolleys charge through the fog with lights. The sidewalks and roadway of Petrikow Street are mobbed. People are buying and selling. Yellowish-white water flows along the gutter, steaming in the cold. I leaf through a newspaper as I walk: "The impending holiday crush forces everyone to look before it is too late for a source that guarantees that one can be opportunely provided with all the necessary products of the best quality and at moderate prices—because of the ostentatious advertising in the local press." They're already thinking of Christmas; it's scary.

Reymont was awarded the Nobel Prize; what good is it: who knows Polish? Such terrible nonsense—the plethora of languages. It would strike me as progress if all nations agreed to teach the same second language in all their schools, along with the national tongue: everywhere English, Esperanto, or whatever. Everywhere an arbitrary, but always the same second language. It would be a simple agreement, at a conference on education; like a conference on postal service or a conference on railroads. We could finally ride the same rails everywhere.

This street is dominated by Jews; and the further north I go, the more Jews there are: in high fur caps and black fur coats, black skullcaps, with long, thick beards, their hands in their pockets, their feet in top boots; furrowed brows. As in Warsaw, scores of them emerge from deep courtyards. Very crowded side streets. Young women come along on high heels, their coats snugly hugging their shoulders and buttocks. A stooped old man with a puffy, malevolent face grumbles past. Bales of red, yellow, blue cloth, packages of linen, calico are driven on wagons, lugged one by one. New Ring, a shabby, round, wide square; to the left, the old town hall; to the right, scaffoldings, a colorful building; the new town hall. The old city, narrow streets, crumbling small houses. I step into a dreadful house, cross the courtyard, pass through a door, find myself in a different street. It's teeming with kids; the ground sinks in waves. Lots of slaughterhouses for geese. A small synagogue is open. They stand in a circle in the vestibule, praying; I wonder why they don't go in. I hear a woman weeping and shrieking; what's she doing among the men? She looks pitiful, she pleads with everyone; they have to let her in. Her three children are critically ill; the doctor has little hope. She's managed to get inside, she goes over to the elders; my companion tells me that they're supposed to read *tillim*, psalms of David, prayers for her children.

Outside, I plod laboriously through fog and sleet. The proletarian district. A poster is pasted to a house: "Poles, don't buy from Jews! You can't, mustn't charge more than the Jews. This is not just for your benefit, it's your patriotic duty." The message is signed by a Development Committee. "Support Polish commerce and industry. Then you'll truly be children of the Fatherland."

The young woman who speaks to me teaches Polish and Jewish children together in a Polish school. "The little Poles are better in writing, in composition and handicrafts; but the little Jews are better in language and comprehension." However, the questions asked by the little Jews are dreadful; at times you're absolutely horrified. Recently, they were talking about Jesus, when a Jewish child asked very calmly: "Did he really exist?" And the Polish children gaped and gawked. She once told them about a heroic patriotic Pole who allowed his hand to be burned off in the war with the Turks; she demonstrated that he had shown courage. A Jewish child sat there, reflecting, and then remarked: "Yes. But the Turks also showed courage." They analyze a lot: they weigh questions precisely, justly; it's impossible to implant any opinions in them. The children find out all sorts of things at home; when it's taught in class, they say disdainfully: "We've heard all that at home." They're very unabashed in coming out with their opinions. Someone else cheerfully cuts in: He was teaching in a school, and when he enthused about a certain

Russian author, he saw the Jewish pupils smirking. He understood fully: they meant: "What a jerk!"

The Jews have fine editions of Schiller in their homes: they read him; he's got grandiloquence, ethics, determination.

The Poles are far superior to them emotionally, in gentleness.

Northward the houses grow even flatter; the trolleys halt in rain puddles. All the women wear shawls. My companion points out that a narrow side street has the disreputable name of Toilet Street. This is Ballut, a district of Lodz, a suburb. The long thoroughfare is Alexander Street. In an adjacent street, I see a house in ruins: a remnant of the Battle of Lodz. In a wretched lane, I'm told, there are many prostitutes, pimps, and thieves; the lane is badly paved; there are miserable houses. A few of the prostitutes are Jewish, he tells me (I've already encountered some in other Polish cities); there are pious girls among them; they're scared of the rabbi. A dog market. At a street corner, a policeman sways on a high rock. Another bombarded house. This Alexander Street, this epitome of a village street, runs on forever. Lots of blonde women roam along the dripping houses.

Then the trolley carries me back near my hotel on modern Petrikow Street. It stops by a big lovely flower shop. Three elegant children with long legs are gazing at the unbelievable, strength-swollen orchids; then they wander over to the poultry stores. On the outside, amid chickens, pheasants, a long deer hangs with its legs bound on top. Reluctant, filled with fear and curiosity, the three children stare into its open dry mouth.

A young smart refined acquaintance reads to me from a Polish literary journal—a report on German literary output: along with another title, it says, one of my books was the "most important book of the past year." You can spare your breath, dear friend! Ah, books. Next year will bring others; the world has a big stomach: everything just keeps on going. I've become rather hopeless during my wanderings. What is writing books all about? And yet I know, lonesome or not: feelings have to be poured out over human beings, even if over just a few, and even if the feelings ooze away a hundred times. One doesn't have the right to bury oneself. I don't know whether the world, the great world-being has any purposes; but I do know that I feel purpose. And I think of the years that have waned, my contacts with tremendous forces, enclosed in a book,[39] pushed away from me —and I can think no more. I am still solemn inside, as solemn as can be.

In the evening, through the fog, I accompany the old woman, his wife's mother, to her home. She's lost her other daughter, "such a beautiful woman." The daughter died giving birth, the sickly child now lives with her. "The pain has been terrible, it happened fourteen years ago, and you can't get over it. . . . How nice the two of them look together, the young people. It's a pure love match. My daughter has to go a long way to school every day, but he can easily work outside now."

I have to hear music, so I go to Szymanowski's concert. I spoke to the Polish composer earlier. An elegant figure, a beautifully carved face. He didn't want to talk about modern composers, but then he said a few things after all. Richard Strauss used to be his idol; Wagner made him weep, now he can't stand him. I asked him what he thought of *Lohengrin*; he nodded: Yes, *Lohengrin* was particularly impossible. He said he has a friend in the literary Skamander Circle; his friend wrote a libretto for him, *King Roger*, which takes place in three different cultures. But, he said, it's awful spending years slaving over a work; a horrible, horrible strain, a strain. (Literati and art historians talk about the intoxication of creativity; poor authors, impotent creatures, pretend there's no such thing. There *is* such a thing, but what comes next is labor, anguish, and tedium.) Mahler: a brilliant eclectic. Richard Strauss's later works are empty, he said. Stravinsky is epoch-making—not Schönberg, the psychologist and the continuation of Wagner; Schönberg falls flat in the essential rhythms. And then the young earnest man formulated his musical credo, while a little girl entered the room and curtsied: "The crux isn't psychology or expression, it's construction and dynamics. Making music means: filling out time constructively with notes; absolute music. We are moving toward a new classicism." He chain-smoked, talked honestly, modestly, vividly.

The Philharmonic is located on a badly lit street. His sister will be singing his songs; I can't understand the lyrics; the final songs have Arabic subjects. He goes to the podium, limping slightly; in a tux, handsome, his eyebrows very close together. She stands next to the piano: rich, shimmering reddish hair, tall, slender; her head back, her bare left arm on the back of her brother's chair. During her deep, sonorous singing, she presses her head even further back. She's wearing a black ankle-length gown; a scarf with particolored dots is wrapped around her neck. Atonal music comes from his piano and her throat, a yearning sostenuto; no tonality can speak like that. Yes, speak like that. Time is not only constructively filled; there is a person here who constructs; what does he have to know it for? How passionately the woman's voice can awaken; how female she is in her tone. What lies behind this voice, what has this person experienced? Consequences of the Allah chants, drawing, summoning. Funny, burlesque trifles. There's something remote, ungraspable in this modern music. The old woman whom I accompanied through the drizzle wouldn't like this music; it appeals to me, excites me. It is a fiery glance from half-closed eyes. The old musicians get bogged down in "tonality" and harmonic laws.

Girls with braids and big green bows get red cheeks in the concert hall; men in tuxes kiss women's hands. Elderly men and women huddle with their families. Adolescent boys dance attendance in groups.

I'm in Lodz: factories, the Wild West, the sticks.

Industry. Supposedly, they've got not just gigantic factories, but also the old hand-weaving places, run by Germans. I hunt for them along Alexander Street. When I knock on a door and speak German, they question me and then guide me gladly. I thought I'd find a poor, shabby room, I pictured homework; and, in a back wing, I come upon a real factory, small, with male and female workers. The boss is a veritable entrepreneur. He tells me about their guild of German craftsmen, five hundred members. He said I shouldn't imagine their doing anything unprogressive. The whole grand mechanization of weaving has not made handlooms superfluous. Machines can't do everything. When his father came to Lodz, everything was still

German; it's amazing, he says, how quickly Polish has spread. I walk with him through the banging, battering low rooms. Hand-looms, warp beams. Some things look very primitive; a stone tied on as a weight. The workers stand at apparatuses, in front of tenters; making tablecloths, bedsheets. Bobbins whirl. Warp and woof are moving; the cloth is wrapped around the beam. I'll never forget that tableau: a girl standing in front of a bobbin frame, reaching in, guiding, ordering, her left foot treading. She treads and treads and treads at an utterly even beat. After observing her for a while, I ask her how long she keeps treading like that: eight or nine hours a day. She's German, eighteen years old. I can't believe that she can tread like that for eight hours. She's been doing it for many months now. But she laughs, her boss laughs too: one can do it. Now I believe it and now I know: one can do it. But it's—deeply disturbing. When I chat with a worker (I'm delighted that I can finally converse without an interpreter), the master, the owner, grows very quiet when the worker starts talking very vociferously about the bad times, about salaries. I go downstairs, there's a cool good-bye. I would have liked to reenter his place: it had a German homey-ness about it, warm, clean, with bright curtains, lots of flowers and pictures.

There's a big textile factory in Widzeb. A modern office building receives me in the center of town. They enlighten me: there's a whole system of factories out there: a weaving mill, a spinning mill (everything on a grand scale, with the latest equipment), the printing, dyeing, bleaching, sizing, storing facilities, the mechanical workshop, the steel foundry, the power plant, the engine house. I ride the trolley for a long time, past a gigantic square: this is where the huge workers' demonstrations take place. Now, in the morning, the dense fog is still gathering and thickening. Little schoolboys and schoolgirls on the trolley whisper and smile because I don't understand them. Afterward, two of them give me their little paws and then watch the trolley rattling off.

In the industrial park, two large factory buildings lie side by side. Bales of cotton, Egyptian, are being transported along a stairway. The fragile, frothy fibers cling to my coat, delight me.

Inside the building they have machines for picking the bales to pieces. Rollers drive the cotton onto a drum; the drum loosens the raw material, then it's cut up by beating machines; additional beaters cut it up and refine it some more; the dust is trapped by sieve drums. Now they've made a broad roll of cotton. This phase is performed by lapping machines, which pull out the fiber slivers, combing and unraveling them. And these are the loose round bands, white bands, looking like gigantic sausages, which rise into the circular pots. It all extends through many rooms, across vast floors. Rollers press bands together into a thick absorbent cotton; the fleece is stretched out, the threads are placed parallel; this is known as "doubling the thread." Thus they produce a refined band. The roving frames twirl each thread around its own axis, making it solid; then the threads run around spools. And this is a tremendous spectacle: the roving threads twisting and running around the bobbins. The bobbin wagon carries the spools, as many as one hundred twenty. But this sight is nothing compared with the tableau of the spinning-machine rooms. Yarn is made: threads are pulled from the fiber mass, twisted together into a screwlike shape, and drawn. Bobbin wagons armed with slanting bobbins slide to and fro along rails. It's a drawing frame. The spindles whirl; the yarn glides from their tips to the bobbin stand.

What cunning inventions! A poor weaver named James Hargreaves from Standhill, England, invented the first spinning jenny. He died in Nottingham—in the workhouse. Later, a man named Richard Arkwright improved on the jenny, thereby raking in three million pounds sterling. Samuel Crompton, who improved the machine even further, wound up with a tiny pension. That's how this industry evolved. There's an old saying in politics: A state can survive only by means of the energy that it creates. Industry, therefore, by means of genius and evil.

The weaving mill processes the yarns. It runs one hundred twenty thousand spindles. How few people in these gigantic rooms. The whole place is squeaky clean. The long drive belts in the middle—a whirring boulevard. The bales of cotton, white, soft, lie in front of roaring machines. Everywhere, the white tubes, the bands rising from the pots. The rooms vibrate with the rolling and whistling, the wagons glide on wheels, the threads draw out, long and still. The weaving mill has three thousand looms. A banging and crashing as at a shooting. Bands slowly roll off; bundles of yarn, twitching strokes: the woof. I stand on the stairway, stone-deaf; it takes me a few minutes before I venture into another hall. This area is all a-steam. One huge watering-down. The workers dash around barefoot, sit on beams. There's washing, boiling. I see bands everywhere, they're being drawn, pressed between cylinders. The linen bands are dried, beaten, laid out, flattened out over rollers. Heating rooms, stretching rooms. They full, dye, print. I am flabbergasted by a singeing machine. A row of gas flames is burning, and the linen is pulled through the fire by rollers. The linen doesn't burn; the surface is merely refined. It's driven through the fire four times. The flattening machines, the stamping of the bales, the measuring machines. The steam boils in the dyeing room, the bands and strips enter white, they drop down green; everything is full of water and steam. The threading room, the refuse-spinning room for poorer-quality yarns.

Now we're finally outdoors again. I look into the power plant. Two or three men are moving about inside. The giant machines are working, the people are watching them. The coal slides in from outside, mechanically; an incredible sight, this glow of the heating room, the coal trucks tipping in from time to time. An old boiler room is being dismantled. Foundry, carpentry shop, smithy, sawmill. The factory owns two hundred acres of land; it's got its own agricultural setup. I cross a bridge: ponds have been built for filtering the waste water. They let the hot water spurt out freely into the air, but the fog and steam are so thick that I can't see anything. They've got 186 houses for workers.

Western nations have suffered a great misfortune. For centuries now, an old emotional structure has been perishing here; it's been supplanted by enlightenment, science, politics, government. But—who dares deny it?—new emotions, new raptures are appearing. We are glowingly rooted in the earth; people are realizing this slowly, distantly. But many have an eye out only for the dissolution of the old, the emptiness replacing it. And they see very clearly the machines, industries, the wars of plunder, wars of expansion, scores of wage earners and masses of pack animals. Things can't go on like this. This era will not remain the technological one. People will be complaining about materialism for a long time. It contains emptiness; anyone can see it. But this emptiness heralds the future; that's why I don't like the romantic bellowing. We'll get the weeds underfoot in time and trample them. The new ways of thinking will require far more time to become knowledge and feeling than to become a machine.

I praised Cracow, the Church of St. Mary, the Hanged Man, the Righteous Man. They are alive. The ancient is always the newest. But these machines here are also genuine, powerful—living steel. They've won my heart. I'm not concerned about their connection with the Hanged Man and the Righteous Man.

I—and if the contradiction gapes all the way to nonsense and all the way to hell—I praise both of them.

Once again I am summoned to the dark lanes. A rebbe lives here, the Rebbe of Strzegom. I'd like to speak to him.

Why don't I speak to any Catholic priest, any monk? I'd really like to. I don't know Polish, I can't ask for directions to reach one; however, the people whom I speak to, and who know what I want, are no help. If I say I'm interested in culture, they think I mean art galleries. I complain. My will is good: a scoundrel that gives more than it has.

The great Rebbe of Gura Kalwarja wouldn't accept me; this one sits down with me at the table. He lives in a tenement, his *bes-medresh* [synagogue] is small. A couple of men pray and study in it. Then the rebbe stands there in his round hat, a tall figure with a powerful gray beard. They tell me he is Reb Sadye, a grandson of the great Rebbe of Gichlin. They take his wet umbrella and his silk overcoat. He sits down at the head of the table in the parlor. He has to live here, I was told; he was forced to abandon his home in Strzegom, a nearby village, during the war; now someone else is occupying his home, and the rebbe is trying to get back in. The men coming from the *bes-medresh* settle gradually around the table. When I ask questions, and the rebbe answers, they join in, giving me explanations; meanwhile,

251

the rebbe sits wordless, self-absorbed, sometimes listening, nodding. I've heard that he's fighting to keep the Sabbath holy and he's head of an organization that's also active in other countries: it's aimed particularly at industrialists and businessmen. I ask him about the Sabbath.

"The Sabbath and its observance are a major principle of religious Judaism. The Sabbath is a rope that God has thrown to the Jews, for them to hold on tight."

During the war, the religious and ethical feelings of the Eastern European Jews were weakened, the love of material things gained control. But eventually, Jewish life stabilized. And he, the rebbe, took on the task of propagating the religious and moral life of the Jews, the sanctity of the Sabbath. He encountered great difficulties among the employers. They refused to permit Jewish workers, say, the packers in the textile industry, to take off on the Sabbath. In 1922, the rebbe founded the Organization to Observe and Maintain the Holy Sabbath. Its activities are practical, it sends delegates out into the streets.

It's not easy for me to ask questions. But I take heart when the rebbe, that tremendous figure with a gray beard, responds calmly and kindly, in a highly intelligible way. I've seen a lot of Jews, I say, I've visited synagogues, prayer rooms, and cemeteries, and learned a lot. But there's one thing I still don't understand: Why do the pious Jews form factions, according to their rebbes? Why are they devoted to their rebbes? In the West, I heard that there is only one Judaism, one faith. They smile amiably at the table; one man nods by way of confirmation: "A good question." The rebbe ponders deeply, then gazes at me with his very gentle eyes:

"All people have the same goal, which leads to God. There is a great land. A king rules the land. But the king cannot rule the land all by himself; he needs soldiers and generals. Those are the rebbes. How do the rebbes differ from one another? They all hold to one and the same thing. A rebbe can understand the Torah harshly or leniently. One can construe the Torah in different ways. There is a Torah of *Middas haddim*, I command, to a Torah of *Middas horakhim*, I commiserate. It's a matter of interpretation. The rebbe who understands the Torah harshly

252

has his followers; and the one who understands it leniently has his followers. And that is what makes for the number of followers. The rebbes are pious and the sons of pious fathers. Each man chooses the rebbe with whom he sympathizes."

At the table, they tell me: At a rebbe's grave, his followers shake hands with the son or grandson who has proved capable and worthy, they congratulate him.

While the mild, lovely words resonate within me, the men sometimes get into violent, chaotic disputes. They sit or stand around; so do the rebbe's two sons, one with a full downy beard, the other softer. They smile a lot. The rebbe's brother is also present; he attends to me and tries to read my thoughts. "One has to study a lot," he says. "I was far from being as good a student as my brother, I wasn't up to it." He whispers reverently: "And then teaching children. He never allowed himself to sleep. And these men here are no scholars. They're all businessmen and simple people. They just come here."

The rebbe, with his tremendous beard, sits at the narrow side of the table, huddling, his head sinking into his chest. He has deep, very calm eyes, which do not gaze out of him, but are turned inward. They are windows peering inside him. There is something sad and still about him; under his beard, his face looks pinched. He's modest, kindly. He's a very poor man. What a contrast with that rich autocrat, the Rebbe of Ger. And soon, as I sit among them, I notice that this rebbe has almost an excess of softness and gentleness; a childlike silence rests upon him. When I open my lips to ask another question, he looks across the table without sitting up: "Quiet—a question."

How does the rebbe, I ask, feel about Orthodoxy and Zionism? "The Orthodox Jew does not alienate himself from Erets Israel [the Land of Israel]. Zion and the Torah belong together. Without the Torah, Zionism is not a Jewish movement." He talks lovingly about the Zionist Jews: He is no enemy of Zionism. But in the eyes of God, a man is a Jew if he keeps nation, country, and Torah together. Without this, there is no Zion. And that is what the Jewish people must remember.

In his pronouncements, the words "Talmud" and "Torah" keep recurring. When I talk about the Western European Jews, he points to Poland: many Western Jews have turned their backs on the Talmud and the Torah, so that their children have no Jewish upbringing. A child must first study the Talmud and the Torah, and then have a secular education. If a child has a good mind, then he can learn secular things anyway.

And how do the old sacred writings relate to modern science and scholarship; can they be made compatible with one another? The rebbe sits there and shrugs. His hobby is astronomy. And he comes up with the following statements:

"The Torah is the source that makes everything fruitful. Science is only a single body of water deriving from it. It cannot survive without the source; it would have to dry out. There are natural phenomena that transcend the highest power, the most cunning calculation. There is a divine supervision that can foil anything."

A marvelous conversation, a perfect treat.

I avoid a Zionist agitator with whom I've made an appointment. While preparing for my final departure, I receive a visitor, a young Yiddish writer. Again, one of them sits with me in a Polish hotel, in a warm room, and I reflect about their concerns with him.

"Before the war," says the young man on the sofa, "the intelligentsia of our people was largely assimilated. Then the intellectuals returned: the middle classes became Zionists, others joined Poale Zion. The Socialists sidestepped the Jewish question." When I talk about the Rebbe of Strzegom, he tells me about a rebbe in a village near Warsaw: for forty years now, he has been weeping, freezing, praying for the entire world, for its sins. Another rebbe has been singing his own songs for many years, he enjoys eating and he eats a lot—an optimist: "Life is wonderful."

And now, what is your situation today? I've heard the name Bialik.[40]

"Oh, a partisan issue. He writes in Hebrew, that's all it takes. He's mediocre, weak, philistine. There are artists who are Jews and there are Jewish artists. You have to distinguish. The difference exists in all nations. Poles or Germans or Jews who depict a piece of Polish or German or Jewish life are not necessarily 'of the people.' We have many artists who are Jews. They paint ghetto pictures, historical motifs. It doesn't mean a thing. You have to have talent and rely on talent; that's all."

The lively man speaks skeptically but not sharply about Palestine; I can hear notes from my conversation yesterday:

"Perhaps they'll succeed in establishing a state there. Perhaps; for how many? And what will they have achieved? They'll provide soldiers, statesmen, and industrial workers; the world will then have more of them. But they will never breed a Spinoza, a Bergson.

"That's not where the future of the world lies. Zionism is a physical movement. The world has to be humanized. Things are horrible not only for the Jews. The Germans, the Poles, the French, the Americans, the British are also badly off. What's so great about their culture anyway? We're not impressed. We saw a lot of things in the war. Everything has to be humanized. Slowly. That will also solve the great problems confronting the Jews. Without destroying our substance."

It feels good hearing such voices without moving my own lips. How clear it becomes that one is not alone in the world. No utterable feeling. The feeling of all feelings.

# DEPARTURE

*There is an independence ordained by God.*
*In the individual.*
*Each man carries his own head between his shoulders.*


Back in Warsaw in the bouncing train. For the third or fourth time. Once again through the streets that I dote on, that I roamed for weeks on end. Marshal Street, Cracow Suburb. I've said hello to people, visited movies and restaurants. I feel wistful, grateful. Everything flashes. I enjoyed being here, I'm enthralled; what kind of human breed is this, human mixture; what seething life, powerful stimuli. I would have loved to get deeper into everything; but I remained deaf and dumb. And now, farewell. This land exists. I realize it from the bottom of my heart.

Before midnight, I was sucked in by the terminal and blasted toward Danzig. A bad night. I sit alone in my compartment with a young gentleman. I see that he reads Polish national-democratic newspapers. The conductor endlessly examines my ticket, I can't communicate with him, I show him my passport, I try German, French. The young gentleman intercedes. And once everything is cleared up, he remarks in good German without an accent: "You won't win any popularity contest if you speak German in Poland." He says I really ought to speak

French. And then, as we stretch out horizontally, each on his own side, he begins speaking French. We talk until deep in the night; he, across from me, does most of the talking. He's large, strong, with a full face. He says he was an officer in the war, first on the side of the Central Powers (I don't know whether it was the Prussians or the Austrians), then for Poland with the Allies. He must come from the former Prussian territory. He says about the Germans:

"They think that might makes right. Russia and Germany are our most dangerous enemies. Industrially, Germany is once again the strongest country."

However, through several intellectuals, the Germans are propagating the idea of a United States of Europe. This isn't sentimentality, it's insidiousness. No one aside from German industry is interested in the notion. For a long time, he talks about Germany with fear and admiration. He knocks the old methods that Prussia used against the Poles:

"They gave us the name 'Slavs,' from 'slaves.' But now they realize they made a mistake."

I point out that, so far as I know, "Slav" comes from the [Slavic] word for "voice," and that it refers to the person who can speak as opposed to the German, who can't speak. He ignores my comment. In Warsaw, I felt that Poland's crisis demands superhuman prudence, coolness, energy. Hearing the young nationalist, I dream about it in the dark railroad carriage.

His hatred of Germans is tied up with fear. He expresses pure hatred of the Jews, a hatred intensifying into disgust. One can't do anything to them, he declares. "No amount of suppression does anything to the Jew. On the sabbath, he sits there again, like a king, and makes himself secure." The Pole in my compartment admits that he doesn't even know whether it makes any sense to wipe them out completely, smash them and suck them up. He has a tremendous horrible phantasmagoria about them. As he spends hours pouring out this hatred, I am forced willy-nilly into the role of observer. He complains in despair:

"They're not individual persons in Poland. They're a nation, a people. They own large areas of the cities. They were allowed into Poland. And what do they live off now? Here and every-

where else? They live off the defective development of a people.
They won't allow my people to climb any higher; otherwise the
Jews would perish. If a nation is poorly developed, they prevent
it from recovering. And our nation is poorly developed. You
must have observed how much commerce is in their hands.
How wealthy they grow, with our wealth. They're nothing but
saprophytes, mushrooms growing from putrescence, fungus living on decaying matter, parasites. They're a race of bacteria. In
high cultures, like America, Western Europe, they're insignifi-
cant. But here, where everything is only just starting. . . ." He
repeats, woebegone: "They're colossally dangerous," and dwells
tirelessly on the theme in order to convince me. He asks
whether I've read a book by the Tharaud brothers, two French-
men who spent a long time studying the court of an East Galician rebbe. Those rebbes are filthy rich, they have real royal
courts; they hold the Jews together. The Jews are jacks of all
deceptive trades, to the detriment of the peasants and townsfolk, who can't keep up with them. They're white slavers; they
kidnap Polish girls and girls of other nations. And outsiders can't
get at them, internally. Because they have their Talmud. It
contains everything for them. And the Talmud teaches a double
ethics: one toward Jews and one toward other nations.

This educated man is simply beside himself with revulsion,
with horror. He must be a patriot. I'm already half asleep, and
he still keeps talking. In the darkness, the door flies open, and
someone shouts something in Polish. The gentleman translates
for me: the stranger has warned us that there are thieves on the
train. And after a while, I'm awoken by a nightmare, I sit up
straight and see a man looming by the window. He's fiddling
with my baggage. And the man is—my fellow traveler! I moan
in terror, my legs drop from the cushion. But now, in the light
of dawn, I realize that he's only rewrapping himself in his blan-
ket. Smiling at me, he lies down again. But I stay awake all
night, too upset to sleep. The train rolls to a beat, three, four
quick strokes: "Wind like the wind, wind like the wind, strike
them dead, strike them dead, wind like the wind." An "oh" and
"ah" runs round the train, swelling into a long amazed
"oooooh!" Suddenly, near bridges, tunnels, the din bursts into

loud shrieks; next comes derisive applause. In the morning (the Pole left the train before the border), I lumber across an enormous railroad bridge. A huge, huge torrent pours underneath. Battered, I roll into the pretty terminal in Danzig.

An obelisk stands in a meadow: "Danzig, in memory of its fallen sons." In the middle of a street, an armed uniformed man lifts and lowers his arm; he holds a signal, he seems to be beckoning to vehicles. He's a traffic cop. He directs the traffic, even when there isn't any. I walk past elegant boutiques, whole rows of them. Old-fashioned dwellings flatter my eyes. The vegetable market is in an absolutely splendid building, with gold emblems; elegant stores are on the inside. Cleanliness, cleanliness everywhere, prosperity. Middle-class life moves along the streets. Good breeding, consistent order, peace and quiet. Many shiny cars drive by. The department stores are having Christmas sales.

I gaze into a photographer's window—and, I think of the photos on Florian Street in Cracow. A woman was sitting there, in a white satin gown that elegantly revealed her bosom; a sinking evening coat, a coquettish hat over her forehead; she smiled voluptuously, very knowingly. Ah, Cracow. Am I glad to be walking here? There's order and cleanliness here. The building façades aren't crumbling. The roadway surface is impeccably intact. Here, respectable well-nourished faces hang in the photographer's window. They're comfortable, with a light and sometimes thick powdering of self-complaisance. This is—*Herzenstod*, the death of the heart! Why does this word haunt me now—I'm no poet. It haunts me doggedly: death of the heart! Dullness, blankness on the faces of the sitters. And not just in the photographer's vitrine; he caught them expertly. The faces of the people walking the street next to me like that: efficient hardworking creatures, but all the same. So much the same. I see no individual person. There's something antlike about them. They're a mass, it acts, it works. Does it know why? But it acts. It's something vegetative, empty. I have to lower my eyes, I don't want to look. Why not? I'm embarrassed, I feel terribly abandoned.

And this, dear heart, also awaits you in Germany. Here you

have cleanliness, order, prosperity. Here you're at home. Not everything—will be like this. It only crashes down on you during the first moment.

I follow the trolley route, I let the rails pull me along to an ancient rectangular tower, through a beautiful gate into Long Street. Ah, a main thoroughfare. During this cold morning, a solid bourgeois public strolls past fine boutiques, department stores. They've got lots of bourgeois people, well dressed. The commanding post office bears the legend "Imperial Post Office." The street is pointedly dominated by a church or town hall. The names of these side streets make me feel good: Milk Can Street.

A long, peaceful bourgeois life expresses itself; in Poland, the young state, hotheaded, politicized in every limb, cast names upon all cities—the names on which the state erects itself. Behind the Long Market, the cozy picture changes; ships steam, a medium-wide river flows past. Ships covered with high masts and smokestacks, half-timber houses with pointed gables wait along the riverbanks. Warehouses after warehouses. A violent wind is blowing, the water glitters greenish, a broad wooden path runs down below.

Where was I last walking along a riverbank? In Cracow, again in Cracow. In Podgorze, the working-class district. Packs of dogs played in the miry side streets, sniffing the garbage. I heard scolding from basements. As if a storm had grabbed hold of me. As if I were about to die. As if I were doing wrong by walking here. How impatient I am, how deeply I yearn, what sorrow I feel in my heart. It is the sharp sorrow of parting, of dying.

I haven't noticed the women and girls here, the serious faces, pale, unkempt. A mother trudges by with her four-year-old daughter; her white panties are drooping from under her calico skirt down to her knees. The New Mottlau: an iron bridge, the green flittering water. And a new breed of man: cocky workers and seamen wearing caps, taking broad strides. Behind the wide thoroughfare, which is named Pepper Street, my route takes me across a large square to the shipyard. And right at the start, when I enter Workers' Street, I have before me the splendid modern tableau, the black mathematical construction of a daring crane as high as a house. Now, very close by, a ship's siren blasts terribly deep. And broad calm water lies before me; I sail across, next to wagons and horses, on a ferry. Rattling, shattering comes over the water from all sides. They're riveting and hammering in the factories. A row of cranes along the bank. Each one stretches out two iron arms from which chains dangle with hooks and handles. I've reached the opposite bank, I walk up the avenue, and the higher I get, the more colorfully the tableau of the other bank flows along. Whole stretches lie swathed in black smoke. Huge steam hammers roar across; an even humming and rattling of the riveters and borers. How alive the cranes become, turning, dropping slender arms. An enormous chimney releases an absolutely colossal mass of black slanting fumes. I follow the swampy road over the island. From the top, I see the silent water spreading out. And what is on the water beyond the island? Four small Polish warships, their guns covered. One ship is named *General Haller*, another *Sea Gull*. This Danzig is no longer a part of Germany, it's a strange sovereign hybrid. I was already astonished by the Polish ticket windows at the terminal. This freak was created for "political" reasons—a free city against its will.

As I turn around, the roaring, rolling, whirring on the other bank are tremendous. Now, all chimneys belch black. Red fires glisten in the factories, the hammering occasionally pauses, but the ear-splitting whirring keeps on.

Egypt offers reparation for the assassination of the British general; Jaurès is lying in state at the Pantheon in Paris. The German chancellor in regard to the Nathusius Case: "The big hit isn't here, the big hit is missing, where is the big hit?"

"We're going to see who gets further: we, who comprehend everything and want to work for the good of the people, or the Marxists, who've got followers only because they use the wildest terrorism, according to that lovely old saying: If you don't want to work with me, I'll smash your head in, one two three! So hands off our honest intentions! We'll stick steadfastly to our course. The man who betrays his Fatherland stigmatizes himself! Germany has to live even if we must die!

"German true, through and through!"

"Found: a wooden crosstie; a handbag containing about two

261

guldens and a key; three pairs of children's panties; a German passport made out to Frieda Dirks; a young large sheepdog; a white terrier with brown spots."

At the café, sour exhausted bespectacled bald heads of families play dance music. What stories are told at the tables: three elegant ladies cackle: Can you dance in roller skates, and is that an art; any street urchin can do it. For this discussion, the ladies offer steely tones.

I'm in the theater, watching *Tristan*. For two acts, I can't get into it. In the third act, Tristan, mortally wounded, lies under a tree by his castle. Then he leaps up, half crazy:

> *In laughter and weeping,*
> *In rapture and wounds,*
> *I have found the poison*
> *In the potion.*

Now I've found the key. How intensely my eyes open, how eagerly I lean forward. . . . This isn't theater. My mind is over-illuminated, I've been hit. All I can feel is: This is true. This is true.

During the intermission, the people chew and suck in the corridors. A fat lady stands at the buffet, opening beer bottles; they laugh and toast. One man takes an open sandwich, egg with anchovies, bites, tears; the egg falls on his boot. They pull sandwiches out of their pockets the instant the auditorium doors are opened; then they station themselves at pillars, walls, and eat stupendously, with rustling paper in their hands. A fat married couple wanders by; the man keeps bowing incessantly right and left. An officer with an Iron Cross and a full face. A short mother with her timid gangly daughter. A grouchy husband with a pince-nez, fat torso, baggy trousers; his wife, awkward and short, waves her handbag aggressively. Two men shake hands, scratch their heads. Three cheese-colored adolescents walk together, discussing the singers like schoolmasters. A young slender pretty girl; her legs are long and straight, and now she staggers, and she doesn't know what to do with her arms.

These women go to fat very quickly, their hips slide away from them, they don't know how to dress, many faces have pimples. And here, an elderly woman stands in front of her daughter, wearing an appalling white blouse; a colossal necklace hangs down to her pubic bone; they gabble away at each other unclearly; their cheeks are fat: full of rolls.

And then the doors reopen. Inside, the shepherd's flute is blowing. And Tristan zooms up:

> *In laughter and weeping,*
> *In rapture and wounds,*
> *I have found the poison*
> *In the potion.*

And he sings—German music . . . music of these Germans.

Death of the heart? Not death of the heart. Music and goodness knows what else in the hearts of these people. Pimply faces; baggy trousers; their minds hemorrhage into music. Music here, faces and actions there.

I want nothing in this city. I only want to spend an hour by the sea. In the morning, I've got sand under my feet; in the morning, I'm by the sea. It's so cold. I passed the lovely ocean resort of Zoppot, I was astonished by the Russian posters, Russian books in the shop windows. Then I walk toward the beach. Deserted. Behind me lies the spa, the house where they gamble; they're building a gigantic hotel next door.

Ah, now I'm walking in the soft white sand. What a boon. I'm wearing the same clothes I wore in teeming Lodz and in the Tatra mountains, in the blizzards; my valise is already floating homeward. I'm very light. The gushing swell of the water, I hear it roll up and crash down. White conches, black shells, beautifully twisted scallops, tangled in seaweed. Now, the horizon is finely etched. The curving and vaulting of the sea. The shore in a soft milky haze. And there's the gray playful surface. I see the ocean. It flaps and comes running. Music to my ears. A lapping: small swinging boats. All waves scud to the right with the wind. I walk through a huge mass of light—sky and mirroring ocean.

The sun emerges white from the fog. What a tableau on the

water: the shine and glow dissolving, carried far away, raised high by the waves. I am right by the water. The splendid wall of the surf arrives in a black line, whitecaps upon it; it tumbles over, spouting and spurting, floods out, billows back in its foam.

A huge motorboat is out there, the din is sometimes very near. It's got foam at its bow, the sniffing chewing running animal, with saliva flowing down its snout and whiskers.

All at once, a lone woman in a long mourning veil comes toward me very slowly. She wanders past me, toward the bridge, without raising her eyes from the sand. The sun shines very bright. The water becomes greenishly iridescent, playing with colors. The colors blend marvelously, yellow stripes, a milky violet, quivering reddish tones, and in back, everything turns blue.

Just ponder, dear heart, what the mightiest thing in the world is. You're by the sea; the journey through the strange land is over.

What I view here strikes me as the mightiest thing: immense nature. Always nature. I don't have to correct myself. A piece of nature lies before me: the ocean, the liquid garden full of plants and animals; the wind breathes upon it.

And the other, the second strongest thing? The—soul. The human spirit, the human will.

I've seen courageous herds of human beings. Oppressed herds of human beings. It's infinitely clear to me that you mustn't surrender to worship. You can alter, shift, tear up, you have to tear up—that's clear to me. The spirit and the will are legitimate, fruitful, and powerful.

There is an independence ordained by God. In the individual. In every individual. Each man carries his own head between his shoulders.

BALTIC SEA

LITHUANIA

*Dvine*

*Nieman*

Zoppot■
Danzig■

Eydtkuhnen•

■Wilno

*Wilja*

•Oszmiana

Stettin•

GERMANY

Bromberg•

•Grodno

Minsk

*Szczara*

RUSSIA

•Ostrolenka

•Berlin

Frankfurt•

Poznan•

*Netze*

*Vistula*

*Warthe*

*Oder*

Warsaw•  ■Praga
■Gura Kalwarja

POLAND

VOLHYNIA

*Pripet*

Lodz■

Radom •

Lublin•

*Bug*

*Elbe*

Breslau•

Czestochowa•

*Vistula*

*San*

Katowice•  Cracow•

Jaroslaw•

■Lwow

Prague•

Wieliczka•

Przemysl•

Zakopane■

CZECHOSLOVAKIA

■Drohobycz
■Boryslaw

■ Places visited by Döblin

HUNGARY

*Theiss*

CARPATHIANS

*Dniester*

Borders in 1924

Poland - - - - -     other countries — — —

Km       100        200        300

*Pruth*

ROMANIA

## I Leafed Through

Adam Mickiewicz: *Histoire populaire de Pologne*

Erdman Hanisch: *Geschichte Polens*

Brückner: *Geschichte der polnischen Literatur*

Emil Knorr: *Polnische Aufstände seit 1830*

Tetzner: *Die Slawen in Deutschland*

Anne de Bovet: *Cracovie*

Dubnow: *Neueste Geschichte des jüdischen Volkes*

Horodezky: *Religiöse Strömungen im Judentum*

C. Bloch: *Die Gemeinde der Hasidim*

## I Read Very Carefully

Bernhard Guttmann: *Tage in Hellas*

## I Neither Read Nor Leafed Through

The national libraries in Berlin, in Warsaw, in Cracow,
and in Lwów.

# NOTES FOR THE INTRODUCTION

1. The first edition, indicating its year of publication as 1926, was printed in a run of 3,200 copies. According to the files of S. Fischer Verlag, Frankfurt am Main, there was no further edition of the book.
2. See Notes for Text, note no. 1.
3. *Die Zeitlupe; Kleine Prosa* (Slow Motion: Short Prose Pieces). Olten and Freiburg i. Br., 1962 p. 59. According to Dr. Gottfried B. Fischer, we may assume that Döblin had his trip to Poland financed by the publisher, as he did in all other cases.
4. Cf. *Die Zeitlupe*, pp. 110, 161, 166.
5. *Schicksalsreise: Bericht und Bekenntnis*. Frankfurt am Main, 1949, p. 164.
6. *Schicksalsreise*, p. 156f.
7. *Jüdisches Lexikon*, vol. 2, 1928, p. 172.
8. "Zion und Europa," in: *Der Neue Merkur*, August 1921.
9. *Alfred Döblin: Im Buch—Zu Haus—Auf der Strasse* (Alfred Döblin: In the Book—at Home—on the Street). Berlin, 1928, p. 32.
10. *Schicksalsreise*, p. 157f.
11. *Schicksalsreise*, p. 156.
12. Linke Poot: *Der deutsche Maskenball* (The German Masquerade). Berlin, 1921, p. 40.
13. Walter Muschg: "Ein Flüchtling; Alfred Döblin's Bekehrung" (A Refugee; Alfred Döblin's Conversion), in *Die Zerstörung der deutschen Literatur* (The Destruction of German Literature). Bern, 1958, p. 121.

14. *Aufsätze zur Literatur* (Literary Essays). Olten and Freiburg i. Br., 1963, p. 17.
15. "Ein Brief" (A Letter), in *Der Jude*, a quarterly periodical founded by Martin Buber. Special issue: *Judentum und Deutschtum* (Judaism and Germanism). Berlin, 1926, p. 102. "Jüdische Erneuerung" (Jewish Renewal), Amsterdam, 1933: revised and expanded version of "Wie lange noch, jüdisches Volk-Nichtvolk?"—How Much Longer, Jewish Nation/Non-nation), in: *Unser Dasein* (Our Existence), Berlin 1933. Olten and Freiburg i. Br., 1964, pp. 355–413. "Jüdische Massensiedlungen und Volksminoritäten" (Jewish Mass Settlements and Ethnic Minorities), in: *Die Sammlung*. Literary monthly. Ed. by Klaus Mann, vol. I, Amsterdam 1933/34, pp. 19–26 (from: "Jüdische Erneuerung," pp. 62–75). *Flucht und Sammlung des Judenvolks; Aufsätze und Erzählungen*. Amsterdam, 1935.
16. Information bulletin no. 1 (4/16/35) of the League for Jewish Colonization (Paris) says among other things: "On 1/21/35, Dr. Alfred Döblin gave a well-attended lecture on 'The End is Nearing.' The speaker's sharp polemics against the assimilated stratum of West European Jews led to an animated discussion; in his final words, Dr. Döblin passionately advocated the idea of the Freeland."
17. "Jüdische Antijuden" (Jewish Anti-Jews), in: *Das neue Tage-Buch*. Ed. by Leopold Schwarzschild. Vol. 3, Paris-Amsterdam, 1935, no. 42, pp. 1002ff (Reply to Ludwig Marcuse: "Döblin greift ein" (Döblin Intercedes), in: *Das neue Tage-Buch*, 1935, no. 33, pp. 783 ff.
18. *Schicksalsreise*, p. 180.
19. Döblin's posthumous papers contain two Polish reviews of the book.
20. Hans Bloch: "Die Reise zu den Juden: Bemerkungen zu Alfred Döblin's *Reise in Polen*" (The Trip to the Jews: Comments on Alfred Döblin's *Journey to Poland*), in: *Jüdische Rundschau*, vol. 24, 1926, p. 44.
21. Klatzkin, Jakob: "Gespräche mit Einstein" (*Schriften* [Writings], Tel Aviv, 1952f.), p. 366.
22. Roth, Joseph: "Döblin im Osten" (Döblin in Eastern Europe), in: *Frankfurter Zeitung*, 1/31/26. Cf. also: Joseph Roth: "Reise durch Galizien" (Journey Through Galicia), in: *Frankfurter Zeitung*, November 20, 22, 1924.
23. Almost half turned up only during the preparation of this book.

# Notes for the Introduction

The various manuscripts by Alfred Döblin—found in a moving and storage firm in Zurich, where the author had evidently left them in 1933 during his flight—included page 67 of the hand-written manuscript of *Reise in Polen*.

24. *Reise in Polen*, in: *Die Neue Rundschau*, 1925, vol. 1, pp. 141–170 (February) under the overall title (book pp. 11–52); pp. 300–322 (March), under the title "Wilno und seine Juden" (Wilno and Its Jews) (book pp. 116–149); pp. 505–520 (May), under the title "Lemberg" (book pp. 181–205); vol. 2, pp. 743–758 (July), under the title "Zakopane" (book pp. 277–296).

25. *Die Neue Rundschau*, 1925, vol. 1, pp. 143f.

26. Loc. cit, pp. 159, 169, 311, 313, 314, 317, 318, 516.

27. In the manuscript the passage goes: "From small provincial Lublin—it welcomed me with a tremendous starry sky, I left on a gray afternoon. . . ."

# NOTES FOR THE TEXT

[Some of the notes in the German edition have been inserted directly into the text. Translator.]

Epigraph: A quotation from Schiller: *Wilhelm Tell*, Act II, scene 2: "For border wields a tyrant's power."

1. "The Triumphal March of the Zeppelin": In September 1924, the airship ZR-III made three trial flights before heading toward its destination, Lakehurst, New Jersey, in mid-October. A two-day flight across Germany took place from September 25 (Thursday morning) to September 26 (Friday evening). The quoted headline presumably refers to that flight, during which the zeppelin also passed over Berlin. The context reveals that this is a Friday-evening edition or a Saturday edition. However, no headline with that wording has been located. Under the title "Zeppelin's Triumph," which comes closest to the quotation, the *Berliner Tageblatt* reported on the landing of the airship in Lakehurst on October 15. By then, Döblin had long since left Poland; the first dated addition to the Warsaw jottings was done on October 3.

2. The Hotel Bristol was Döblin's hotel in Warsaw.

3. Josef Poniatowski, 1763–1813, Polish general.

4. Adam Mickiewicz, 1798–1855, Polish poet.

5. Julius Slowacki, 1809–1849, Polish poet.

6. "Napoleon's death": taken by the editor from the magazine pre-publication.

7. Then warehouses behind fences, decrepit one-story houses. Overlooked by copyist, taken from the manuscript by the editor.

272

8. Stanislaw Wyspianski, 1869–1907.
9. Emile Vandervelde, 1866–1938, Belgian Socialist, leader of the Second International.
10. Rosa Luxemburg, 1875–1919, with Karl Liebknecht leader of the Berlin Spartacus Uprising. Leading characters in Döblin's *November 1918: Eine deutsche Revolution* (November 1918: A German Revolution): vol. III: *Karl und Rosa: Eine Geschichte zwischen Himmel und Hölle* (Karl and Rosa: A Story Between Heaven and Hell), Freiburg, Munich, 1950.
11. Hakatist: Member of the German Ostmark Union. Established in 1894 as an association "for the promotion of German culture in the Eastern provinces." Also called the HKT union after the initials of the last names of its founders (Hansemann, Kennemann, Tiedemann).
12. "The oak forest roars, the clouds race": Schiller: *Wallenstein— Die Piccolomini*, Act III, scene 7.
13. Three rows of clocks: They show the times of the three daily prayers.
14. "Upper body swaying": expression of fervor.
15. Poale Zion: Jewish Socialist Party, founded at the start of the twentieth century when it broke away from the general Zionist movement.
16. *Rov*: Honorary title for leading religious scholars.
17. *Gaon*: Honorary title for particularly venerated non-Hasidic rabbis in Eastern Europe.
18. In 1924, the Day of Atonement occurred on October 10.
19. Yitsik Leib Peretz, 1852–1915, Yiddish writer.
20. Kol Nidre prayer: Named after its opening words, this prayer inaugurates Yom Kippur, the Day of Atonement.
21. Talmud: the compendium of the oral tradition of the exegeses of the Mosaic law. Torah: The Mosaic Law, the first five books of the Bible.
22. That year the Feast of Tabernacles lasted from October 15–22.
23. Cabbala: Jewish mystical tradition.
24. Shulkhan-Orukh: A compendium of the ritural laws, compiled during the sixteenth and seventeenth centuries.
25. Mishnah: The older and fundamental portion of the Talmud.
26. Bundists: members of the Bund, a Jewish-Socialist party.
27. Ganef: Yiddish for "thief."
28. Aleksander Fredro, 1793–1876, Polish playwright.
29. Today: October 24, 1924.

30. The days of All Saints, All Souls: November 1 and 2. On October 29, Döblin had gone to Drohobycz; on October 31, he was back in Lwów. The text fails to point out that his stay in Lwów was interrupted; the excursion to the Petroleum District is covered by a separate chapter ("The Petroleum District"), which follows "Lwów."
31. There are many: Overlooked by the copyist; inserted by the editor from the original manuscript.
32. Four racing farm horses yanking a wagon across ice: Overlooked by the copyist; inserted by the editor from the original manuscript.
33. Shevuos: roughly at the same time as Whitsuntide.
34. The Book of Raziel: An ancient Cabbalistic work made up of diverse components and named after the angel Raziel.
35. *Sefer Yesirah:* A sixth-century work, the first systematic presentation of Jewish mysticism.
36. Something else: Overlooked by the copyist; inserted by the editor from the original manuscript.
37. Grunwald: The Battle of Grunwald, Polish name for the Battle of Tannenberg, 1410, when a Polish-Lithuanian army defeated an army of the German Order.
38. Tefilin: phylacteries, which Jewish men strap on for morning prayers on normal weekdays.
39. Enclosed in a book: *Mountains, Oceans, and Giants.*
40. Chaim Nachman Bialik, 1873–1934, modern Hebrew poet.